3075

THE BEATLES

SIDE ONE
1. **DRIVE MY CAR**—Paul and John (with George)—Paul on piano
2. **NORWEGIAN WOOD** (This Bird Has Flown)—John (with Paul)—George on Sitar
3. **YOU WON'T SEE ME**—Paul (with John and George)—Paul on piano ; Mal 'organ' Evans on Hammond
4. **NOWHERE MAN**—John and Paul and George
5. **THINK FOR YOURSELF**—(Harrison)—George (with John and Paul)—Paul on fuzz Bass
6. **THE WORD**—John and Paul and George—Paul on piano ; George Martin on harmonium
7. **MICHELLE**—Paul (with John and George)

SIDE TWO
1. **WHAT GOES ON**—(Lennon—McCartney—Starkey)—Ringo (with Paul and John)
2. **GIRL**—John (with Paul and George)
3. **I'M LOOKING THROUGH YOU**—Paul (with John)—Ringo on Hammond Organ
4. **IN MY LIFE**—John and Paul—George Martin on piano
5. **WAIT**—John and Paul
6. **IF I NEEDED SOMEONE**—(Harrison)—George (with John and Paul)
7. **RUN FOR YOUR LIFE**—John (with Paul and George)

All titles composed Lennon-McCartney (except *Think For Yourself* and *If I Needed Someone*).
Recording Produced by GEORGE MARTIN   Photography : Robert Freeman   ℗ 1965

TRADE MARK OF
THE GRAMOPHONE CO. LTD.

LONG PLAY 33⅓ R.P.M

E.M.I. RECORDS
(The Gramophone Company Ltd.)
HAYES · MIDDLESEX · ENGLAND
Made and Printed in Great Britain

12   LL   Printed and made by Garrod & Lofthouse Ltd. Patents pending   PMC 1267   PCS 3075

The BEATLES
Rubber Soul to Revolver

Compiled by Bruce Spizer

With additional contributions by

Bill King,
David Leaf,
Al Sussman,
Frank Daniels,
Piers Hemmingsen,
Jude Southerland Kessler,
and other Beatles fans

Copyright ©2022 by 498 Productions, L.L.C.
498 Productions, L.L.C.
935 Gravier Street, Suite 707
New Orleans, Louisiana 70112
Phone: 504-299-1964
email: 498@beatle.net

The Billboard, Cash Box and Record World chart data used in this book was taken from books published by Record Research, including Billboard Pop Album Charts 1965- 1969 and The Comparison Book 1954- 1982. Photography by Robert Whitaker shown on pages 67, 71, 72, 73, 74, 75, 77, 229 and 231 licensed from the family of Robert Whitaker. Other images provided by: Beatles Book Photo Library (pages viii, 68, 199, 201, 204, 208, 211, 218, 225 and 227); BeatlesPhotos.de (pages 78 and 80); Kristen Tash (page 164); Jon Roe (page 170); Bob Schuller (page 171); Bill Badon (page 173); John Bezzini (page 174); and Bruce Spizer (page 215). The Canadian images (pages 110 - 117) were primarily provided by Piers Hemmingsen. Most of the other collectibles shown in the book are from the collections of Bruce Spizer, Frank Daniels, Jeff Augsburger, Tom Grosh of Very English & Rolling Stone, Gary Johnson of Rockaway Records, Gary Hein and Perry Cox.

Print edition ISBN 978-0-9832957-9-2
Printed in U.S.A.
1 2 3 4 5 6 7 8 9 0

Say The Word

In December 1965 I was ten and a half years old. My favorite interests were the Beatles, James Bond, comic books and the American space program. That month two manned Gemini capsules blasted off on Titan rockets from Cape Kennedy (as Cape Canaveral was known from late November 1963 through 1973). The second-launched Gemini capsule tracked down the one that had gone up 11 days earlier and was still in orbit circling the globe. I learned a new word describing the event: "rendezvous," a prearranged meeting at a particular time and place. My teacher told the class that the word was French in origin. Somehow calling it a rendezvous made it seen even more exciting.

That same month I added more French words to my vocabulary, this time from a Beatles song: "Sont les mots qui vont tres bien ensemble." I learned from "Michelle" that the phrase meant "these are words that go together well." Paul's lovely ballad from the new Beatles album *Rubber Soul* was getting nearly as much air play on the radio as the group's fantastic new single, "We Can Work It Out" and "Day Tripper." The album was full of great songs from start to finish, including one of my favorite Beatles songs of all time, "In My Life." In America, the album differed from the U.K. LP, but I certainly did not know that back then. The Capitol disc had a great folk rock sound. The Beatles even had a message for us: "Say the word, LOVE."

In mid-February I began hearing a new Beatles single on the radio titled "Nowhere Man." I loved the song's breath-taking vocal harmonies, bright-sounding guitars and introspective lyrics. By late May "Nowhere Man" was nowhere to be heard, replaced by another different-sounding single, "Paperback Writer." Once again I was captivated by the vocal harmonies at the start of the song. I also loved the churning guitar riff, booming bass and storyline.

In August my family took a car vacation to see the USA. My parents accommodated my desire to play the radio during the long car rides. Everywhere we went, the radio played "Yellow Submarine" on a near-hourly basis. When we got back to New Orleans, I learned that the Beatles had a new album out called *Revolver*. My favorite tracks on the disc were "Eleanor Rigby," "Here, There And Everywhere" and "Good Day Sunshine." Back then, I didn't know what to make of "Love You To" or "Tomorrow Never Knows" although I love both now.

A few yeas later my mother bought me a stereo record player for my bedroom. It was now time for me to begin buying stereo copies of the Beatles Capitol LPs.

One of the first stereo albums I purchased was *Rubber Soul*. I immediately noticed that on most of the songs the vocals were almost exclusively coming from the right speaker. For the most part, the right channel had little, if any, instrumental backing. On some tracks, there was percussion or one guitar throughout the song, while on others the right channel also contained instrumental breaks and solos. The left channel occasionally had backing vocals, but on most songs it only had instruments. Oddly, the first songs on each side had a normal stereo balance with vocals and instruments being heard through both speakers. I later learned that those songs were recorded for the British *Help!* LP, thus explaining why they were mixed differently than the other *Rubber Soul* tracks on the U.S. album.

My record player had a knob that allowed me to alter the balance between the speakers. By turning the knob all the way to the left or right, the sound would come exclusively from one speaker. For *Rubber Soul*, that meant I could focus entirely on a song's vocals or instrumental backing, giving me a greater appreciation of the harmonies or the intricate playing. It also gave me a bit of the giggles when I noticed that the Beatles were singing "tit, tit, tit, tit" in the background on "Girl." I took great pride in pointing out this naughty discovery to my high school friends.

Revolver also sounded great in stereo on my new record player. Because the stereo imaging was more conventional than on *Rubber Soul*, I could not isolate the vocals. But with my equipment upgrade, I could hear everything more clearly now, including the special effects and noises on "Yellow Submarine" and "Tomorrow Never Knows."

Several of the tracks on *Yesterday And Today* also had drastic stereo separation. It was particularly noticeable on "Drive My Car" and "Nowhere Man," which really blew me away when I isolated the right channel and heard the vocals and treble guitar duets. I later learned that those songs were recorded and mixed during the *Rubber Soul* sessions. When I later bought a guitar, I used opening riff on "Day Tripper" to tune the low E2 string and the rest of the guitar.

By my senior year in high school I had learned about the different British pressings of the Beatles LPs from the discography appearing at the back of the Hunter Davies official biography *The Beatles*. I stumbled across a store in the French Quarter of New Orleans that had import albums. Over the next few months, I purchased the British LPs *Please Please Me* through *Revolver*. I did not get the later U.K. albums because they had the same song selections as the U.S. albums.

The British *Revolver* LP, which contained three songs not on the Capitol album, made the U.S. disc obsolete. As for *Rubber Soul*, I continued to play the Capitol disc, giving it slightly more spins than its British counterpart. Although "Drive My Car" was a great opener for the U.K. album (having also served as the lead track on *Yesterday And Today*), I loved how "I've Just Seen A Face" started the Capitol LP. I can't tell you which version of *Rubber Soul* is better. It's like comparing a great red wine to a great white wine.

While I appreciated the extra number of tracks on the British albums, I was disappointed that many of the hit singles were not on the Parlophone discs. I became more interested in what songs the Beatles recorded during each album session and decided to program the sessions onto cassettes. But rather than placing the singles at the end of each album, I got the idea to place the singles between each side of the LP. By doing so I preserved the integrity of the running order of each side while making the singles part of the listening experience.

My favorite "Do It Yourself" 90-minute cassette featured *Rubber Soul* on one side and *Revolver* on the other. My plan worked to perfection, with the fading guitar solo on "Michelle" that ended Side One moving beautifully into the opening guitar riff of "Day Tripper," and "We Can Work It Out" flowing nicely into the Side Two opener "What Goes On." *Revolver* also worked quite well with the guitar dominated "She Said She Said" leading into "Paperback Writer" with its churning guitar and vocal harmonies. And, as luck would have it, "Rain" was followed by "Good Day Sunshine."

When the Beatles catalog finally became available on CD, I recreated my album sessions series on CD. And, of course, I burned new album sessions discs when the catalog was remastered in 2009.

I Want To Tell You

After moving forward through time with the Beatles Album Series books on *Sgt. Pepper* through *Let It Be* and tying up some loose ends with my previous book on *Magical Mystery Tour* and *Yellow Submarine*, I decided to go backwards through the Sea of Time with this latest installment in my Beatles Album Series.

Although I could have justified writing separate books on *Revolver* and *Rubber Soul*, I decided to cover both of those albums in one installment. This worked well with how Capitol reconfigured the Beatles album catalog from December 1965 through 1966. In the U.K., fans got two 14-track albums, *Rubber Soul* and *Revolver*, plus two stand-alone singles. In America, we also had the "Nowhere Man" single and the *Yesterday And Today* album, which featured a combined seven tracks from the British versions of *Rubber Soul* and *Revolver* (along with four songs issued on Capitol singles). By focusing on the Beatles records released from December 1965 through the end of 1966, this enabled the background chapters on the news, music and film of the era to also delve into this fascinating 13-month period.

As you will learn in the upcoming chapters, the Beatles output during this period was all the more remarkable considering the group had just come off a tour of America with no supply of ready-to-record songs for the 1965 Christmas season. Yet they managed to issue a double A-side single and an album containing some of their greatest recordings. And a few months later before heading off on a world tour of Germany, Japan and the Philippines, the Beatles did it all over again, releasing an innovative single and album. The Beatles clearly were at their best when under pressure.

In researching this book, I went through tons of magazines from late 1965 and 1966, with a heavy focus on the British music weeklies and the American music trade magazines. I also returned to Mark Lewisohn's *The Beatles Recordings Sessions* and *The Complete Beatles Chronicle*. I assembled the same team utilized in the previous volumes in this series. Piers Hemmingsen provided the Canadian perspective. Beatlefan editor Al Sussman wrote about the news of the world and music, while Frank Daniels took us through the great films of the era to put it all in perspective. Beatlefan publisher Bill King returned with more fan notes. Jeff Augsburger, Perry Cox, Tom Grosh, Gary Johnson and Gary Hein provided images of memorabilia from their collections and inventory. Sadly, Gary died during the writing of this book and did not live to see his contributions in print. He was one of the truly good guys and will be missed.

The Fan Recollections chapter has always been an important part of my album series books. Once again I was able to compile a wonderful collection of memories from Beatles fans of all ages, including wonderful essays from music journalist David Leaf, and Jude Southerland Kessler, the author of the John Lennon Series.

On the technical side, Diana Thornton worked her magic to make the book look terrific as always and Kaye Alexander coordinated the interactions with our printer in Clarksville, Tennessee. Proofreaders included Diana, Frank, Al, Anthony Robustelli, Beatle Tom Frangione and Warren Huberman. In the tradition, my thanks to my family, Sarah, Eloise, Barbara, Trish, Big Puppy and others too numerous and crazy to name.

And yes, The Beatles Album Series Shall Return...

words About Author

Bruce Spizer is a lifelong native of New Orleans, Louisiana, who was eight years old when the Beatles invaded America. He began listening to the radio at age two and was a die-hard fan of WTIX, a top forty AM station that played a blend of New Orleans R&B music and top pop and rock hits. His first two albums were *The Coasters' Greatest Hits*, which he permanently "borrowed" from his older sisters, and *Meet The Beatles!*, which he still occasionally plays on his vintage 1964 Beatles record player.

During his high school and college days, Bruce played guitar in various bands that primarily covered hits of the sixties, including several Beatles songs. He wrote numerous album and concert reviews for his high school and college newspapers, including a review of *Abbey Road* that didn't claim Paul was dead. He received his B.A., M.B.A. and law degrees from Tulane University. His legal and accounting background have proved valuable in researching and writing his books.

Bruce is considered one of the world's leading experts on the Beatles. A "taxman" by day, Bruce is a Board Certified Tax Attorney with his own practice. A "paperback writer" by night, Bruce is the author of 13 critically acclaimed books on the Beatles, including *The Beatles Are Coming! The Birth of Beatlemania in America*, a series of six books on the group's American record releases, *Beatles For Sale on Parlophone Records*, which covers all of the Beatles records issued in the U.K. from 1962- 1970, and his new series of books on the Beatles albums. His articles have appeared in Beatlefan, Goldmine and American History magazines.

He was selected to write the questions for the special Beatles edition of Trivial Pursuit. He maintains the popular website www.bcatle.net.

Bruce has been a speaker at numerous Beatles conventions and at the Grammy Museum, the Rock 'N' Roll Hall of Fame & Museum and the American Film Institute. He has been on ABC's Good Morning America and Nightline, CBS's The Early Show, CNN, Fox and morning shows in New York, Chicago, Los Angeles, New Orleans and other cities, and is a frequent guest on radio shows, including NPR, BBC and the Beatles Channel.

Bruce serves as a consultant to Universal Music Group, Capitol Records and Apple Corps Ltd. on Beatles projects. He has an extensive Beatles collection, concentrating on American, Canadian and British first issue records, promotional items and concert posters.

contents

1   The Music of Lennon & McCartney & Harrison: Bruce Spizer
A British Perspective of *Rubber Soul* & *Revolver*

36   Yesterday And Today: An American Perspective of   Bruce Spizer
the Beatles Records in 1966

64   "Mommy, did Capitol butcher the Beatles?"   Bruce Spizer
The Truth Behind the Butcher and Trunk Covers

110   *Rubber Soul* Through *Revolver* in Canada   Piers Hemmingsen

118   The Beatles Rendezvous with Greatness   Al Sussman
(As 1965 Spins into 1966)

140   A Song for Every Purpose Under Heaven   Al Sussman

154   A Funny Thing Happened in 1966 in Film & Comics   Frank Daniels

160   Picture Sleeves

164   Fan Recollections

179   In My Life With The Beatles   Jude Southerland Kessler

182   A Fan's Notes: Summer of '66–A Quiet Revolution   Bill King

184   I Love the America *Rubber Soul* More   David Leaf

188   The *Nowhere Man* EP   Bruce Spizer

190   *A Collection Of Beatles Oldies*   Bruce Spizer

192   Two More Innovative Covers   Bruce Spizer

198   The *Rubber Soul* and *Revolver* Sessions   Bruce Spizer

228   Promotional Videos   Bruce Spizer

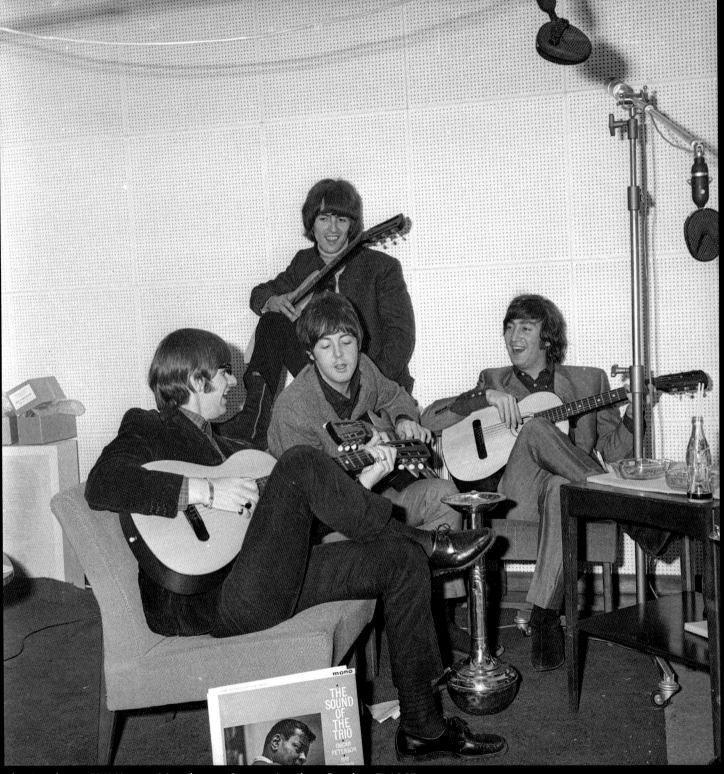

The Beatles at EMI House, Manchester Square, London, October 5, 1965

The Music of Lennon & McCartney & Harrison: A British Perspective of *Rubber Soul & Revolver*

Readers of the October 1965 issue (No. 27) of The Beatles Book learned that the group was getting ready to record a new single and album. In the issue's Editorial, editor Johnny Dean (actually publisher Sean O'Mahony) told fans that John and Paul had to write an entire new batch of songs, including a new single, by the end of month (meaning September). Paul indicated that they had discussed it on the plane coming back from the group's North American tour (landing in London on September 2, 1965), telling Dean: "We have nothing up our sleeves at the moment, the cupboard is definitely bare." Dean assured readers that the Beatles had never let us down and that he knew they wouldn't this time either. The issue's Beatle News section reported that John and Paul hoped to have enough new songs ready to record a new single at the end of October, for release in November, and an LP out before Christmas.

The fan magazine's November 1965 issue (No. 28) had more information. In his Editorial, Dean told readers that the Beatles had been recording new songs at EMI's "famous No. 2 studio in St. John's Wood" [now known as Abbey Road Studios] since October 12 with recording manager [producer] George Martin and balance engineer Norman Smith. Dean indicated that he had heard the group run through some of the songs they were going to record before they went into the studio. He assured readers that the numbers were "really terrific." He speculated that the songs would be "even more fabulous when [the group] finished adding that special Beatles magic to them." Dean told readers that John and Paul had been working very hard on ideas, having written seven new songs in a week's time. The Beatle News section reported that George had been working hard on ideas for new songs since the group's return from America and that he had two ideas that he hoped would "turn out well enough to record."

The magazine's next issue contained a report on the filming of a Granada TV spectacular honoring the songwriting skills of John and Paul (see page 228). The show would air on December 17 under the title The Music of Lennon & McCartney. The Beatles lip-synced two new songs, "Day Tripper" and "We Can Work It Out."

In addition to the monthly publication The Beatles Book, British fans could also read about the group in several music magazines published at the end of each week. The October 22, 1965 New Musical Express ("NME") reported that the Beatles were currently recording several new tracks for their Christmas season album and single. When asked if the new album would have any surprises like "Yesterday," Paul answered, "We've written some funny songs—songs with jokes in. We think that comedy numbers are the next thing after protest songs." McCartney added that the group didn't like protest songs "because we're not the preaching sort." He mentioned that George had written a song for the album which was the best he's done. Although the group hadn't decided what the next single would be, they had a couple recorded which could be A-sides. They wouldn't pick the single until the end of the sessions. The following week NME reported that the Beatles planned recording sessions for the week were called off "because the group ran out of songs!" George Martin said: "The boys have gone away to write more, and we hope to resume next week. We are not waxing songs by other composers—we want this to be an all-Lennon-McCartney album." [Apparently Martin was so focused on John and Paul's songwriting skills that he overlooked Harrison's compositions.]

The November 6 Disc Weekly ("Disc") ran an article on the group's Granada TV special in the which Paul said that the band would perform two numbers they had just written, "Day Tripper" and "We Can Work It Out." These songs would probably go on the new album, still without a title. John and Paul flippantly tossed out a few ideas for the name of the LP while sitting in their dressing room for the TV show, including *It's The Bloody Beatles* and *Eight Feet Away* (perhaps a play on an early considered title to the Beatles second film, *Eight Arms To Hold You*).

That same week Melody Maker interviewed Paul about the upcoming album. McCartney indicated that they were "in the midst of recording sixteen tracks" and were not sure what the next single would be. Once the songs were completed, they would decide which to issue as a single and which to be on the new LP. George Martin added that the group had ten songs of a planned sixteen on tape and that he hoped to get a single from the sixteen tracks. He indicated that the group might release more than one single in America because the Beatles needed more singles over there than in Britain. Martin said that the group would be doing two new numbers for the TV show, "We Can Work It Out" and "Day Tripper." He added: "These two might be the next single. On the other hand, they might not."

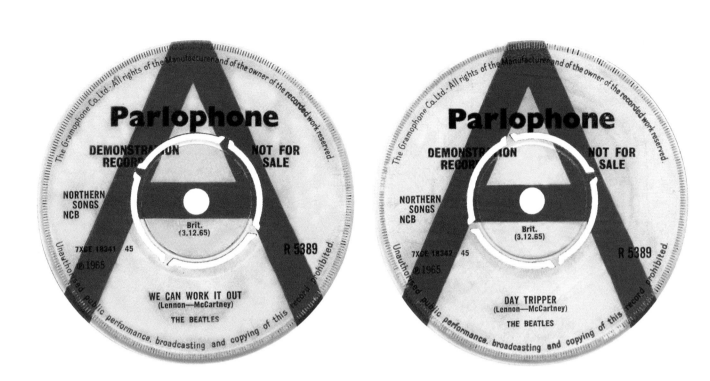

In mid-November EMI made it official, announcing that "We Can Work It Out" would be the A-side, coupled with "Day Tripper." John, however, insisted that "Day Tripper" be plugged as the top side. George Martin told NME in its November 19 issue that: "After we gave both titles to EMI the boys decided they preferred 'Day Tripper,' but both sides are extremely good and worth a lot of plays. As far as EMI's official policy is concerned, there is no A-side—both will be promoted equally on the company's Radio Luxembourg programmes, for example." This double A-side campaign was unique to the British market at that time, although EMI had previously planned on marketing the Beatles single "A Hard Day's Night" c/w "Things We Said Today" as a double A-sided disc before abandoning the idea shortly before the single's release. NME speculated that the split promotion could prevent the disc from instantly topping the charts. If fans requested different songs, record stores would make separate sales figures for each song. While this could result in two chart placings, it would divide the points. [This did not happen because the music magazines chose to list the songs as a single disc entry.] "Day Tripper" was described as an "out-and-out rock 'n' roll number" sung by John (double-tracked) with backing vocals by Paul and George, while "We Can Work It Out" was a medium-tempo song sung by Paul (double-tracked) and John. The instrumental backing included a harmonium.

The November 20 Disc reported that the Beatles were excited about their next single featuring "Day Tripper" and "We Can Work It Out." It would be released on December 3, with the new LP, *Rubber Soul*, due about the same time. The group considered the single their best ever, with George saying, "We're all made up about it." Disc described "Day Tripper" as a rock 'n' roll song with some good guitar work, featuring a double-tracked John lead vocal backed by Paul and George. Although the disc was a double A-side, Harrison explained, "After a lot of talk, we decided 'Day Tripper' is really the top track." That same week Melody Maker told its readers that the Beatles were coming back with a new assault on the hit parade with a new single. Paul sang lead on "We Can Work It Out," while John sang double-tracked on the other side. Record Mirror also gave basic information about the new single and album.

The music weeklies reviewed the group's new single the week before its December 3 release. The November 26 NME contained a review by Derek Johnson, who wrote that "Day Tripper" opened with a repetitive guitar phrase that persisted throughout the song, joined by tambourine to "establish the steady rocking shake beat." The song, sung by John (double-tracked) and joined by Paul and George, had "an impressive drum roll and tambourine rattle" between each chorus. While the tune was not one of the boys' strongest melodically, "it generates plenty of excitement—complete with their falsetto trademarks." Johnson found "We Can Work It Out" to be "more startling in conception." The song featured Paul (doubled-tracked), with tambourine and "additional depth of sound provided by John on harmonium." It was a "mid-tempo shuffle rhythm, except where the pace suddenly slackens in a fascinating way." Johnson joked, "I'll stick my neck out and tip it for a hit."

The others ran reviews in their November 27 issues. In Disc, Penny Valentine found "We Can Work It Out" to be arresting, wonderfully made and an obvious number one. "Day Tripper" was aggressive, masculine and very much John Lennon. Although it was the one getting all the radio air play, she found it somewhat disappointing. Melody Maker's Chris Welch thought the disc lacked spontaneity. Both songs were the product of hard work, but did not have the closeness or the lyrical importance of songs such as "Yesterday" and "She Loves You," songs so wonderfully complete they could never be improved upon. He also preferred "We Can Work It Out," but thought "Day Tripper" would probably be the number one hit. Record Mirror also noted that the new Beatles single, released as a double A-side disc, was an obvious number one. "Day Tripper" was called a rock-tempoed beater, with John on doubled-tracked vocal coming in after a strong guitar intro, and Ringo gradually whipping up a percussive storm. Upon first hearing, it seemed a bit jerky, lacking continuity, but soon settled down. George and Paul provided vocal fill-ins on the track, which featured strong lead guitar. "We Can Work It Out" had Paul double-tracked in places. The song had maracas boosting the rhythm, with harmonium swells and swings in the background. There was a curious change of tempo, slowing down, in one part. Although the track was not so rocky, it was in some respects more commercial than "Day Tripper." The magazine wondered which side would register more with fans.

The single debuted in the December 9 Record Retailer as "Day Tripper"/"We Can Work It Out" at number two behind the Seekers' "The Carnival Is Over" and ahead of the Who's "My Generation." The next week it moved up to number one, where it remained for five weeks before giving way to "Keep On Running" by the Spencer Davis Group. The Beatles record charted for 12 weeks, including nine in the top ten. Disc also listed both sides with "Day Tripper" first. The single debuted on December 11 at number one and remained there for five weeks during its ten-week run.

Melody Maker reported the single as "We Can Work It Out"/"Day Tripper." The record debuted on December 11 at number three, infuriating Brian Epstein, who was livid that the disc was not an immediate number one. "The chart must be made up of returns from inferior shops—fish shops and the like." The magazine reported that people liked both sides of the disc. It noted that the single sold out on Saturday (the day after its release), but that the chart-topping Seekers' disc had sales from the entire week. The next week the Beatles single moved up to number one, where it remained for four weeks. It spent 11 weeks on the charts, including nine in the top ten. NME also listed the single as "We Can Work It Out"/"Day Tripper." The disc debuted at number one in the magazine's December 10 issue and held down the top spot for five weeks. That same issue reported that the new single was one of the Beatles "fastest-ever selling records!" NME observed that it was impossible to determine which side of the disc was the most popular because customers were asking for "the new Beatles single." The BBC also reported the single at number one. The record shipped over 750,000 units by December 8 and reached the one million mark on December 20. In recognition of this achievement, Disc presented the group with a gold disc award, the fifth for the band.

As part of its 1965 Beatles Christmas campaign, EMI released an EP on December 6 featuring the group's first four gold discs: "She Loves You," "I Want To Hold Your Hand," "Can't Buy Me Love" and "I Feel Fine." The record was titled *The Beatles' Millions Sellers* on its sleeve, but the labels had the EP's initial title, "Beatles' Golden Discs." The disc charted for 26 weeks in the Record Retailer EP chart, with five weeks at number one and nine weeks at number two.

The November 20 Disc provided some of the first details on the new Beatles LP. George had two compositions on the disc, with the remainder by John and Paul. Ringo sang lead on a five-year-old Country and Western song written by Paul titled "What Goes On." One of George's songs, "If I Needed Someone," would be recorded by the Hollies. Harrison couldn't wait for the album to be released, indicating that the group was pleased with how it turned out. "We all think it's just about our best LP." He also thought the picture on the front sleeve was "pretty good."

Record Mirror provided additional information in its November 27 edition. In his column, Tony Hall wrote that George Harrison had dropped by his flat and played him a bunch of acetates containing songs from the new album. Hall called the songs the "best things the Beatles have ever recorded" and noted that the group's musical development was "quite startling," with their playing and performances having "improved out of all recognition." He found the group's harmony "especially impressive," adding: "Every track has something interesting happening. And the songs cover so much different ground." He admitted he was disappointed with the last LP, but this time was "knocked out."

The Beatles!

That same week Ray Coleman wrote about the album in Disc. *Rubber Soul* had a new Beatles sound. The group was tighter, better and more harmonious. While the band had improved with each new LP, their latest showed the most improvement yet. Coleman was impressed with George's compositions, "Think For Yourself" (his best ever, with harmonies by John and Paul, a great beat and a wild finish) and "If I Needed Someone" (an excellent tribute to the Byrds). Other highlights included: "Drive My Car" (a catchy Chuck Berry-type song, with John and Paul vocals and Paul adding lead guitar); John's "This Bird Has Flown (Norwegian Wood)" [sic] (beautiful, poetic and Dylanesque, with haunting guitar and funny lyrics); and "Nowhere Man" (one of the album's best, with John and George playing matching guitar riffs). He called John's "Run For Your Life" a "happy-sounding tune," apparently overlooking the song's dark and nasty lyrical sentiments. Equally strange, he found "The Word" to be an "angry song." The track featured Paul on piano and George Martin on harmonium. Paul's "Michelle" was a very catchy French-sounding song, while John's "Girl" was a soft and lilting tune. Paul's "I'm Looking Through You" was another rocker. John's "In My Life" was a pretty ballad. "You Won't See Me" was a hard-driving song with Paul on lead vocals and piano. "What Goes On" was a Country and Western number sung by Ringo. Coleman thought *Rubber Soul* was the Beatles best album yet, brilliantly played and sung.

Allen Evans reviewed *Rubber Soul* in the December 3 NME, giving the disc five stars and telling readers that "the Beatles are still finding ways to make us enjoy listening to them." The LP was a "fine piece of recording artistry and adventure in group sound" with "plenty of tracks you'll want to hear again and again, liking them better each time." Side 1 opened with "Drive My Car," a light-hearted song with a catchy "beep-beep-beep, yeah" motif sung by John and Paul. "Norwegian Wood" was a "folksy-sounding bit of fun by John, with Arabic-sounding guitar chords." "You Won't See Me" had Paul double-tracked, singing without his scouse elocution [Liverpool accent], and playing piano with the group providing "la-la"s in the background. "Nowhere Man" was another elocution piece sung by John, Paul and George, with some "exciting guitar sounds." It had a "plaintive, attractive sound," at times reminiscent of the Everly Brothers. George's "Think For Yourself" had a "good tempo and vocal sound." "The Word" was an exciting track with a "gospelish sound" and "good harmony singing." The first side closed with "Michelle," a memorable track with a "bluesy French sound" with wistful singing by Paul in French and English.

Side 2 opened with "What Goes On," a tuneful Country and Western track sung by Ringo with a catchy instrumental backing. Ringo was given credit as co-writing the song with John and Paul. Evans described "Girl" as a "sigh song," apparently referencing John's audible, sigh-sounding deep breath taken on the chorus following the word "girl." The song was about a "difficult illogical girl he likes in [a] slow, deliberate way." The track had a soft acoustic guitar backing and "some amusing vocal effects" (most likely referring to the "tit-tit-tit-tit" backing vocals). Paul's "I'm Looking Through You" was a "quiet, rocking song about a girl who has changed after letting her boy down." It sounded like earlier Beatles songs and had Ringo on organ. "In My Life" told of reminiscences of life, a slow song with a beat and a "spinet-sounding" solo by George Martin. "Wait" was a "jerky song, with pauses giving more effect to the short lines of the lyric," sung by John and Paul. It gives "advice to someone who has to wait for a loved one who's been away." George's "If I Needed Someone" was a quick-tempoed track with effective harmony backing vocals by Paul and John that make up for its ordinary backing. The album closed with "Run For Your Life," a happy-sounding raver sung by John, who advises a little girl that she "had better run for her life, because if he catches her with another man, that's the end."

Melody Maker

December 4, 1965   9d weekly

BEATLES BOUNCE BACK

—tour, TV, single, LP!

THIS is National Beatles Week! Once again the star-studded quartet hit the pop headlines as they roar back into action.

Within seven short days they undertake their first British tour for over a year, release a new single and LP and make TV appearances.

● THE SINGLE: "Day Tripper" coupled with "We Can Work It Out" is released tomorrow (Friday). Will it burst through all opposition to number one in the MM's Pop Fifty?

● THE LP: "Rubber Soul", containing 14 tracks all written by Lennon and McCartney and George Harrison and featuring vocals and solos from all four millionaires. It includes George playing sitar, Paul on piano and singing in French and Ringo playing Hammond organ.

The album, reviewed on page 12, is released next Friday (December 10). Watch it fill those Christmas stockings.

Glasgow kick-off

● THE TOUR: The Beatles new British tour kicks off tomorrow (Friday) at the Glasgow Odeon, moving to Newcastle's City Hall on Saturday and the Liverpool Empire on Sunday.

The rest of the itinerary is: Apollo, Manchester (December 7); Gaumont, Sheffield (8); Odeon, Birmingham (9); Odeon, Hammersmith (10); Astoria, Finsbury Park (11); Capitol, Cardiff (12).

The Moody Blues and Beryl Marsden are also on the bill.

● TV SHOWS: The promotional TV appearances so far set for the Beatles are: Top of the Pops tonight (Thursday), Thank Your Lucky Stars on Saturday (December 4); The Lennon and McCartney Granada TV Spectacular (17) and Top of the Pops Christmas Show (23).

The cover of the December 4 Melody Maker ran the headline "Beatles Bounce Back" and told of the group's new single, LP, British tour and TV appearances. It was "National Beatles Week!" with the "star-studded quartet" roaring back into action. The cover blurb for *Rubber Soul* stated that the LP featured "vocals and solos from all four millionaires" and included "George playing sitar, Paul on piano and singing in French and Ringo playing Hammond organ." The magazine listed its release date as December 10, telling readers to "Watch it fill those Christmas stockings."

Inside, the album got mixed reviews in an article titled "Mixed Beatles." The magazine stated that *Rubber Soul* was not their best on first hearing and predicted that it probably wouldn't receive much acclaim when compared to the group's earlier albums such as *Please Please Me*, *With The Beatles* and *Help!* "It isn't apparently filled with Lennon-McCartney classics although one or two tracks should stand out in a few months." The magazine noted that the Beatles sound had matured, but unfortunately had "become a little subdued," with several songs, such as "You Won't See Me" and "Nowhere Man," almost getting "monotonous—an un-Beatle like feature, if ever there was one."

As for the positive, "Drive My Car" was singled out as one of the best, an "active rocker, with nice bluesy piano and guitar." George's "Think For Yourself" was another of the better tracks, with Paul's fuzz bass, a double-tempo middle eight and a "good chugging marraca [sic] beat." The vocals in "The Word" had "more urgency in their phrasing, a quality lacking on the other tracks." The magazine described the punchy "I'm Looking Through You" and the up tempo "Run For Your Life" as tracks to watch. Melody Maker ended on a positive note: "A record certainly worthy for a place in your collection—maybe it's just that we expect too much from the Beatles!"

While the review found the album's songs sub-par, Mike Hennessey, writing in the issue's "Colour Section," praised the group's songwriting: "The Beatles are TOPS—because they have Talent, Originality, Personality and Style. But unquestionably the biggest single factor in their unprecedented success is the superb songwriting partnership of John Lennon and Paul McCartney." He continued: "Allied to their natural ear for harmony is an entirely original concept of song construction which has reinvigorated contemporary popular music...It is the Beatles' ability to produce this fresh, young, vital and essentially melodic music which keeps them way out in front of their challengers."

The December 4 Record Mirror ran a joint review by the "RM Disc Jury." The magazine noted that *Rubber Soul* was the most eagerly awaited of the albums released in time for Christmas, with EMI pressing 750,000 copies. It was bound to be a massive success. "Drive My Car" had a medium tempo and very solid beat, with good guitar work and tambourine. Paul added piano to "break up the sound picture." The magazine joked that the title "isn't an invitation to take over the Beatles Rolls." "Norwegian Wood" was melodic, with a folksy feel, gentler tempo and beat. It was sung by John and featured George on sitar. "You Won't See Me" had a happy medium tempo, with good harmonies and road manager Mal Evans on organ. "Nowhere Man" was described as slow, melodic and pleasant. The magazine called the track a "stand-out" that could make a fine single. [It would later be a U.S. 45.] Although George's "Think For Yourself" was a nice song, it had a "sameness about some of the melody-construction ideas." "The Word" was a mid-tempo track with a strong beat that chugged along nicely. It had excellent lyrics and an "excellent blend of voices" by John, Paul and George. George Martin played harmonium. The magazine thought that Paul's "Michelle" was slightly similar to "Yesterday" in its general approach. It was "another stand-out performance" with great lyrics.

"What Goes On" had Ringo singing in a "strong Country and Western flavour" and doing so, very well. John's "Girl" was called a "dramatic sort of number" with "plenty of sadness and feelingfulness" and George and Paul "in the background create tremendous atmosphere." It was another stand-out track that could have been a single. Paul's "I'm Looking Through You" had plenty of beat and "top-notch guitar work." Ringo added Hammond organ, "maintaining this spirit of everybody having a go at everything." "In My Life" was described as a slowish, effective "nice song" with stand-out harmonies and George Martin on piano. "Wait" was a song that "bounds along, cuts out for a slow vocal bit, then bounds off again, with guitar filling in." Tambourine effectively filled out the sound of the track. The magazine noted that George's "If I Needed Someone" was the new Hollies single and that the two recordings were very different. "Run For Your Life" was "fast, exceptionally strong, with John in his best voice... pushed along by some great guitar work." It was one of the most exciting tracks on the album and a "fine old curtain-closer." The RM Disc Jury marveled at the "constant stream of melodic ingenuity stemming from the boys, both as composers and performers," and their fantastic "pace of creativeness." While perhaps not their best in terms of variety, "instrumentally it's a gas!"

The following week Record Mirror's Richard Green expressed his disappointment with the new album. He speculated that if Beatles fans bought their idols' records only if they liked them, then *Rubber Soul* would not do as well as previous Beatles LPs. He argued that: "Over half the tracks, if recorded by anyone but the Beatles, would not be worthy of release." He found "You Won't See Me," "Think For Yourself," "The Word," "What Goes On" and "If I Needed Someone" to be "dull and ordinary," with "none of the old Beatles excitement and compulsiveness about them." "Think For Yourself" was only lifted from the doldrums by its "Duane Eddy-type guitar work." Other tracks were just OK: "Drive My Car" (saved by an "almost pop art guitar break"); "Norwegian Wood" (helped out by the "originality of a sitar"); and "Wait" ("little to offer on any count"). "Nowhere Man" was a good track, as was "Michelle" (a "plaintive little ditty with clever harmonics and instrumental work"). Green liked two of the songs with John lead vocals. "Girl" was "very sad and weepy," proving John is a singer "whose voice can be full of emotion at its height." He thought "Run For Your Life" was the best track on the album.

Green thought previous Beatles albums were well above average, with *Help!* and *Beatles For Sale* being in a class of their own. *Rubber Soul* was "nowhere near as good." Green added: "Someone must know the reason why, certainly I don't." He ranked recent LPs by Manfred Mann, the Beach Boys and Jerry Lee Lewis high above *Rubber Soul*.

Rubber Soul made its debut in the Record Retailer album chart at number 12 on December 9, 1965, while the Beatles *Help!* LP was at number three. The next week it moved up to number two, sandwiched between the soundtracks to *The Sound Of Music* and *Mary Poppins*. On December 23 *Rubber Soul* hit the number one spot, where it remained for eight weeks before being replaced by *The Sound Of Music*. The Beatles LP spent 42 weeks on the charts during 1965 and 1966, including 11 weeks at number two, 26 in the top five and 30 in the top ten. *Rubber Soul* debuted in the December 11 Melody Maker at number one, where it remained for 13 straight weeks followed by seven straight weeks at number two. The magazine charted the LP for 31 weeks. The album performed similarly on the NME charts, debuting at number one on December 10 and remaining at the top for 12 straight weeks before dropping to the second spot for seven weeks. Disc debuted *Rubber Soul* at number one on December 11 and charted the LP at the top for 15 weeks. The magazine also reported the LP on its singles charts for five weeks with a peak at 16.

In his editorial in the March 1966 issue (No. 32) of The Beatles Book, Johnny Dean noted that not all record reviewers liked *Rubber Soul*, with a few critics thinking that the new album "wasn't up to the boys' usual standard." Dean pointed out how wrong they were as evidenced by the number of artists rushing to record their own cover version of *Rubber Soul* songs. He explained that from the start the Beatles refused to release recordings that weren't up to their high standards. Before the Beatles, pop albums typically had one or two top-quality songs, with the rest being just "reasonable." But with the Beatles insisting on "nothing but the best," buying one of their albums was like getting "seven separate singles!"

The magazine's Beatle News section indicated that the Beatles would be going to EMI Studios in early March to record songs for their next film. If the movie was indeed a Western, then some of the songs would need to have a "Country and Western flavour." The magazine noted that group was still discussing what songs to do and "anything can happen once they get in the recording studios." In the April 1966 issue, Dean indicated that work on the next Beatles single and album had been delayed because Paul wanted some rest before they went back into the studio as he had spent the past three months working nearly non-stop on new song ideas. The Beatle News section reported that the group was considering flying to Memphis on April 11 to record their new single. The reason given was that the Beatles had "heard so much about the American technicians and sound engineers—so they wanted to see for themselves whether it makes any difference." George Martin was slated to accompany them. The magazine added that George Harrison had written a great song for the new recording session, which could be a B-side or album track.

In the March 11 NME, John gave an intriguing answer as to what would come out of the next recording sessions: "Literally anything. Electronic music, jokes." He assured readers that the next LP was going to be very different. The group wanted a continuous album with no space between tracks, but EMI "wouldn't wear it." [The group's 1967 LP, *Sgt. Pepper*, would be continuous.] He added that he and Paul were keen on electronic music: "You make it clinking a couple of glasses together or with bleeps from the radio, then you loop the tape to repeat the noises at intervals. Some people build up whole symphonies from it." John thought it would have been better than the background music from the last film, which he described as "All those silly bands." He emphatically stated, "Never again!"

In the May 1966 issue (No. 34) of The Beatles Book, Johnny Dean informed readers that the group's plans to go to America to record their next single were scrapped. The Beatles decided it was best to stick to the studio they knew best, EMI's No. 2 in St. John's Wood. As for the new single, the boys promised that, once again, "it would be something different from anything they had done before," with "New Sounds" seemingly the new golden rule in the recording studio. Dean predicted the new single would become the "song of the Summer." He indicated that he had heard several of the group's new songs in half-finished form, saying "they're different, original and fab! fab! fab!"

The May 7 Disc (now called Disc and Music Echo after merging with Music Echo) announced that the new Beatles single would feature two Lennon-McCartney songs, "Paperback Writer" and "Rain," and be released on June 10. "Paperback Writer" featured Paul singing lead (double-tracked) backed by John and George. Its lyrics were in the format of a letter. The song was an upbeat rock tune described by George Harrison as a "joggerty-rogalong song." "Rain" was a slower song, with John's lead vocal double-tracked. George Martin told Disc: "Of several numbers recorded, these two titles were the obvious and immediate choices for the new single. The rest will go on the new Beatles LP." That week Melody Maker gave its spin on the new disc. "Paperback Writer" was the story of a man trying to get a paperback novel published. "Rain" drove home the point that whatever the weather, people will complain.

Ray Coleman previewed the new Beatles single in the May 14 Disc. Both songs were excellent, leading Coleman to predict that there would be controversy over which side should be the A-side when "Paperback Writer" and "Rain" went on sale. After playing the new record for Coleman, George Harrison said the group thought the disc would turn out like their last single where several people prefer the B-side. He explained: "But it takes time to get some of our stuff across—and anyway, if they think the B side is better than the A, it means we produced two good songs." Coleman described "Paperback Writer" as fast and catchy, "with Paul taking a good vocal on some exceptionally clever words." Paul plays a "heavy guitar riff which helps punch the song across." George said it was Paul's story line. The song opens with Paul, John and George singing "Paperback Writer" in chorus, "sort of Beach Boys style," according to George. Coleman described "Rain" as "more plaintive and pretty, and a typically attractive slow Beatles melody," with John singing lead. The lyrics were based on the fact that "whatever the weather, somebody will always complain."

When asked if the Beatles were worried that the disc wouldn't hit the top spot at first, George said: "We just know we are making better records...The fact that they sell a lot isn't enough any more. We're interested in getting better sounds, and if the new sounds of the group don't go down so well as the OLD sound, well I don't know what to say... We've made the record. Now it's up to the people who buy it." He hoped the Beatles new single would reach the top over the Rolling Stones' new disc ("Paint It Black") and called the new single the Beatles best so far, even better than the last one. "The sounds are better and the songs are, too." George thought there were several songs recorded for their next LP which could have been a single, but "Paperback Writer" had the "best single sound." He admitted the Beatles took too long between singles, "but we'd rather wait and be sure." Coleman found the wait worthwhile, calling "Paperback Writer" and "Rain" both "excellent Beatles songs which will give the summer a hot start."

The June 1966 issue (No. 35) of The Beatles Book gave Johnny Dean's personal account of the second and final day of the recording session for "Paperback Writer." The basic track had already been recorded, so John and Paul were working out what to add to the recording. Paul overdubbed his bass part while the backing track played through the studio speakers. George Martin exited the control room and came into the studio to share ideas with the band. Paul told Dean, "The trouble is that we've done everything we can do with four people, so it's always a problem to ring the changes and make it sound different." The group tried out different ideas until Paul came up with the "Frère Jacques" backing vocals. It was a long ten-hour session because the Beatles insisted on working at it until completely satisfied. Fans would appreciate the song even more knowing what it took to achieve that really great sound.

The music weeklies reviewed the new Beatles single a week before its release. The June 3 NME titled its review "Startling, even for the Beatles!" Derek Johnson stated that the "top side swings along at a thundering pace, with Paul double-tracking the lyric, aided by some of the most startling harmony chanting even the Beatles have ever come up with." Great cymbal-bashing by Ringo emphasized the drive, and the sudden breaks in tempo increased the impact. "Rain" was a medium-paced philosophic ditty with a Lennon vocal "enhanced by background harmonies and a shuffle beat." NME and Disc ran an ad for the single (shown on the next page) that was equally startling, even for the Beatles! The ad marked the first publication of a photo taken during the controversial butcher session.

THE BEATLES
PAPERBACK WRITER
RAIN

PARLOPHONE
R5452

RELEASE DATE
10 JUNE

In its June 2 issue, Record Retailer called the disc "an obvious number one hit—but one which will puzzle fans." "Paperback Writer" was described as fast-paced with "American-style falsetto harmonies, with Paul taking lead vocal on a very clever set of lyrics." "Rain" was characterized as "slower, more Beatle-ish, and a damned good contrast." The magazine concluded that the record "shows the boys' development, musically." The June 4 Melody Maker's review by its pop panel wrote that the Beatles "subtly follow the trait towards Indian pop using wailing harmony and dipping bass lines" on a "very swinging track with a lot of impact, some vicious sounds, and almost disconcerting vocal harmonies." The magazine added that George Martin had "obtained a very powerful overall sound with some excellent timing on the vocal echo." The panel surprisingly misidentified the lead singer as John, adding that he "sings in rather a strained, urgent cry about a man who wants to be a paperback writer with George and Paul soaring behind him." The review also mistakenly attributes the song's "heavy, churning guitar" to George. The panel concludes that the disc is "right up to the Beatles standard and needless to say—a huge hit."

Norman Jopling and Peter Jones reviewed the new single in the June 4 Record Mirror, stating that it was obviously a number one hit and a "single that will stir up plenty of controversy." The song's opening was a "group vocal, with high falsetto chords" that "hardly sounds like the Beatles," but rather a "sort of Anglicised Beach Boy sound." The track had a "fast-tempoed, hard-rock rhythm" with a "swinging guitar riff" and "moments of compelling jerkiness in the melody line." The recording was "positively different" with clever lyrics and a "marvelous sense of style." The flip side, "Rain," was described as a "slower, more melodic" tune, with John's vocal "giving it much more of a typical Beatles' sound." With its interesting lyrics, great "whining guitar sound" and "droning group vocal," the B-side might be as popular as the top side. The reviewers emphatically stated that "the Beatles aren't relaxing one whit in their attempts to come up with something startlingly different." The judgment was now "up to the million plus buyers."

The June 4 Disc ran the comments of eight fans who were given an advance opportunity to hear the new single at the magazine's offices. The disc did not get the "usual rave reception," with a few saying it was not as good as their previous hits, while others didn't like it. Only one fan thought it was as good as most of their hits. Nearly all agreed that "Rain" dragged and was boring, although one fan thought "Rain" had more of a tune to it. Singles reviewer

Penny Valentine felt people were expecting too much from the Beatles. There seemed to be a new Beatles sound "vaguely mid-way between the Beach Boys and Byrds with a smattering of Hollies harmonies." "Paperback Writer" was striking with a "marvelous dance beat," while "Rain" was very pretty and could "grow on you." Mike Nevard of The Sun wrote that if "Paperback Writer" had been recorded by another group, it would have gone in the junk pile.

The June 17 NME ran Alan Smith's interview with George Martin on the "Paperback Writer" recording session. Martin observed that the group now spent more time in the studio than before. "The Beatles have come to accept that recording is their way of life. They accept the voluntary imprisonment of being in the studios for as long as 14 hours on in." He said that "Paperback Writer" was not specifically recorded as a single and that there were other tracks he preferred. Martin thought that the song had an ordinary rock beat, but added "there's nothing ordinary about the style." He liked the use of answering voices, one against the other. He joked that The Times' critic [William Mann] would describe it as "polyphonic!" Martin said that this was the first time they had used echo that way on a Beatles track. He also liked the song's "Frère Jacques" refrain. He described the backwards vocals at the end of "Rain" as an in-joke. "The Beatles weren't quite sure what to do at that point, so I took out a bit of John's voice from earlier on and played it backwards. They all thought it was marvelous...it had a sort of unexpectedly Eastern sound. So we kept it in." He added, "We often like to do that for a giggle, particularly as they so often work out."

"Paperback Writer" entered the Record Retailer chart at number two on June 16, while Frank Sinatra's "Strangers In The Night" was topping the charts. The following week it moved into the top spot for two weeks before being replaced by the Kinks' "Sunny Afternoon." Record Retailer charted the Beatles single for 11 weeks, including five in the top ten. "Paperback Writer" debuted at number one in the June 18 Melody Maker and held down the top spot for four weeks during its ten weeks on the charts. In Disc, the song debuted at number two before moving up to the top spot on June 25 for its first of two weeks at number one during its eight-week chart run. The single performed similarly in NME, debuting at number two before spending two weeks at the top during its eight weeks on the chart. "Paperback Writer" also topped the BBC chart. The single shipped 300,000 copies by June 15 and 500,000 by June 22. Disc announced that the single had been awarded a silver disc on June 25, 1966.

The picture selected by the Beatles to promote their new single (see page 17) created a quite a stir when it appeared in color on the cover of the Beatles American album *Yesterday And Today* (as shown on the Capitol Records promotional poster on page 107). In contrast, the U.K. advertisement failed to elicit any serious concern, most likely because it appeared only in the interior pages of Disc and NME and was in black and white rather than color, which softened its graphic depiction of raw meat and flesh-colored baby parts. A week later, on June 11, Disc ran another photo from the session, this time in color and on the magazine's cover. Although the picture combines raw meat with false teeth and eye balls, it is missing the highly offensive decapitated baby dolls. The photo is printed in reverse. It is not know whether the magazine intentionally flipped the transparency or simply made a mistake. Based on reader responses, many thought it was the Beatles who made the mistake.

The caption to the picture opted for British humor, boldly stating "**BEATLES: WHAT A CARVE-UP!**" The article also recognized the satirical nature of the photo: **BEATLES WEEK!** They're back with a single Paperback Writer and Rain, out tomorrow (Friday). **BUT WHAT'S THIS?** The Beatles as butchers draped with raw meat! Disc and Music Echo's world exclusive colour picture by Bob Whitaker is the most controversial shot ever of John, Paul, George and Ringo. **THE PLACE:** A private studio in Chelsea, London. Whitaker is taking some new pictures of the Beatles, and decides that a new approach is needed. "I wanted to do a real experiment—people will jump to the wrong conclusion about it being sick," says Whitaker. "But the whole thing is based on simplicity—linking four very real people with something real." "I got George to knock some nails into John's head, and took some sausages along to get some other pictures, dressed them up in white smocks as butchers, and this is the result—the use of the camera as a means of creating situations." [These photos and more are shown in the Butcher cover chapter starting on page 65.]

PAUL'S comment after the session: "Very tasty meat!" GEORGE: "We won't come to any more of your sick picture sessions." JOHN: "Oh, we don't mind doing anything." RINGO: "We haven't done pictures like THIS before..."

The magazine then asked, "Well, what's YOUR verdict? Sick—or super? Six LPs for the best six captions—of no more than 12 words—to the picture above."

DISC
and MUSIC ECHO 9d

JUNE 11, 1966

USA 25c

MERSEY UPROAR

after 'Whole Scene' attack

SEE PAGE 6

SANDIE
TV miming no CRIME!

Page 7

MERSEYS
jealous of the Hollies!

Page 8

CILLA
I just can't stop myself GIGGLING!

Page 8

BEATLES: WHAT A CARVE-UP!

BEATLES WEEK! They're back with a single, "Paperback Writer" and "Rain"—out tomorrow (Friday).

BUT WHAT'S THIS? The Beatles as butchers, draped with raw meat! Disc and Music Echo's world exclusive colour picture by Bob Whitaker is the most controversial shot ever of John, Paul, George and Ringo.

THE PLACE: A private studio in Chelsea, London. Whitaker is taking some new pictures of the Beatles, and decides that a new approach is needed.

"I wanted to do a real experiment — people will jump to wrong conclusions about it being sick," says Whitaker. "But the whole thing is based on simplicity — linking four very real people with something real.

"I got George to knock some nails into John's head, and took some sausages along to get some other pictures. Dressed them up in white smocks as butchers, and this is the result—the use of the camera as a means of creating situations."

PAUL'S comment after the session: "Very tasty meat."

GEORGE: "We won't come to any more of your sick picture sessions."

JOHN: "Oh, we don't mind doing anything."

RINGO: "We haven't done pictures like THIS before . . ."

Well, what's YOUR verdict? Sick—or super? Six LPs for the best six captions—of no more than 12 words—to the picture above. Send your entry to "Beatles Picture," Disc and Music Echo, 161 Fleet Street, London, E.C.4, before next Friday, June 17.

● PAUL in his own write—exclusive interview: Page 9.

The following week Disc ran a story on the initial reaction to the picture under the headline "Fans Slam 'Sick' Beatles Picture." The article began, "Oh dear! That front-page full-colour picture of the Beatles 'in the raw' last week certainly triggered off some harsh comments from readers." The negative comments included: "Help! Beatles victims of sick photography." "How disgusting! From now on, I am a vegetarian." "The Beatles' reputation is risked by indulging in this kind of disgusting publicity." "It's a horrible picture and a sick idea. I love the Beatles and was sorry to see them in a photo like this." "Any civilized cow would die of fright if it saw that picture." Some fans saw it differently: "Super! All their pictures are really fantabulous." "It shows harmony, loyalty and perfect understanding of each other. It's super." "It's great! What's wrong with meat? We see it and eat it every day. It has a certain atmosphere about it!"

No one could deny the picture had atmosphere, but this atmosphere created a storm of controversy. The June 25 Disc reported that the picture "triggered off the biggest reaction since the hydrogen bomb!" The magazine selected the following six winning captions: "BEATLES decorated again—by Order of the Butchers Empire" "PROVES success is a joint effort!" "DEFINITELY no tripe here!" "THEY told us this is one of the best joints in town." "FROM ME to you? More like from ewe to meat!" "THROWING jellybabies is one thing, but this is ridiculous."

Although the Beatles 1966 album would not be released until August, fans began reading about the LP in mid-May. George Harrison provided details about a few of the tracks to Ray Coleman, who included the information in his article on the group's new "Paperback Writer" single in the May 14 Disc. George told Coleman: "One of the songs on our new LP is amazing. It's nothing like a pop song. I wonder how it's going to be received–I've been told that years ago, when Ornette Coleman came along with his new sounds in jazz, everybody thought he was a bit weird. Perhaps we can do that as well–change the scene a bit and start some new sounds." [The song discussed by George would be titled "Tomorrow Never Knows" by the time of the album's release.] George said he had written two songs for the LP and played sitar on one. He talked about the track "I'm Only Sleeping" ("we try to get the vocal to sound like somebody's asleep, which is very difficult!"), which led Coleman to falsely conclude that George had written the song. As for the cover, Harrison indicated that photographer Bob Freeman was working on a revolutionary cover for the album. "He's talking about having it done in silvery colour, or put out just like a photo negative."

That same week Tony Hall wrote about a few of the new songs in his column appearing in the May 14 Record Mirror. Having had the privilege of hearing songs from the yet-to-be-completed album, Hall boldly stated: "SOME OF THE TRACKS ON THE NEXT BEATLES LP ARE THE MOST REVOLUTIONARY EVER MADE BY A POP GROUP! They shatter every convention ever laid down. And could well have fantastic and far-reaching effects on the whole future of the music...." The track that had the greatest effect on him was without title and referred to by the boys as "The Void," although he doubted that would be its name. [The song would later be titled "Tomorrow Never Knows."] It had the weirdest, wildest electronic effects that Hall had ever heard. "Sound-wise, it's like a hypnotically horrific journey through the dark never-ending jungle of someone's mind. Indian instruments are cleverly utilised. And the effect is of shapes and sounds and colours looming over and above one and zooming in and out of a monotonous drone." The track had great drumming by Ringo. In contrast to the music, the lyrics were "beautifully simple and pure and unbelievably truthful." Hall added that Paul had played the track the previous week for Bob Dylan and Brian Jones (of the Rolling Stones). Like Hall, they were "absolutely gassed" because the track was so original, "Unlike anything they'd ever heard before." Hall said that the song was "as revolutionary as Ornette Coleman appeared to the jazz scene a decade ago." [George made the same reference in his interview with Ray Coleman in the May 14 Disc.]

Hall also singled out two other tracks: a marvelous McCartney song about lonely people, with a drumless backing of ominous strings; and a fascinating George Harrison song on which he plays a "long exotic solo on sitar." While listeners might prefer some of the album's less complex songs, those with ears and imagination would "get a tremendous kick out of the ones...cited above." The Beatles were "progressing musically at an unbelievable rate... making their own musical rules as they go along." Hall found it exciting, noting the group was "so far ahead."

More information about the new album was revealed in Alan Smith's interview with George Martin appearing in the June 17 NME. Martin indicated he was hoping for an August release, but noted that there were still a couple of songs to record. The album was "far more varied than anything they've done before." One track included jazz musicians, with Paul trying to achieve a trumpet sound "in the James Brown band style." Martin didn't think there was anything particularly weird on the album, except for one track on which he played an instrument he just bought.

Fans learned even more about the new LP a few weeks later in a Ray Coleman article on the Beatles tour of Germany appearing in the July 2 Disc. Coleman indicated that the group played him songs from the album on a tape machine with terrible reproduction. Although John complained "It brings me down, listening to things that sound so bad on rotten machines," Coleman didn't mind, calling it a "fascinating new LP." The group was still trying to come up with a title for the album, passing on *Magic Circles*, *Bubble And Squeak*, *Beatles On Safari* and *Freewheelin' Beatles*.

Coleman then provided brief descriptions of nine of the songs. "Good Day Sunshine" starred Paul on vocals, with George Martin on honky tonk piano. Ringo sang a "sea-shanty styled 'We All Live In A Yellow Submarine,'" which Coleman mistakenly thought was written by John. "Love You To" was a tremendous sitar showcase for George, who wrote that song and another one titled "I Want To Tell You." Paul sang beautifully in a sensational moody song, "For No One," which had terrific French horn effects. The Beatles favorite track was "Tomorrow Never Knows," described as "pop-free-form, with incredible electronic sounds." Coleman noted: "Even the Beatles are amazed how revolutionary this has turned out." "Doctor Robert" was a good-sounding song. John, apparently joking, told Coleman, "It's all about a queer." George's "Tax Man" [sic] was nice, while Paul's "Eleanor Rigby" was special, with "surprise violins." The song was "another 'Yesterday.'" Overall, the album was glorious and superb.

The next week Alan Walsh gave his report on the upcoming album in the July 9 Melody Maker, telling readers that the Beatles were "about to send the British, and possibly the world pop scene off on a tangent." He predicted that their new album would "set a new direction for popular music," noting that "a wide range of musical influences have been absorbed into the [album's] tracks." In addition to the usual three guitars and drums, instruments included French horn, trumpets, sitar, violin, Clavichord, viola and piano. The songs reflected "Paul's love of classical music and George's involvement in Indian sounds, rhythms and counterpoint." Walsh was aware of 11 of the 14 tracks.

"Good Day Sunshine" had a "sort of a street band sound at times; vaguely reminiscent of a sea shanty at others." "Yellow Submarine" was a children's song sung by Ringo, with laughter and noises like clinking glasses. In George's "Love You Too" [sic], he "plays sitar as a traditional Indian instrument and not as a weird 'new' guitar sound."

George was also the writer and vocalist on "I Want To Tell You," which featured Paul on piano. According to George: "It's regularly irregular. But I didn't realize this until the others told me." "For No One" was a ballad with "classical overtones," featuring Paul on piano and a "beautiful French horn passage that's brilliant." "Eleanor Rigby" was another track with a classical sound, this time with a string quartet backing Paul's vocal. Walsh wondered if the song would be another "Michelle." The Beatles favorite track was "Tomorrow Never Knows," which featured the "electronic sounds that have had so much publicity." Other known tracks were "Doctor Robert," "Tax Man" [sic], "And Your Bird Can Sing" and "I'm Only Sleeping." Walsh closed by asking if the album was: "A new direction? A new meaning to pop? Perhaps the catalyst that could lift the Beatles out of pop music into a league of their own?" He observed that the sound on the LP would "defeat the bandwagon-jumpers," quoting Paul's challenge: "They'll never be able to copy this!"

In a separate article, Walsh reminded Ringo that the new album took about ten weeks to record and asked the drummer if the group could "face up to this tremendous effort for every new single or album?" Ringo admitted it could only get harder, but thought they had achieved a high standard and did the best they could. They insisted on having the time to do what they wanted to do. Because of their success, EMI didn't argue. They no longer had to do an LP in ten hours the way they previously did. Ringo emphasized, "The important thing is to get it right."

The July 8 NME contained Beatles press officer Tony Barrow's personal account of the Beatles frightening tour incident in Manila (see page 130). Barrow disclosed that the title of the Beatles new LP, set for August release, was *Revolver*. The magazine provided a list of the album's tracks in their correct running order.

In the August 1966 issue (No. 37) of The Beatles Book, Johnny Dean told of getting a preview of the new album's tracks during the group's German tour. He was completely knocked out by the sheer originality of the numbers, telling readers that the group had "done it again and produced an album full of great tracks, most of which would smash right up the charts if they were ever released as singles. No oldies rehashed or poor material served up as new. Just great tunes sung by the boys in their own magic way. Marvelous!" Paul came up with the title, *Revolver*.

The music weeklies ran their proper reviews of *Revolver* the week before the disc's release on August 5, 1966. Writing in the July 29 NME, Allen Evans stated that the LP had "new sounds and new ideas, and should cause plenty of arguments among fans as to whether it is as good as or better than previous efforts." Evans then gave a track-by-track breakdown. George's "Taxman" was a fast rocker with "twangy guitar" with lyrics about "dealing with the tax inspector, something near to all wealthy Beatles' hearts." "Eleanor Rigby" was a "folksy ballad sung with very clear diction by Paul" backed by violins. It was the wistful tale of the lonely Miss Rigby. "I'm Only Sleeping" had a "very human lyric" about not wanting to get up in the morning. Evans liked the song's false-endings and bass playing. "Love You Too" [sic] was described as an "Oriental sounding piece" with George on sitar and singing a "Kama Sutra type lyric," while Paul's "Here, There And Everywhere" was a "slow, soft, wistful song." "Yellow Submarine" was a simple song that "should become a nursery or college or public house sing-song classic" and a "household favourite." It was skillfully sung by Ringo and had "fooling around" in the backing. As for "She Said She Said," Evans thought that John's "high, nasal tones" worked well with his song "about a girl with morbid thoughts being put right by boy."

"Good Day Sunshine" was a "bright, airy, light-hearted love song" with a great vocal by Paul and piano and drums opening. "And Your Bird Can Sing" had "strident, vigorous guitars," philosophical lyrics and a "high-pitched, raving vocal, led by John." Paul's "For No One" had a good horn sound by Alan Cavil. John's "Dr. Robert" was a straightforward beat song "about a doctor who does well for everyone." George's "I Want To Tell You" was a "neatly lyriced" song about an everyday occurrence: "Boy wants to tell girl, but can't, how much he likes her." The song had prominent guitars and drums. "Got To Get You Into My Life" was a "rollicking rocker" with a "rich backing" from jazz musicians sung well by Paul. Evans apparently thought "Tomorrow Never Knows" was a bit of a contradiction. John's vocal tells you to: "turn off your mind and relax and float downstream. But how can you relax with the electronic, outer-space noises, often sounding like seagulls? Even John's voice is weirdly fractured and given a far-away sound. Only Ringo's rock-steady drumming is natural." Klaus Voorman's cover was clever, with "pictures planted into the Beatles hair."

The July 30 Record Mirror provided "in depth" coverage of the new LP, noting that the magazine's Tony Hall had raved over some of the tracks, describing them as "easily the most ambitious yet by the incredibly consistent quartet."

The review was co-written by Richard Green, who disliked *Rubber Soul*, and Peter Jones. The 14-track disc was full of musical ingenuity, but would be controversial, with parts of the album that would "split the pop fraternity neatly down the middle." But, as the authors observed, "whoever made progress without running the risk of criticism?"

The pair then gave their individual views of each track. Jones described the "deliberately untidy opening" and "saga of sadness of how the tax collector keeps 19 bob of a Beatle-earned pound." He loved the wild, strident guitar, but found the song a bit repetitive. Green liked the song, calling it "big beat rock 'n' roll." Green called "Eleanor Rigby" the "Michelle" of the album. The strings gave the backing an 18th-century sound. Jones praised the strings and found the track pleasant, but "rather disjointed." He liked more meat from the Beatles. Jones liked the lyrics and backing harmonies on "I'm Only Sleeping." He wondered what the funny string sound was, tossing out, "Electric bagpipes?" [It was actually backwards guitar.] Green thought its musical content was pretty ingenious. As for "Love You To," Green noted it started out like an Indian recital before switching to a normal beat. The song was great and different, judged by him to be the best so far. Jones thought it was a good tune, but would need to "hear it a few more times before getting it." After only four songs, he observed, "This is a really different album–already." Both found "Here, There And Everywhere" to be very romantic, with Jones observing that "Paul's voice is dead right for it. The stuff that standards are made of." Green thought it was sung with great feeling. "Yellow Submarine" was described by Green as a "sort of Beatle 'Puff The Magic Dragon.'" Jones thought the track was OK, showing Ringo's good personality and the group's versatility. Both liked "She Said She Said," with Jones praising the guitars and construction of the song and Green finding it "rather bluesy" with "heavy accept on guitars for the atmosphere."

"Good Day Sunshine" was also well-received, with Green calling it "subdued ragtime" and Jones being reminded of the Lovin' Spoonful. Paul sang with "character, power and subtlety." Jones found "And Your Bird Can Sing" to be different, while Green thought it was typical Beatles and one of the stronger tracks on the album with Paul's bass reminding him of "Paperback Writer." Green found "For No One" to be semi-classical with a marvelous French horn, while Jones, who also liked the French horn, appreciated the gentleness of approach to the melodic song. He interjected that this was a "really unusual album."

Neither particularly cared for "Dr. Robert," although Jones thought it had strong lyrics. Green praised "I Want To Tell You" for being well-written, produced and sung. He loved the harmonizing and unusual piano. Jones liked George's vocal and noted: "The deliberately off-key sounds in the background add to a toughly romantic number." "Got To Get You Into My Life" was one of Jones' favorites. They both liked the song's "big band brassiness" backing. Both expressed admiration for "Tomorrow Never Knows," with Green calling it very weird and the most off-beat track. Jones observed: "You need some sort of aural microscope to get the message...darned compelling listening...Very advanced." They both liked the album, finding it "pretty dead well right" and "an excursion...into the realms of musical fantasy" with parts of it "ridiculous...in the nicest way."

The following week Tony Hall continued with his praise of the album in the August 6 Record Mirror. He thought "Tomorrow Never Knows" was not only the album's most outstanding track, but also the "most progressive ever recorded by a pop group." Its sound was incredible, effectively using electronic "loops." Its lyrics were extracted from "The Tibetan Book of the Dead." John's performance was "just beautiful." "Yellow Submarine" was a giggle—a children's song with the Beatles just "having a ball." "Eleanor Rigby" was "possibly the most mature Paul has yet written." Of George's songs, he found "Love You To" to be the "most ambitious and successful." Hall also dug "I'm Only Sleeping." In fact, he dug all of the album's songs, calling it "an album that even sounds good at breakfast!"

Hall lamented the rush of other artists to record cover versions of songs from the Beatles last two albums, *Rubber Soul* and *Revolver*. There would be 15 different singles with songs from the LP, with four or five of "Good Day Sunshine" and multiple versions of "Here, There And Everywhere," "For No One" and "Got To Get You Into My Life." As to whether these hits were the singer or the song, he put his money on the song. Although the Overlanders had a number one hit with "Michelle," they hadn't been heard from since.

Hall indicated that while critics were busy analyzing the songs on *Revolver*, the group had "virtually 'forgotten' them." The *Revolver* phase was the past. The group was already thinking ahead to the next album, "which will be something entirely different again."

BUY A BEATLES LP

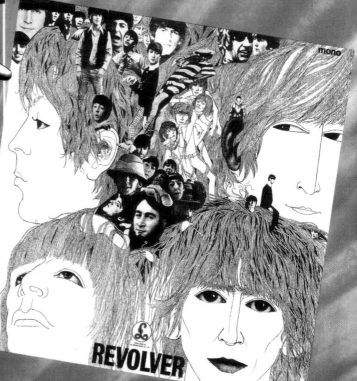

REVOLVER

Melody Maker's July 30 review opens with: "Paul was right — they'll never be able to copy this one!" The magazine noted it wasn't "the electronic effects, George's stunning use of the sitar, or Paul's penchant for the classics" that made copying impossible. It was that "the Beatles individual personalities are now showing through loud and clear," with only a few of the LP's songs really being Beatle tracks. "Most are Paul tracks, John tracks, George tracks, or in the case of 'Yellow Submarine,' Ringo's track." The magazine observed that there are "still more ideas buzzing around in the Beatles' heads than in most of the pop world put together." Many of those ideas are found in *Revolver,* resulting in, like *Rubber Soul,* "a veritable gold mine of ideas which the lesser fry will frantically scramble over." While each individual Beatle enjoys the "heady freedom of being able to translate their every whim onto record," this "freedom is not abused," with "George's fascination for Indian music, Paul's liking for classical effects, and the discriminate use of electronics...put to good use." Although the Beatles won't be able to perform most of these songs live, it doesn't matter. *Revolver* is a brilliant album that proves "the Beatles have...broken the bounds of what we used to call pop."

"Taxman" has a "strong backbeat with heartfelt lyrics." "Eleanor Rigby" features Paul singing against a "firm, rhythmic string backing" in a charming song that is one of the album's best. "I'm Only Sleeping" has "intriguing harmonies" and clever yawning effects. George goes "whole Indian hog" on "Love You To," one of the disc's most striking tracks, with "straight Indian sound, complete with tabla drummer, and tremendous sitar part by George." "Here, There And Everywhere" has a "gentle, languid sound with Paul's voice leading on quite a beautiful melody." "Yellow Submarine" is a disarming "song for the kiddies, with catchy...singalong bit." "She Said She Said" has a great John vocal, Eastern influence and "odd bits of chord-bending in the backing." "Good Day Sunshine" features "Paul in good-time mood over pub piano," while "And Your Bird Can Sing" is a "beaty mid-tempo track with another fine John vocal." Signs of Dylan are present in Paul's vocal on "For No One," which has a horn solo "playing counterpoint with the melody." "Dr. Robert" has mysterious lyrics that are "partly obscured by [an] obtrusive, but firmly swinging backing." "I Want To Tell You" has a "touch of the bitonalities with a piano figure which resolves into tune for nicely spread harmonies." "Got To Get You Into My Life" has an urgent vocal from Paul backed by riffing trumpets. "Tomorrow Never Knows" has "an Indian opening...electronics and a superb rhythmic figure." John's voice "sounds as if it's coming from Abbey Road." [The reference to Abbey Road apparently being the street outside EMI Studios, not the studio itself.]

Disc turned over the task of reviewing *Revolver* to Ray Davies of the Kinks, who provided track-by-track summaries. "Taxman" was a "cross between the Who and Batman" saved by "sexy double tracking." "Eleanor Rigby" sounded like John and Paul were "out to please music teachers in primary schools," although it was commercial. "I'm Only Sleeping" was a "jolly old thing" and the album's best track. "Love You To" was "well performed which is always true of a Beatles track." "Here, There And Everywhere" was a nice song with a "lot of busy chords in it." Davies described "Yellow Submarine" as "absolute rubbish," while "She Said She Said" was included "to restore confidence in the old Beatles sound." "Good Day Sunshine" was "back to the real old Beatles." Davies thought that fans didn't like the newer electronic stuff. "The Beatles are supposed to be like the boy next door only better." "And Your Bird Can Sing" was "too predictable." "For No One" was better than "Eleanor Rigby," with the French horn being a nice effect. "Dr. Robert" was good and had clever bits, but "I Want To Tell You" was "not up to the Beatles standard." "Got To Get You Into My Life" was "the most vintage Beatles track on the LP" with Paul sounding like Little Richard. As for "Tomorrow Never Knows," he predicted it would be popular in discotheques with "all those crazy sounds!" While Davies thought that *Rubber Soul* had better songs, overall the "balance and recording technique are as good as ever" on the new LP.

Edward Greenfield's August 15 review in The Guardian was titled "Thinking pop." Greenfield described "Tomorrow Never Knows" as: "Musically most original, starting with jungle noises and Eastern-inspired music which merge by montage effect into the sort of electronic noises we associate with beat music." He appreciated the compassion in "Eleanor Rigby" and praised Paul's "understanding of emotion" in "For No One" and "Here, There And Everywhere."

Revolver entered the Record Retailer LP chart at number one on August 11, replacing *The Sound Of Music*. The new Beatles disc charted for 34 weeks, including seven weeks at one (before *The Sound Of Music* reclaimed the top spot) and six weeks at number two. *Revolver* debuted at number one in the August 13 Melody Maker, remaining there for nine weeks before dropping to two for five weeks during its 20-week run. *Revolver* entered the NME album chart on August 12 at number one, where it remained for seven weeks before dropping to two for seven more weeks. NME reported the LP on its singles chart for four weeks with a peak at number 18. Disc charted the album at number one for eight weeks. *Revolver* had advance orders of over 300,000, and sold over a half million copies by year's end.

The Beatles and EMI surprised both the music industry and fans by rush-releasing a double A-side single featuring two songs from Revolver, "Yellow Submarine" and "Eleanor Rigby," on the same day as the album's release. The August 4 Record Retailer called it an unusual move, but noted that "it should at least prevent others getting in on the lovely 'Eleanor Rigby,' featuring Paul's expressive voice." "Yellow Submarine" was described as a children's sing-along. The magazine concluded: "A hit, this LP-extract, of course." In the August 6 Disc, George Harrison explained why the group had broken its rule about not releasing singles from albums. "We just thought we may as well put it out instead of sitting back and seeing dozens of cover versions all getting hits. Well, we might as well cop the hit as well as anybody else." Harrison thought it was a good commercial single and liked both songs. He made light of Ray Davies' comments on the tracks by adding "'Yellow Submarine' will appeal to old-age pensioners and that kind of mob, whereas 'Eleanor Rigby' will probably only appeal to Ray Davies-types." The September 1966 issue (No. 38) of The Beatles Book informed readers that it was first decided that the songs would be the single in America and that the idea of the same UK single was not made until a fortnight (two weeks) before its August 5 release date.

Penny Valentine raved about "Eleanor Rigby" in her "Penny picks the pops" column in the August 6 Disc, calling it an "outstanding beauty" and "the best song the Beatles have written." The words showed "remarkable insight into the life of the lonely," portraying "a desolate and moving picture of utter loneliness." The song was miles above "Michelle" and "Yesterday" in "poetic quality." She was befuddled why both sides are top sides when "Eleanor Rigby" was such a superior song. She assumed that "the nutty 'Yellow Submarine' with John having a fit in the background and Ringo singing his heart out was added to stop us all from jumping off Waterloo Bridge." The August 6 Record Mirror described the disc as "nicely contrasting sides" from the new LP, noting that "Yellow Submarine" was sort of sub-teen slanted. "Eleanor Rigby" was "excellent, marvelously arranged, and possibly the most ultra-commercial of all the tracks on the album." The magazine stated it would be a hit, but added that it would "be interesting to see how big a hit." NME reviewed the disc in its August 5 issue. Derek Johnson acknowledged that either side could be the hit, but had no doubt that "Ringo's 'Submarine' party-piece would catch on big." The song was "enormous fun, so different from the usual Beatles, and a compulsive singalong." "Eleanor Rigby" was a "quality ballad" with lasting value, beautifully sung by Paul backed by baroque-type strings.

The August 6 Melody Maker provided separate reviews for each song. "Yellow Submarine" was described as a "cute" and "highly humourous song sung in a non-highly humourous fashion by Mr. Starr," leaving it to "the rest of the Beatles plus anybody else loafing about in the studio to make all the funny noises behind Ringo, while he's seriously attempting to sing about life inside a yellow submarine." While the "potty song" would be "number one on children's requests for years and years," the magazine envisioned "drunks being thrown out at twenty past eleven bawling out this singalong with the Beatles minor classic." "Eleanor Rigby" was one of the Beatles "finest achievements" that "has all the urgency and finality of any great classic." The reviewer noted: "You feel something tremendous has to be said, and they say it simply and starkly." The song is the "consummation of Beatle sadness and bitterness."

"Yellow Submarine"/"Eleanor Rigby" entered the Record Retailer chart at number eight on August 11. The following week it replaced the Troggs' "With A Girl Like You" at number one, where it remained for four weeks. The Beatles disc spent 13 weeks on the charts, including six in the top five. NME also reported the single for four straight weeks at number one after its debut on August 12 at number two during its ten-week run on the charts. The single entered the Melody Maker chart at number four on August 13 before spending the next three weeks at the top. The disc charted for 12 weeks, including seven in the top five. The record performed similarly in Disc, debuting at number four before topping the charts for three weeks during its 12-week run. The magazine awarded the single a silver disc on September 3, 1966. The BBC also charted the single at number one. The record reportedly had advance orders of 250,000 and sold 455,000 by the end of the year. The sales were respectable considering that many fans who normally would have bought the single chose not to do so because they opted to buy the *Revolver* album instead.

Unlike past years, there would be no new Beatles album and single issued during the 1966 Christmas holiday season. The only Beatles release would be the LP *A Collection Of Beatles Oldies* (see page 190), which contained only one recording new to England, a cover of Larry Williams' song "Bad Boy." But fans could continue listening to *Rubber Soul* and *Revolver*, two remarkable albums that featured well-crafted songs, instruments well beyond the two guitars, bass and drums lineup, and sounds unlike anything previously heard on pop or rock discs. These albums and their concurrent singles truly showcased the incredible songwriting skills and music of Lennon & McCartney & Harrison.

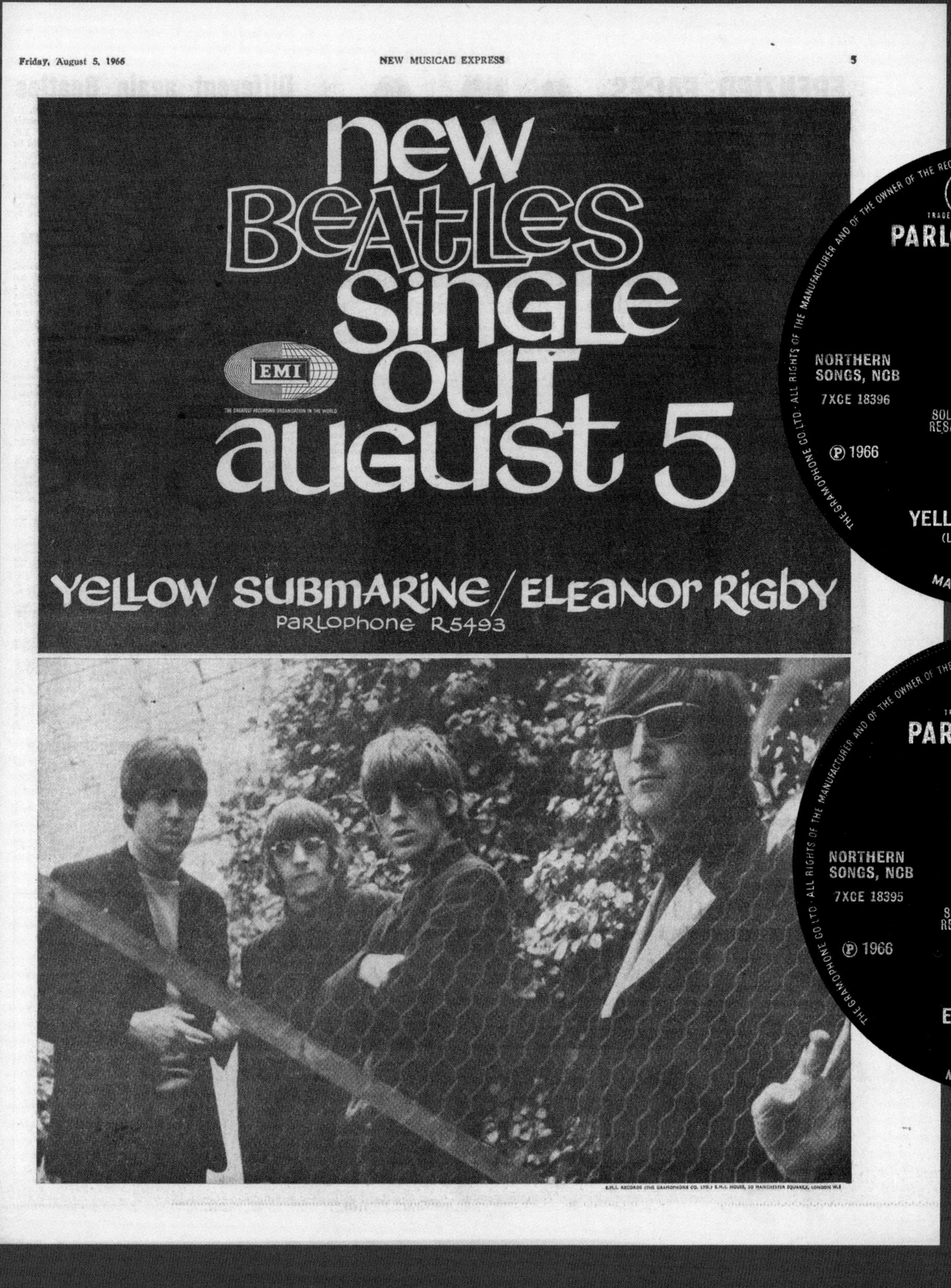

Friday, August 5, 1966 NEW MUSICAL EXPRESS 5

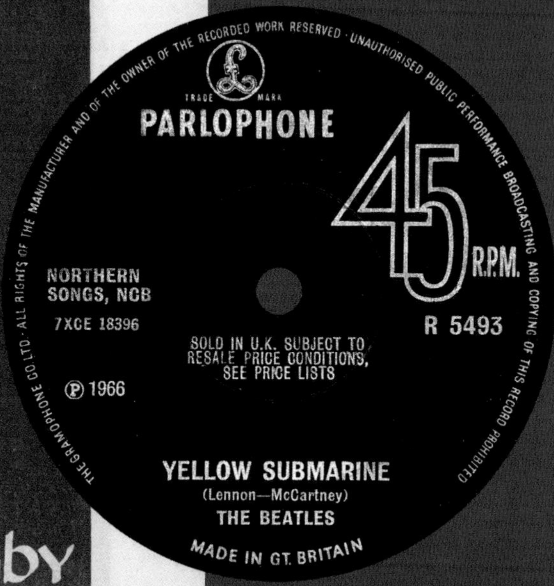

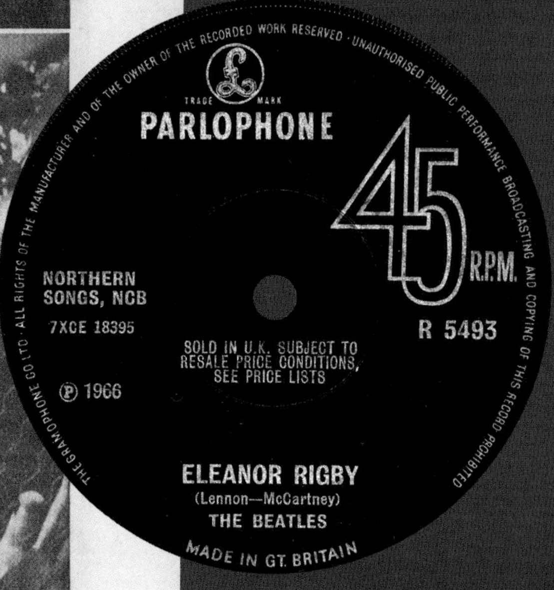

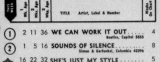

Billboard

HOT 10

★ STAR performer—Sides registering greatest proportionate upward progress this week.

Wks. ago			TITLE Artist, Label & Number	Weeks on Chart
①	2 11	36	WE CAN WORK IT OUT — Beatles, Capitol 5555	4
②	1 5	16	SOUNDS OF SILENCE — Simon & Garfunkel, Columbia 43396	8
★	16 22	32	SHE'S JUST MY STYLE — Gary Lewis & the Playboys, Liberty 55846	5
★	12 13	21	FLOWERS ON THE WALL — Statler Brothers, Columbia 43315	9
★	8 9	12	EBB TIDE — Righteous Brothers, Philles 130	6
⑥	5 1	2	OVER AND OVER — Dave Clark Five, Epic 9863	9
⑦	3 3	3	I GOT YOU (I Feel Good) — James Brown, King 6015	9
⑧	11 16	23	FIVE O'CLOCK WORLD — Vogues, Co & Co 232	7
★	4 2	1	TURN! TURN! TURN! — Byrds, Columbia 43424	12
⑩	18 28	56	DAY TRIPPER — Beatles, Capitol 5555	4
⑪	6 4	4	LET'S HANG ON — 4 Seasons, Philips 40317	14
⑫	7 7	9	FEVER — McCoys, Bang 511	9
⑬	22 33	52	NO MATTER WHAT SHAPE (Your Stomach's In) — T-Bones, Liberty 55836	5
⑭	48 79	—	AS TEARS GO BY — Rolling Stones, London 9808	3
⑮	27 48	—	A MUST TO AVOID — Herman's Hermits, MGM 13437	4
⑯	21 23	30	YOU DIDN'T HAVE TO BE SO NICE — Lovin' Spoonful, Kama Sutra 205	7
⑰	10 6	7	MAKE THE WORLD GO AWAY — Eddy Arnold, RCA Victor 8679	13
⑱	24 29	38	THE DUCK — Jackie Lee, Mirwood 5502	8
⑲	25 30	37	SPANISH EYES — Al Martino, Capitol 5542	6
⑳	9 8	8	ENGLAND SWINGS — Roger Miller, Smash 2010	10
㉑	14 14	19	PUPPET ON A STRING — Elvis Presley, RCA Victor 0650	9
㉒	13 17	17	ONE HAS MY NAME — Barry Young	
㉓	28 38	45	JUST LIKE ME	
㉔	57 80	—		
㉕	29			

㉝	37 42	46	YOU'VE BEEN CHEATIN' — Impressions, ABC-Paramount 10750	8
㉞	20 21	26	THE LITTLE GIRL I ONCE KNEW — Beach Boys, Capitol 5540	7
㉟	40 53	65	LIES — Knickerbockers, Challenge 59321	6
㊱	15 10	6	I CAN NEVER GO HOME ANY MORE — Shangri-Las, Red Bird 043	10
㊲	45 49	63	SANDY — Ronny & the Daytonas, Mala 513	6
㊳	50 57	71	A WELL RESPECTED MAN — Kinks, Reprise 0420	6
㊴	49 50	55	LOOK THROUGH ANY WINDOW — Hollies, Imperial 66134	8
㊵	31 26	14	A TASTE OF HONEY — Herb Alpert & the Tijuana Brass	
㊶	44 54	58	I'VE GOT TO BE SOMEBODY — Billy Joe Royal	
㊷	38 43	44	HARLEM NOCTURNE — Viscounts	
㊸	19 15	11	HANG ON SLOOPY — Ramsey Lewis Trio	
㊹	42 32	35	APPLE OF MY EYE — Roy Head	
㊺	56 61	79	CRYING TIME — Ray Charles, ABC-Paramount	
㊻	60 74	90	UNDER YOUR SPELL AGAIN — Johnny Rivers	
㊼	58 77	—	IT WAS A VERY GOOD YEAR — Frank Sinatra	
㊽	52 58	66	ARE YOU THERE — Dionne Warwick	
㊾	59 76	82	SECOND HAND ROSE — Barbra Streisand, Columbia	
㊿	54 66	76	IT'S GOOD NEWS WEEK — Hedgehoppers Anonymous	
51	55 56	62	A YOUNG GIRL — Noel Harrison	
52	74 90	—	MY LOVE — Petula Clark, Warner Bros.	
53	63 68	84	BROOMSTICK COWBOY — Bobby Goldsboro, United Artists	
54	47 47	57	JEALOUS HEART — Connie Francis, MGM	
55	51 51	54	CRYSTAL CHANDELIER — Vic Dana, Dolton	
56	67 82	—	ZORBA THE GREEK — Herb Alpert & the Tijuana Brass	
	78 95	100	UP TIGHT — Stevie Wonder, Tamla	
			BARBARA ANN — Beach Boys, Capitol	
			...TO A GO-GO — Miracles, Tamla	
			...N'T FIGHT IT — Bobby, Desi & Billy, Reprise	

GARY LEWIS & THE PLAYBOYS

SHE'S JUST MY STYLE

THE BEATLES
WE CAN WORK IT OUT
DAY TRIPPER

5555

Capitol RECORDS

PRINTED IN U.S.A.

THE BYRDS

COLUMBIA
45 RPM
NOT FOR RESALE
RADIO STATION COPY

HOT 100—A TO Z

4-43424
JRZSP 72734

TURN! TURN! TURN!
(To Everything There Is A Season)
—Words from the Book of Ecclesiastes—
Adaptation and music by Pete Seeger
Produced by Terry Melcher

OVER AND OVER
OVER AND OVER

EPIC

Yesterday And Today: An American Perspective of the Beatles Records in 1966

For American Beatles fans, 1966 started like 1965. The Beatles had the number one song, "We Can Work It Out," a Top 10 flip side, "Day Tripper," and the number one album, *Rubber Soul*. The January 8 Billboard showed "We Can Work It Out" at number one in its fourth week on the charts, having dislodged Simon & Garfunkel's "The Sounds Of Silence." Billboard charted the Beatles single for 12 weeks, including three nonconsecutive weeks at the top. Cash Box charted "We Can Work It Out" for 12 weeks, with four straight weeks at number one starting on January 1. Record World charted the single for 13 weeks, including two at the top. Cash Box's Radio Active Chart indicated that by December 1, 1965, 42% of its reporting stations had added the song to their play lists. By December 8, this had grown to 97%. The single was certified gold by the RIAA on January 6, 1966, for sales of one million units.

The Top 10 of the Billboard Hot 100 for January 8 was bookended by the new Beatles single, with "We Can Work It Out" at one and "Day Tripper" at ten. The flip side charted for ten weeks, peaking at number five on January 22. The other music trades also charted "Day Tripper" for ten weeks, with Cash Box showing a peak at number ten and Record World at 12. Cash Box indicated that by December 25, 82% of its reporting stations were playing the song.

The other songs in the Billboard Top 10 for January 8, 1966 showed the variety and excellence of the music of the times. Gary Lewis and the Playboys were at number three with "She's Just My Style," a rocker with Beach Boys-styled harmonies. The Statler Brothers, who were then working with Johnny Cash, had the number four song with "Flowers On The Wall," a country-flavored humorous tale of woe highlighted by "playing solitaire till dawn with a deck of 51" and "watching Capt. Kangaroo." The Top 5 was rounded out with the Righteous Brothers' version of the pop standard "Ebb Tide." The remaining songs in the Top 10 were: "Over And Over," an R&B cover by the Dave Clark Five; "I Got You (I Feel Good)," an R&B classic by James Brown; "Five O'Clock World," an exciting vocal pop number by the Vogues; and "Turn! Turn! Turn!," a folk-rock classic by the Byrds. A time for every purpose, indeed.

The Beatles were also number one in the January 8 Billboard Top LP's chart. *Rubber Soul* reached the top in three weeks, replacing *Whipped Cream & Other Delights* by Herb Alpert's Tijuana Brass (which dropped to three) and holding off the soundtrack to *The Sound Of Music* (at two). The Top 5 was rounded out by the Rolling Stones' *December's Children* and *Going Places* by Herb Alpert and the Tijuana Brass. The remaining albums in the Top 10 were: *The Best Of Herman's Hermits*; *My World* by veteran country singer Eddy Arnold; the Elvis Presley soundtrack album *Harum Scarum*; *My Name Is Barbra, Two* by Barbra Streisand; and the comedy LP *Welcome To The LBJ Ranch!*

Rubber Soul topped the Billboard Top LP's listing for six straight weeks. The magazine charted the album for 59 weeks, including 14 in the Top 10. Cash Box reported *Rubber Soul* at number one for seven straight weeks, with 17 in the Top 10. Record World charted the album at number one for six straight weeks, with 15 in the Top 10. Within nine days of its release *Rubber Soul* was certified gold by the RIAA, with Capitol reporting sales of 1,192,000 units, including 200,000 copies in New York City alone. As of January 10, 1997, the RIAA had certified sales of 6,000,000.

Although Capitol Records demanded that radio stations not play the new Beatles single until November 29, Miami's WFUN jumped the gun by airing "We Can Work It Out" on November 23. Other stations soon followed suit. While both sides got significant air play, U.S. radio stations and their listeners had a slight preference for Paul's infectious "We Can Work It Out" over John's riff-driven rocker "Day Tripper." The Capitol single was officially released on Monday, December 6, although it was most likely in stores the prior Friday. The December 4 Billboard reported a December 1 release date and gave both sides a favorable review: "Two powerhouse rhythm sides featuring the entire group this time. Both have strong dance beat backing." The "entire group this time" language was to contrast the disc with the group's prior American single, "Yesterday," on which Paul (vocal and acoustic guitar) was the only Beatle. The other music trades also reviewed the disc in their December 4 issues. Cash Box observed: "The Fab Four should quickly trip the charts fantastic for the umpteenth time with this new Capitol stand tabbed 'We Can Work It Out.' The cut is a rhythmic, medium-paced affair about a determined fella who is sure that he can solve his romantic problems. 'Day Tripper' is a hard-pounding, raunchy ode all about a gal who is somewhat of a tease." Record World predicted: "The Beatles' new one will fascinate teens with its change of pace 4/4-3/4 timing and potent lyric."

Record World was the first of the music trade magazines to review the Beatles new album, noting in its December 11 issue that the group's "new Capitol package is called 'Rubber Soul,' which seems to indicate that they're singing soul music with a bounce." The magazine found the tunes "even more inventive than usual and the George Martin arrangements, using sitar, fuzz bass and organ, are tops. Past-mastery." A week later the others had their say. The December 18 Billboard proclaimed that the Beatles had "done it again with this No. 1 chart contender." *Rubber Soul* was called "one of their best programmed LP's," in which listeners would hear the group "run the gantlet from swingers to folk-rock to the beautiful solo ballads of Paul on 'Michelle' and John on 'Girl.'" After observing that the Beatles were "currently one of the most successful groups to hit the American music market, both in singles and album product," Cash Box stated: "The grand-daddies of all the mop-tops, this British foursome has concocted one of their most interesting and potent albums to date." Highlights included "You Won't See Me," "Girl" and George Harrison's "Think For Yourself." Retailers were advised: "Stand back and watch it go."

American DJs quickly gave one of the new album's tracks substantial air play, with Cash Box indicating that by January 1, 76% of its reporting stations were playing "Michelle—(From Rubber Soul LP)—Beatles." Boston's WMEX listed three songs tied for number one on its December 17, 24 and 31 charts: "We Can Work It Out"/"Day Tripper"/"Michelle." WAAB in neighboring Worcester listed its top three songs for December 19 as "Michelle," "We Can Work It Out" and "Day Tripper" in that order. WHOT in Youngstown, Ohio had the trio of Beatles songs tied at one on January 10, 1966. "Michelle" topped the KRUX Phoenix chart on January 7. WPTR in Albany listed "Michelle" at number one on January 7, with "Nowhere Man" from the U.K. *Rubber Soul* at 14. In Denver, KBTR listed four songs at number one on its December 17 and 24 surveys: "Michelle" and "Girl" (requests) and both sides of the new Beatles single. Syracuse's WOLF had "Michelle" at number one on its charts for January 1 and 8, with "Girl" at four and six for the two weeks. KJR in Seattle debuted "Michelle" at number two behind both sides of the group's single on its survey for January 7. After remaining there for an additional week, "Michelle" spent its first of two straight weeks at the top on January 21. The station also charted "Norwegian Wood" for six weeks, with a peak at five. Although KJR listed "The Beatles" as the artist for "Michelle" in its earlier charts, beginning January 21, the artist was shown as "Beatles & Others," acknowledging requests, airplay and sales for cover versions of the song by other recording artists.

The December 25 Record World showed the labels to five cover versions of "Michelle" on its front cover under the banner "Sleepers of the Week." The magazine explained: "Because deejays pulled 'Michelle' out of the Beatles *Rubber Soul* album, but the Beatles refused to do it themselves, five artists and companies have seized the opportunity to supply the suddenly created single demand for the soothing and stupendous ditty." Record World noted that "Buyers and programmers will buy and program according to the bag they prefer most; but, one thing for sure, they'll buy and program." The most successful was the George Martin-produced David & Jonathan recording, which peaked at 18 in Billboard and Cash Box and at 12 in Record World. Bud Shank's moody instrumental version of the song peaked at 65 in Billboard, 86 in Cash Box and 74 in Record World. The jazz arrangement of "Michelle" by Billy Vaughn, His Orchestra & Chorus also charted, peaking at 77 in Billboard, 61 in Cash Box and 52 in Record World. The Spokesmen's recording charted at 106 in Billboard, 116 in Record World and 124 in Cash Box. The Les Baxter single was the only one that failed to make any chart impact. Cash Box reported the following percentages of reporting stations adding the cover versions: David & Jonathan (91%); Billy Vaughn (55%); and Bud Shank (23%).

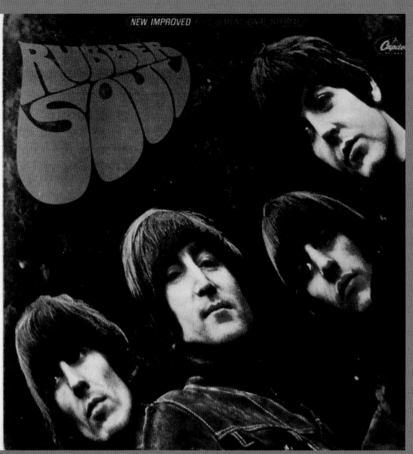

RUBBER SOUL

JOHN LENNON, PAUL McCARTNEY, GEORGE HARRISON and RINGO STARR

T-2442
(T-X-1-2442) 1

1. I'VE JUST SEEN A FACE (BMI-2:04)
(John Lennon-Paul McCartney)
2. NORWEGIAN WOOD
(This Bird Has Flown) (BMI-2:00)
(John Lennon-Paul McCartney)
3. YOU WON'T SEE ME (BMI-3:19)
(John Lennon-Paul McCartney)
4. THINK FOR YOURSELF (BMI-2:16)
(George Harrison)
5. THE WORD (BMI-2:42)
(John Lennon-Paul McCartney)
6. MICHELLE (BMI-2:42)
(John Lennon-Paul McCartney)

MFD. BY CAPITOL RECORDS, INC. U.S.A. T.M. • MARCA REG. • U.S. PAT. NO. 2,631,859

RUBBER SOUL

JOHN LENNON, PAUL McCARTNEY, GEORGE HARRISON and RINGO STARR

T-2442
(T-X-2-2442) 2

1. IT'S ONLY LOVE (BMI-1:53)
(John Lennon-Paul McCartney)
2. GIRL (BMI-2:26)
(John Lennon-Paul McCartney)
3. I'M LOOKING THROUGH YOU (BMI-2:20)
(John Lennon-Paul McCartney)
4. IN MY LIFE (BMI-2:23)
(John Lennon-Paul McCartney)
5. WAIT (BMI-2:13)
(John Lennon-Paul McCartney)
6. RUN FOR YOUR LIFE (BMI-2:21)
(John Lennon-Paul McCartney)

MFD. BY CAPITOL RECORDS, INC. U.S.A. T.M. • MARCA REG. • U.S. PAT. NO. 2,631,859

Although the January 1, 1966 Beat magazine featured an article on the British *Rubber Soul*, very few Americans at the time knew that the Capitol version of the *Rubber Soul* album differed from its U.K. counterpart. In programming the record, Capitol went with the American standard of 12 songs rather than the British norm of 14 tracks. The company had a pair of songs from the British *Help!* LP that had yet to be released in America: "I've Just Seen A Face" and "It's Only Love." Capitol added these songs to the program and dropped four songs from the Parlophone *Rubber Soul* LP: "Nowhere Man," "What Goes On," "Drive My Car" and "If I Needed Someone." The overall quality of the songs led Capitol to program the record without a hit single, a first for a Capitol Beatles album.

The American *Rubber Soul* opens with "I've Just Seen A Face," with its intricate acoustic guitar intro grabbing the listener's attention. John's "Norwegian Wood (This Bird Has Flown)" features interesting lyrics, John on acoustic guitar and George on 12-string acoustic guitar and overdubbed sitar. "You Won't See Me" is a return to the girl group sound, at least as to its "la-la-la" backing vocals. It features Paul on lead vocals and piano. George carries the lead vocal on his composition "Think For Yourself," which is followed by John, Paul and George spreading "The Word" of love. Side One closes with Paul's ballad "Michelle." As with many of the songs on the album, it is dominated by acoustic guitars, this time with Paul on six-string, George on 12-string and John on nylon-string. Side Two opens with John's "It's Only Love," once again featuring acoustic guitar. "Girl" is another acoustic guitar song with John on lead vocal. It features a Greek-influenced instrumental passage and naughty "tit, tit, tit, tit" backing vocals. Paul's bitter love song, "I'm Looking Through You," also features acoustic guitar. John's ballad, "In My Life," is one of the album's highlights with its introspective lyrics and baroque-influenced piano solo played by George Martin. Although "Wait" was recorded during the *Help!* sessions, it did not appear on the album. The track was given overdubs and added to the *Rubber Soul* line-up. The album closes with "Run For Your Life," featuring John on lead vocal and acoustic guitar.

While not exactly what the Beatles and George Martin had in mind, Capitol's version of *Rubber Soul* is still a great album that influenced many American artists, including Brian Wilson of the Beach Boys, to strive for even greater studio achievements. Many people actually prefer the Capitol version of the album over the British LP. This is because the American record has more acoustic and less rock songs than the British disc, giving it a cohesive folk-rock sound.

The December 11, 1965 edition of KRLA Beat featured the Capitol version of *Rubber Soul* on its cover; however, there was nary a word about the new album found inside. It wasn't until the magazine's January 1, 1966 issue that the album got reviewed in Eden's DISCussion column. Nikki Wine (her real name) assured readers that the Beatles had "produced another unbelievably sensational album" and that "once again they're setting trends in this world of pop." But rather than writing about the 12-song Capitol version of the album that nearly all Americans were getting familiar with, Wine instead chose to cover the 14-track British LP with a "little review of the whole Elpee."

"Drive My Car" was described by her as a medium-tempo song sung by Paul and John, with "Paul cutting up on the piano in the background." "Norwegian Wood" was a "sort of John Lennon-type folk, with the inimitable John-John lead vocalizing" and George on sitar. The song's second title, "This Bird Has Flown," caused her to incorrectly speculate that the song was an adaptation. She called "You Won't See Me" one of the disc's best, with a great arrangement and blending of melodies. "Nowhere Man" was "melodic and nice to listen to," with John, Paul and George combining their "golden tones" on the tune. George's "Think For Yourself" had a "good, strong, driving beat" with a wonderful fuzz-bass sound effect by Paul. "The Word" was a great song and one of her favorites, with the "harmonies and special tune-and-word blendings...absolutely out of sight!!" "Michelle" was a "beautiful ballad" and "tender love song, sung as only Paul could sing it."

Wine thought the Side Two opener, "What Goes On," would surprise most Americans with Ringo singing in his "favorite Country and Western sort of style." She noted that Ringo assisted John and Paul in writing the song, which sounded "pretty good." John's "Girl" was a "sad and wistful ballad" with an atmospheric background and a "good deal of feeling coming through." "I'm Looking Through You" was described as a "really swingin' cut" belted out by Paul. The rocker was "wonderful fun" and had an "almost bluesy sound." "In My Life" had "philosophical sounds," good harmony and a "strong over-all feeling.""Wait" was described as a "rough-edged up-tempo tune" with excellent guitar and tambourine. George's "If I Needed Someone" had a good sound and John's "Run For Your Life" was "one of the most energetic and exciting tracks on the album." Wine concluded her review with: "Another Beatle album has been released, so what? SO...WOWWWWWWWWWW!" Or as Capitol proclaimed, "JUST GROOVY LISTENING!"

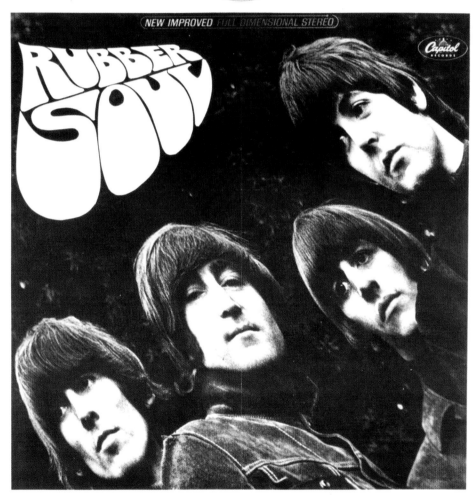

By mid-February 1966, "We Can Work It Out" began falling out of the Top 10. To fill the void and its cash coffers, Capitol issued a new Beatles single on February 15. The record paired two of the tracks withheld from the U.S. version of *Rubber Soul*, "Nowhere Man" and "What Goes On." Capitol's holding back "Nowhere Man" proved to be a shrewd move. Although it would have fit perfectly on the acoustic-dominated American version of *Rubber Soul*, the song had all the markings of a hit single: clever lyrics, a catchy melody, tight harmonies and a bright treble sound that would burst through radio speakers. Fans took notice, quickly flocking to stores to buy the new single, which sold 744,000 copies within eight days of its release. The initial labels printed for the single failed to give Ringo co-songwriter's credit for "What Goes On." Later labels correctly credited the song to "Lennon-McCartney-Starkey."

"Nowhere Man" debuted in the Billboard Hot 100 at number 25 on March 5. It worked its way up to number three on March 26 during its nine-week run, but could not get past SSgt. Barry Sadler's "The Ballad Of The Green Berets" and the Rolling Stones' "19th Nervous Breakdown." The song performed better in the other trades. Cash Box charted the song for nine weeks, with a peak at number two. Record World listed the song for ten weeks, including two weeks at number one. "What Goes On" was charted by Billboard for two weeks, peaking at 81. Record World charted the B-side for one week at 99. Cash Box reported that by February 23 "Nowhere Man" had been added by 68% of its reporting stations and "What Goes On" by 31%. The single was certified gold by the RIAA on April 1, 1966.

The trade magazines reviewed the new Beatles disc in their February 26 issues. Billboard described the songs as "two powerhouse rhythm numbers to fast follow up 'We Can Work It Out' and 'Day Tripper.'" The magazine mistakenly listed "What Goes On" as the A-side, noting that it "features a Ringo solo...a first." This was also a mistake as Ringo had sung solo on two previous Capitol singles, "Matchbox" and "Act Naturally." Cash Box predicted that the Fab Four's latest should "zip them up the charts with their usual supersonic speed." "Nowhere Man" was characterized as "an easy-going rhythmic ode all about a real myopic fella who has a great deal to learn." The B-side was a "twangy, medium-paced country-ish tearjerker." Record World described "Nowhere Man" as a "meaningful song about what happens to a fellow afraid to be himself." The flip was "nice, too." Noting that the "boys are still infallible hitmakers," the magazine stated that "Nowhere Man" was "going somewhere" (presumably to the top of the charts).

NOWHERE MAN
(John Lennon-Paul McCartney)

Capitol
RECORDS

Maclen
Music, Inc.
BMI-2:40
5587
(45-X45406)
Recorded
in England

THE BEATLES

MFD. BY CAPITOL RECORDS, INC., U.S.A. • T.M. Capitol MARCA REG.

WHAT GOES ON
(Lennon-McCartney-Starkey)

Capitol
RECORDS

Maclen
Music, Inc.
BMI-2:44
5587
(45-X45407)
Recorded
in England

THE BEATLES

MFD. BY CAPITOL RECORDS, INC., U.S.A. • T.M. Capitol MARCA REG.

NOWHERE MAN
b/w What Goes On

CAPITOL RECORDS
5587

Capitol released its second Beatles single of 1966 on May 30. The disc, pairing Paul's riff-driven harmonic rocker "Paperback Writer" with John's heavy-sounding "Rain," was the same as the Parlophone single later issued on June 10. In contrast to previous efforts, neither song was about love, with Paul singing about an aspiring author on the A-side. Although the song's story line and sound were a drastic departure from the group's previous efforts, stations quickly played the disc, with Cash Box reporting that by May 25 "Paperback Writer" had been added by 30% of its reporting stations and "Rain" by 27%. By June 1 this had grown to 90% for the A-side and 59% for the B-side. By June 8 "Rain" was being played by 89% of the stations. "Paperback Writer" entered the Billboard Hot 100 at number 28 on June 11, 1966. Two weeks later, on June 25, it reached the top, passing Frank Sinatra's "Strangers In The Night" and the Rolling Stones' "Paint It Black." Other contemporary hits included the Cyrkle's recording of Paul Simon's "Red Rubber Ball" and the garage band classics "Hanky Panky" by Tommy James & the Shondells and "Wild Thing" by the Troggs. Cash Box also charted "Paperback Writer" for ten weeks, with five weeks in the Top 5 and two weeks at number one. Record World reported the song for 11 weeks, including one week at the top.

The single's equally innovative B-side, "Rain," also received heavy air play and chart action, peaking at number 23 during its seven weeks in the Billboard Hot 100. Cash Box charted the song for five weeks, with a peak at 31. Record World reported "Rain" for five weeks, with a high of 28. With sales of over 750,000 units in its first week, the disc quickly became the tenth Capitol Beatles single certified gold by the RIAA on July 14, 1966.

The trades reviewed the new Beatles single in their June 4 issues. Billboard proclaimed: "The boys have two exciting sides to replace their 'Nowhere Man' smash." The A-side was described as an "up-tempo dance number," while the flip was a "well balanced lyric ballad." Cash Box observed that the Fab Four would have no trouble "adding another blockbuster to their long list of super-smashes." "Paperback Writer" was described as a "rhythmic, pulsating ode with an infectious repeating riff all about the creative urge." "Rain" was called a "soulful, medium-paced, effectively-rendered blueser." Record World told retailers that the rush was on for the new Beatles cut, a fast one in which the lads "try out interesting electronic effects to great effect." Color clips of the Beatles miming "Paperback Writer" and "Rain" at Abbey Road Studios were shown on the June 5 Ed Sullivan Show (see page 230).

Heading into the summer of 1966, Capitol continued its quest for dollars from eager Beatles fans by releasing a new album of Fab Four tunes while "Paperback Writer" was moving up the charts. But unlike its predecessor, *Rubber Soul*, which contained 12 songs never before available in the U.S.A., *Yesterday And Today* contained only five songs new to America. In compiling the 11-track LP, Capitol selected six songs that had been issued on Capitol singles, but had not been on any U.S. album: "Yesterday," "Act Naturally," "We Can Work It Out," "Day Tripper," "Nowhere Man" and "What Goes On." The company had two songs from the British *Rubber Soul* that had yet to be issued in America, "Drive My Car" and "If I Needed Someone." To get to 11 tracks, Capitol requested that EMI provide three recordings from the group's next LP due for release in August. The album was titled *Yesterday And Today* in recognition of the hit single "Yesterday" and the other older tracks, as well as the new songs representing the Beatles sounds of today.

Copies of the new LP were available for sale in a very limited number of stores on Friday, June 10, a few days ahead of the album's scheduled release on June 15. However, all copies of *Yesterday And Today* were quickly removed from record bins and racks when Capitol recalled the album due to the overwhelmingly negative response to its cover, which depicted the Beatles in white butcher smocks surrounded by slabs of raw meat and decapitated baby dolls. Capitol quickly came up with an alternate cover design. The company's employees worked at a frenzied pace to destroy or paste over the offensive covers and insert the vinyl discs into covers showing the group hanging around a steamer trunk. By June 21, copies of the album in its new Trunk Cover began appearing in stores. Although many fans had heard or read about the provocative Butcher Cover, others were oblivious to the controversy. The story behind both covers can be found in the following chapter on the Butcher and Trunk Covers starting on page 65.

Yesterday And Today entered the Billboard Top LP's chart at number 120 on July 9, 1966. It reached the top in its fourth week on July 30, replacing Frank Sinatra's *Strangers In The Night* and holding off *Aftermath* by the Rolling Stones. After five weeks at the top, the album dropped to number two behind *What Now My Love* by Herb Alpert & the Tijuana Brass. Billboard charted the Beatles album for 31 weeks, including nine in the Top 10. Cash Box charted the album for 16 weeks, including two weeks at one, four weeks at two and ten weeks in the Top 10. Record World reported the album 19 weeks, including three weeks at one, four weeks at two and ten weeks in the Top 10.

BUY BEATLES HERE!

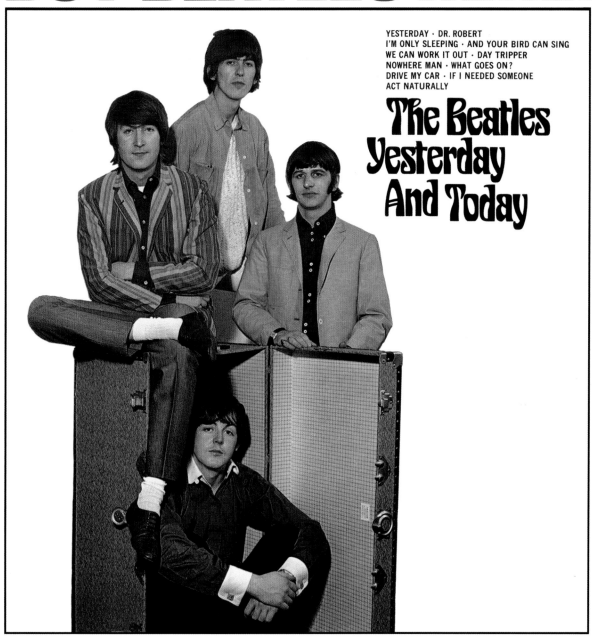

YESTERDAY · DR. ROBERT
I'M ONLY SLEEPING · AND YOUR BIRD CAN SING
WE CAN WORK IT OUT · DAY TRIPPER
NOWHERE MAN · WHAT GOES ON?
DRIVE MY CAR · IF I NEEDED SOMEONE
ACT NATURALLY

The Beatles Yesterday And Today

Once again Record World was the first trade to review the new Beatles album. Its June 25 issue reported that the disc had a number of recent hits plus "some rousing new ones like 'Drive My Car.'" The other magazines ran their reviews a week later. The July 2 Billboard alerted retailers of the "hot album release from the Beatles" that included big singles hits. The five new cuts all had "singles potential with the strongest sounds coming from 'Drive My Car' and 'And Your Bird Can Sing.'" Cash Box raved that "the Fab Four outdo themselves with this stunning set" of hit singles and a "selection of top notch new numbers" including "Dr. Robert" and "Drive My Car." The magazine concluded the "top of the charts is the place for this one."

Yesterday And Today opens with one of the new selections, "Drive My Car." The song is a clever attention-grabbing rocker that had served as the lead track on the British *Rubber Soul*. A soulful-sounding Paul shares the lead vocals with John. Next up is the first of the songs that would appear on the British *Revolver* LP, John's "I'm Only Sleeping," which features backwards guitar parts played by George. This is followed by "Nowhere Man," with its beautiful harmonies and introspective lyrics. John is featured again on another track slated for *Revolver*, "Dr. Robert." The guitar-driven rocker is about a doctor who freely gives his patients pills and shots to keep them high. Side One ends with both sides of the group's September 1965 single featuring Paul's solo ballad, "Yesterday," and "Act Naturally," with Ringo on lead vocals. The second side gets off to a rousing start with the last of the *Revolver* preview songs, John's "And Your Bird Can Sing." The song's most striking feature is its harmonic electric guitar runs. "If I Needed Someone" is the last of the new songs. The Harrison composition features George on his Rickenbacker 12-string electric guitar. The album's last three tracks were previously issued on Capitol singles. Paul's "We Can Work It Out" provides both lyrical and musical counterparts by Paul and John, while "What Goes On" is Ringo's second lead vocal on the disc. The album closes on a high note with "Day Tripper," one of the group's more effective riff-driven rockers.

Yesterday And Today was programmed by Bill Miller, who took over Dave Dexter's role of compiling the Beatles American releases. Although the LP is a pieces-parts collection of Beatles songs, it is effectively programmed, pulling tracks from three British albums (*Help!*, *Rubber Soul* and *Revolver*). For American fans, the disc delivered five new numbers and six songs from singles, four of which were huge hits. All in all, a very solid and enjoyable album.

SCHOOL'S OUT!

NEW IMPROVED FULL DIMENSIONAL STEREO

YESTERDAY - DR. ROBERT
I'M ONLY SLEEPING - AND YOUR BIRD CAN SING
WE CAN WORK IT OUT - DAY TRIPPER
NOWHERE MAN - WHAT GOES ON?
DRIVE MY CAR - IF I NEEDED SOMEONE
ACT NATURALLY

The Beatles
Yesterday
And Today

GET READY!

"YESTERDAY"...AND TODAY

THE BEATLES
(Recorded in England)

T-2553
(T-X-1-2553)

1. DRIVE MY CAR (BMI-2:25)
   (John Lennon-Paul McCartney)
2. I'M ONLY SLEEPING (BMI-2:58)
   (John Lennon-Paul McCartney)
3. NOWHERE MAN (BMI-2:40)
   (John Lennon-Paul McCartney)
4. DR. ROBERT (BMI-2:14)
   (John Lennon-Paul McCartney)
5. YESTERDAY (BMI-2:04)
   (John Lennon-Paul McCartney)
6. ACT NATURALLY (BMI-2:27)
   (John Russell-Voni Morrison)

"YESTERDAY"...AND TODAY

THE BEATLES
(Recorded in England)

T-2553
(T-X-2-2553) 2

1. AND YOUR BIRD CAN SING (BMI-2:02)
   (John Lennon-Paul McCartney)
2. IF I NEEDED SOMEONE (BMI-2:19)
   (George Harrison)
3. WE CAN WORK IT OUT (BMI-2:10)
   (John Lennon-Paul McCartney)
4. WHAT GOES ON? (BMI-2:44)
   (Lennon-McCartney-Starkey)
5. DAY TRIPPER (BMI-2:47)
   (John Lennon-Paul McCartney)

The Beatles next single, officially released on August 8, contained two songs from the group's new *Revolver* album. The top side, "Yellow Submarine," is a joy-filled sing-along featuring Ringo on lead vocal aided and abetted by his bandmates and others on the infectious chorus, sound effects, brass instruments and John's vocal shenanigans, while "Eleanor Rigby" is a stirring story of loneliness and isolation beautifully sung by Paul over a strident string arrangement. Cash Box reported that by August 3, 40% of its reporting stations were playing "Yellow Submarine." By August 10 this had grown to 97% with 44% of the stations adding "Eleanor Rigby." The B-side continued to gain spins and by the next week it was being played by 62% of the stations. By August 24 this had grown to 92%.

"Yellow Submarine" began its nine-week run in the Billboard Hot 100 at number 52 on August 20, 1966. The following week it moved up to number eight. Three weeks later, on September 17, it moved past Donovan's "Sunshine Superman" to the second spot, but could not knock the Supremes' "You Can't Hurry Love" from the top of the charts. The other trade magazines disagreed with Billboard's assessment. Cash Box charted the song for ten weeks, including five in the Top 5 and one at number one. Record World also charted the song for ten weeks with one week at number one. The song's failure to top the Billboard charts was probably due to the splitting of consideration between "Yellow Submarine" and its flip side, "Eleanor Rigby," which spent eight weeks in the Billboard Hot 100, peaking at number 11. Cash Box charted "Eleanor Rigby" for eight weeks, with a peak at number 12. Record World reported the song for nine weeks, with peak of 16. The September 24 Billboard reported sales of 1,200,000 during its first four weeks on the market. The single was certified gold by the RIAA on September 12, 1966.

The trades reviewed the new disc in their August 13 issues. Billboard observed: "With Ringo taking the lead, and everything in the arrangement but the kitchen sink, the group has their most unusual easy rocker to date." The flip side was called "an offbeat baroque ballad with equal potential for the No. 1 spot." Cash Box predicted that the Beatles would reach "that special spot with this unique outing." The A-side is a "thumping, happy go lucky, special effects filled highly improbable tale of joyous going on beneath the sea." The flip side is a "powerfully arranged, haunting story of sorrow and frustration." Record World stated: "The Beatles are out for a whacking good time on the jolly nonsense song sparked by all sorts of sideshow sounds. 'Yellow Submarine' is top drawer."

YELLOW SUBMARINE

(John Lennon-Paul McCartney)

Capitol RECORDS

Maclen Music, Inc. BMI-2:40
5715
(45-X45619)
Produced in England by George Martin

THE BEATLES

MFD. BY CAPITOL RECORDS, INC., U.S.A. • T.M. Capitol MARCA REG.

ELEANOR RIGBY

(John Lennon-Paul McCartney)

Capitol RECORDS

Maclen Music, Inc. BMI-2:11
5715
(45-X45616)
Produced in England by George Martin

THE BEATLES

MFD. BY CAPITOL RECORDS, INC. U.S.A. • T.M. Capitol MARCA REG.

b/w Eleanor Rigby

 Capitol RECORDS **5715**

The single performed well despite a ban by several American radio stations, primarily in the south, on playing Beatles records. The ban was the result of the controversy over John's remark that the Beatles were more popular than Jesus. Most radio stations continued playing the Beatles because failure to do so would be "ratings suicide." Miami's WFUN made its decision to play records by the Beatles based "solely on the group's proved musical talent."

The album that spawned the single, *Revolver*, was officially issued on August 8, less than two months after Capitol's *Yesterday And Today* hit the stores. While the close proximity in releases may have weakened ongoing sales of the earlier LP, *Revolver* was not adversely affected, entering the Billboard Top LP's chart with a bang at number 45 on September 3. The next week it shot to the top, knocking out *What Now My Love* by Herb Alpert & the Tijuana Brass and holding off the *Dr. Zhivago* soundtrack LP. After six weeks at the top, it was replaced by *Supremes A' Go-Go*. Billboard charted *Revolver* for 77 weeks, including nine in the Top 5 and 14 in the Top 10. Cash Box reported *Revolver* at number one for eight straight weeks from September 3 through October 22, before dropping it to two behind the Monkees' self-titled debut LP. The magazine charted the Beatles disc for 24 weeks, including 14 in the Top 10. Record World also reported the album at number one for the same eight weeks. The magazine charted the disc for 31 weeks, including 11 in the Top 10. The RIAA certified sales of five million units as of July 25, 2000.

Cash Box was the first music industry magazine to review *Revolver*, calling it a "power-packed, groovy release by the four young men from Liverpool" in its August 13 edition. The disc was "another fantastic sales item" featuring their new single "enhanced by very inventive black and white cover art." The magazine noted that Harrison wrote three songs and that "sitar is used to advantage on 'Love To You [sic].'" The others ran reviews in their August 20 issues. Billboard called the album "another sure-fire sales winner, timed perfectly with their U.S. concert tour." In addition to the single, the collection contains "well done and unusual performances such as George's solo, 'Love You Too [sic],' the plaintive ballad 'Here, There And Everywhere,' which features Paul, and John's raucous, off-beat number, 'Tomorrow Never Knows.'" Record World described the new Beatles album as "stunning," noting that it was released "in the midst of controversy and their American tour." It contained the single along with "other diverse sounds," and was "intriguingly packaged in stark black and white and intriguingly titled 'Revolver.'"

stereo

REVOLVER

(S)T 2576 Capitol RECORDS

including and Eleanor Rigby

The Capitol version of *Revolver* was identical to its British counterpart except for one significant difference. The Capitol album has 11 tracks while the British disc has 14. This was due to Capitol placing three songs from the *Revolver* sessions on its *Yesterday And Today* LP, knowing it could get away with having only 11 tracks on its release. The "Capitolization" of *Revolver* has the unfortunate effect of shifting the creative balance of power within the group. On the British LP, John and Paul each sing lead on five songs. George has three of his compositions on the album, while Ringo is given the spotlight for his usual one track. On the American release, John is under-represented as all three of the songs pulled from *Revolver* were sung by him, leaving John with only two songs on the U.S. album.

George's emergence as a songwriter is evident from the start, with the album opening with his rocking condemnation of the "Taxman." Next up is Paul's "Eleanor Rigby," with its haunting melody and theme sung over a string instrumental backing. This is followed by George's full-throttle excursion into Indian music, "Love You To." Paul's "Here, There And Everywhere" is a return to more familiar territory with its sentimental lyrics and beautiful moving harmonies. The side closes with the sing-along single, "Yellow Submarine," and John's hard-rocking "She Said She Said."

Side Two opens with Paul's piano-driven upbeat love song, "Good Day Sunshine." He is also the lead singer for his song of lost love, "For No One." George returns with his final composition, "I Want To Tell You," with its "I've got time" fade-out ending leading into Paul's horn-driven "Got To Get You Into My Life." The album closes with John's remarkable "Tomorrow Never Knows," mixing intriguing lyrics with a hypnotic tribal beat and sound effects. Even without the three songs found on the British disc, it is an impressive collection of well-recorded songs.

Tony Barrow wrote about *Revolver* in the August 13 KRLA Beat. He warned that "some younger Beatle people will find at least three or four of these recordings too complicated, too intelligent (musically) and/or too weird," but predicted that as it also has some great straightforward songs, nobody would likely be disappointed with the album. KRLA would soon chart three of LP's non-single tracks in its Top 40 Requests chart: "Here, There And Everywhere" (#1 on 9/24/1966); "Got To Get You Into My Life" (#3 on 9/24/1966); and "Good Day Sunshine" (#10 on 10/8/1966).

KRLA Beat reviewed *Revolver* in its September 10 issue. The magazine pointed out that in recent months, a number of albums by other artists had been labeled a "*Rubber Soul* in its field," indicating a high achievement. It lamented that there had been relatively few cries of *Revolver* being called a "second *Rubber Soul*" despite being a "musical creation of exceptional excellence...of which the Beatles should be justifiably proud." Even with several of its songs quickly becoming contemporary standards, there was an "amazing absence of fanfare and discussion." [True to this point, Newsweek ran an article on the Beatles in its August 22, 1966 issue that discussed the group's upcoming tour, the Jesus controversy, the "Yellow Submarine" single and John's apology, but failed to mention the *Revolver* LP.]

The review then went through the album's songs. "Taxman" was described as "one of the best, most concise satirical comments on the British society and current tax situation." "Eleanor Rigby" was praised for its haunting melody, beautiful string arrangement and its unforgettable "universal description of the countless thousands of 'lonely people.'" The magazine was frustrated that George's "Love You To" ("well done and musically valid"), "Here, There And Everywhere" ("fantastic vocal arrangement from Paul" and "one of the most beautiful love songs...in many, many years") and "I Want To Tell You" ("unusual, newly-melodic and interesting") were receiving very little comment.

"Yellow Submarine" was referred to as "the satirical 'children's song' that *isn't*." "For No One" was recognized as a "fantastically beautiful and haunting love song, musically sighed as only Paul can." The album's closing track, "Tomorrow Never Knows," was described as a "weird and polished electronic creation from John Lennon." KRLA Beat concluded that "*Revolver* has fired a shot which will be heard around the globe wherever people really care about the music they are listening to" and predicted that "the Beatles won't soon be forgotten either."

The August 12, 1966, WMCA edition of Go magazine bragged that WMCA was the first station in the world to play tracks from the Beatles new *Revolver* album. This air play apparently began on or about August 1, over a week before the record's official U.S. release date of August 8. Within 24 hours, the station received a call from attorneys representing the music publisher demanding that it cease air play. After lengthy telephone calls with Beatles management, the station finally got clearance to play the tracks at 6:11 p.m. on Friday, August 5. DJ Dandy Dan claimed: "The Beatles knew that we didn't want to disappoint our Beatle-fan listeners. So they gave us a full okay."

The station's 4-page insert in Go also provided superficial reviews of the album's 11 tracks, primarily drawing information from the song credits on the album's back cover. "Here, There And Everywhere," "Good Day Sunshine" and "For No One" were all winners. "Love You To" was well performed and "likely to influence the group." "Got To Get You Into My Life" was "vintage Beatles" with Paul sounding like Little Richard over the track's jazz backing. Oddly, WMCA described "Tomorrow Never Knows" as a "sure smash hit for dancers." The station's verdict was that the "recording techniques, the songs and the music are as good as ever." Readers and listeners no doubt agreed.

Richard Goldstein, writing in the August 25 Village Voice, opened with words of high praise: "*Revolver* is a revolutionary record, as important to the expansion of pop territory as was *Rubber Soul*." While *Rubber Soul* was "an important advance," *Revolver* is "the great leap forward." Goldstein advised: "Hear it once and you know it's important. Hear it twice, it makes sense. Third time around it's fun. Fourth time, it's subtle. On the fifth hearing, *Revolver* becomes profound." Just as *Rubber Soul* incorporated baroque progression and Oriental instrumentation, *Revolver* did the same for electronic music with the Beatles "reaching a super-receptive audience with electronic soul."

For Goldstein, the album's key track is "Tomorrow Never Knows," whose overall effect is a "suspension of musical reality" with its "foghorn-like organ chords" and sounds of "birdlike screeching" overshadowing John's voice, which "sounds distant and Godlike." The song "transcends almost everything in what was once called pop music. The boundaries will now have to be renegotiated." He also writes highly of: "Love You To" (a "functioning raga with a natural beat and an engaging vocal"); "Eleanor Rigby" (metaphysical and an "orchestrated ballad about the agony of loneliness"); "Yellow Submarine" ("whimsical and childlike"); "For No One" ("poignant"); and "Taxman" ("political cheek"). While the LP has some mediocre material, there is a "mystique forming around *Revolver.*" Goldstein predicts "we will view this album in retrospect as a key work in the development of rock 'n' roll into an artistic pursuit."

Crawdaddy!, started in February 1966 as a mimeographed magazine of rock and roll criticism, reviewed *Revolver* in its fifth issue dated September 1966. The review was written by Paul Williams, who founded the magazine while a student at Swarthmore College. Williams called *Revolver* "a good album," but thought that *Rubber Soul* was "much, much better." His main criticism of *Revolver* was that it wasn't integrated, that it didn't work the way *Rubber Soul* did "as a somehow unified listening experience in which each song blends into the next without anything feeling out of place." This elusive quality had to do with "layout and balance," not just similarity of material. His disappointment in *Revolver* was that it wasn't "another *Rubber Soul*," which he acknowledged was praise for *Rubber Soul* "rather than disparagement for *Revolver,*" which succeeded as an album because of the "wide range of material it offers."

Williams had three favorites. "Eleanor Rigby" was "thoroughly new and utterly irresistible," a "work of craftsmanship" in which melody, structure, sound of the words and story "all work together as one." While the vocals were "flawless," he didn't particularly care for the strings. (Williams indicated that after the group's last two singles, "Nowhere Man" and "Paperback Writer," he was "beginning to think of 1966 as The Year They Finally Stopped Trying.") "Love You To" was Harrison's attempt at "approximating raga form" that was essentially a western piece with eastern influences. Impressed with George's sitar, he found the song to be a "fascinating musical experiment" that was "surprisingly successful." "For No One" was a beautiful song with gentle and perceptive words, a sensitive and "hauntingly formal" melody and great piano and French horn; a "processional hymn" or "something military; taps for a love affair."

The rest of *Revolver* was a mixed blessing. "Yellow Submarine" was a "horribly stereotyped piece of music." Its verse structure was similar to that of SSgt. Barry Sadler's "The Ballad Of The Green Berets," which was "equally catchy and equally blah." "Taxman" was a "successful attempt at humor...with a touch of bitterness." "Got To Get You Into My Life" did some nice things, but would have been better had the jazz musicians playing been more inspired. "She Said She Said" and "I Want To Tell You" were "fairly attractive," but "minor stuff." "Good Day Sunshine" was "full of good thoughts and fine piano playing." "Here, There And Everywhere" was a pretty and gentle love song, but tended towards being monotonous. Although he applauded the Beatles for trying new directions, he found "Tomorrow Never Knows" to have words that were "unbearably pretentious" and "meaningless" with a tune and structure that were "simply dull." Williams stated that we shouldn't take the Beatles for granted, but to "think of the Beatles as something surprisingly new and refreshing, for this is what they are...and, let us hope, what they continue to be."

In the August 27 British magazine Disc, Derek Taylor reported on *Revolver*'s reception in the U.S. Shindig producer Jack Good said: "It's the only thing at the moment that makes the gramophone meaningful. *Revolver* has all these beauteous things, these surprises in construction, and so many subtle jolts, shocks and jokes." Taylor indicated that the album was the talk of all pop Hollywood, being played at every party and on the air, track by track, day and night.

The 9th Annual Grammy Awards show for 1966 records was held on March 2, 1967. As was often the case in the early years, Frank Sinatra won most of the key categories, including Album of the Year for *A Man And His Music*, beating out *Revolver*, *What Now My Love* by Herb Alpert & the Tijuana Brass and *Color Me Barbra* by Barbra Streisand. His single, "Strangers In The Night," won Record Of The Year and Best Vocal Performance, Male. The Beatles, however, were not shut out. Song of the Year went to John Lennon and Paul McCartney for "Michelle" performed by the Beatles. Best Contemporary (R&R) Solo Vocal Performance, Male or Female, went to Paul McCartney for "Eleanor Rigby." Best Album Cover, Graphic Arts, went to Klaus Voormann for *Revolver*. It was only fitting that *Rubber Soul* and *Revolver* both gained some recognition from the then-generally-unhip music establishment, for they both were truly landmark albums with great songs and sounds. By the time of the broadcast, the Beatles had recently released their fantastic new single, "Strawberry Fields Forever" and "Penny Lane," with *Sgt. Pepper* just three months away.

STEREO

SINATRA
A MAN
AND
HIS MUSIC

AN ANTHOLOGY OF THE MUSICAL CAREER
OF THE MOST EXCITING
ENTERTAINER OF OUR TIME.

reprise
1016

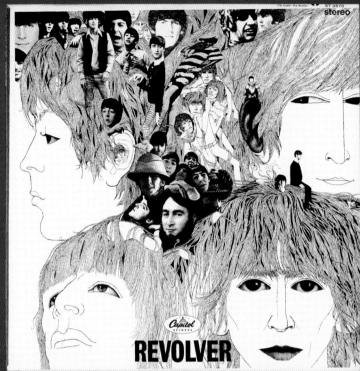

File Under: The Beatles   ST 2576

stereo

Capitol
RECORDS

REVOLVER

Color Me Barbra

STEREO   A&M SP 4114

Herb Alpert &
the Tijuana Brass
What Now
My Love

The Shadow of Your Smile
It Was A Very Good Year
If I Were A Rich Man
Five Minutes More
So What's New
Magic Trumpet
Freckles

A&M
RECORDS

File Under: The Beatles   ST 2228

CAPITOL FULL DIMENSIONAL ◄► STEREO

GREAT NEW HITS BY JOHN • PAUL • GEORGE • RINGO

BEATLES '65

Capitol RECORDS

HIGH FIDELITY

I FEEL FINE • SHE'S A WOMAN • NO REPLY • I'M A LOSER • ROCK AND ROLL MUSIC • I'LL FOLLOW THE SUN • HONEY DON'T • I'LL BE BACK • BABY'S IN BLACK • EVERYBODY'S TRYING TO BE MY BABY • MR. MOONLIGHT

"Mommy, did Capitol butcher the Beatles?" The Truth Behind the Butcher and Trunk Covers

Beatles folklore has long held that the Butcher Cover was the result of the Beatles frustration with how Capitol Records handled their catalog in America. The company took their carefully crafted 14-track LPs and broke them apart. It randomly dropped and added songs and changed the titles and covers of the albums. In an effort to squeeze out more albums, Capitol reduced the number of songs from 14 to either 11 or 12, and padded them with songs already issued on singles. The Beatles resented this treatment of their artistic endeavors, believing that Capitol had butchered their albums. The company even had the gall to modify *Rubber Soul*. When the group learned that Capitol was going to do the same with its upcoming *Revolver* LP and create a "new" album of leftover tracks and singles, the Beatles came up with a plan. They arranged for a photographer to take a picture of them wearing butcher smocks and covered with raw meat and decapitated baby dolls. They would insist that Capitol use the picture for the cover of its latest pieces-parts creation, unleashing a brutal visual pun that Capitol butchered the Beatles. The company reluctantly issued the *Yesterday And Today* LP with the Butcher Cover, but had to recall the album due to the firestorm of controversy it created. The Beatles were forced to get their picture taken for another cover. They couldn't be bothered to come up with something creative, instead just standing around an empty steamer trunk, their faces showing their disappointment that the album would no longer have their chosen cover.

It's a fascinating story and a plausible explanation for the grisly Butcher Cover, but simply not true as will be detailed below. As for Capitol, it didn't butcher the Beatles; it marketed the Beatles. The album *Beatles '65* is typical of the company's strategy. Capitol took eight songs from the group's latest U.K. album, *Beatles For Sale*, matching the running order of the first six songs on the British LP to form its first side. It added the group's then-current single, "I Feel Fine" and "She's A Woman," on its verified belief that hit singles make hit albums. Finally, to get to 11 tracks, it pulled "I'll Be Back" from its inventory of songs unissued in America. It held back "Eight Days A Week" for release as the group's next single, which was later used to anchor the next Capitol Beatles album, *Beatles VI*.

While Capitol's actions may seem callous today, it was typical of the times. We were not living in a global community back in the sixties. Record companies throughout the world reconfigured albums and issued singles as they saw fit to maximize sales and profits in their own market. While British pop albums typically had 14 tracks, American discs normally had 11 or 12 to save money on publishing royalties, which were calculated on a per song basis unlike the U.K. where royalties for an album were fixed, with each publisher allocated its share of the royalties per disc sold.

As for the Butcher Cover, it caused quite a stir when it made its limited appearance in June 1966. The controversial cover marked the first time that the Beatles judgment was severely and universally criticized. The gory picture was a drastic and shocking departure from the group's carefully crafted image of four young mop tops. And despite commonly held beliefs, it was never intended to be an album cover in the first place.

The so-called butcher picture was taken by Bob Whitaker on March 25, 1966, in a rented Chelsea studio located at 1, The Vale, London SW3, as part of an elaborate photo session. Whitaker's previous work with the Beatles included a thematic session held at Farringdon Studio, 23 West Smithfield, London EC1, on October 7, 1964, in which they held everyday props such as umbrellas, brooms, baskets and springs. The pictures, representing the four seasons, graced the front cover of *Beatles '65* (shown on page 64). The Winter photo shows the group holding umbrellas to protect against winter showers. The Spring photo has John holding a stemmed flower while the others hold large springs. The Summer photo has the boys casually dressed for warm weather with sunglasses and a beach towel. The Fall photo has them sweeping autumn leaves. One year later, at a photo session held at West Hampstead Studios on Sherriff Road, West Hampstead, London NW6, on October 28, 1965, Whitaker shot several pictures of the Beatles on a colorful set designed by Stuart Brisley and theater designer Carol Russell consisting of wide colored rolls of cloth (mauve, red and white), silver foil, mirrors, large blocks of white polystyrene board and clear polythene sheets. He also posed them in front of a white backdrop with a Salvador Dali-influenced eye. In one year's time, Whitaker had moved from the ordinary real to the surreal. Thus, when Brian Epstein scheduled another Beatles session with Whitaker five months later in March 1966, the boys may have been expecting something completely different, but certainly not the adventure that would exceed their wildest dreams.

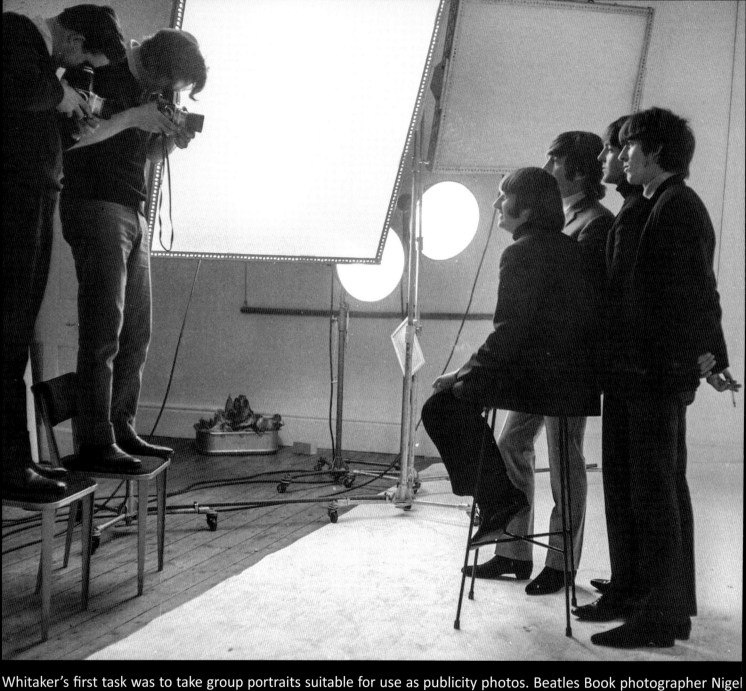

Whitaker's first task was to take group portraits suitable for use as publicity photos. Beatles Book photographer Nigel Dickson was present for the first part of the session and took the above picture of Whitaker and his assistant shooting the portraits. On the floor is a metal container full of meat and sausages that would later serve as props. The picture shown right, which has the Beatles positioned differently than above, was provided to the press and fans during the Beatles 1966 North American tour.

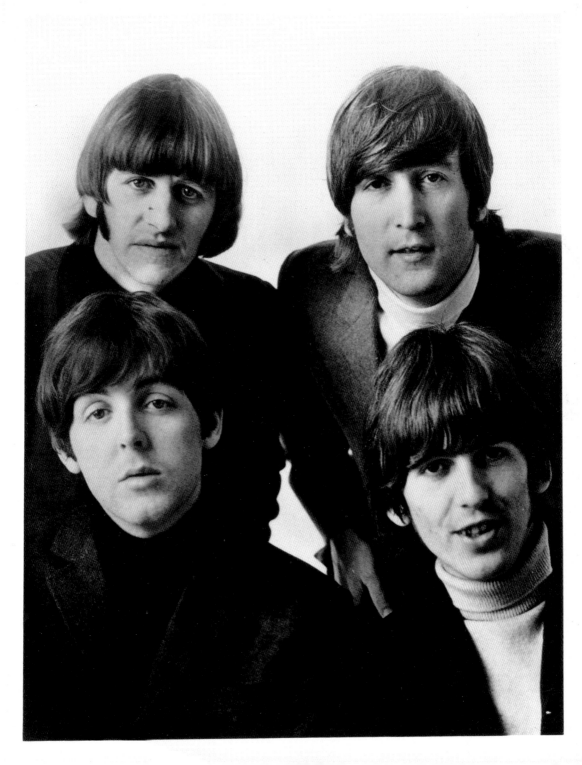

Once the required publicity portraits were completed, it was time for Whitaker's master plan to take shape. According to Whitaker, "The whole thing was quite literally going to be based on the theme of yesterday and today with the overall title of 'A Somnambulant Adventure.'" The past (birth) and present (everyday life) would be mixed with mortality (death). The images would also serve as Whitaker's personal comment on the mass adulation of the group and the illusory nature of stardom. At the time the photos were conceived and taken, Whitaker had no idea that a picture from the most controversial part of the session would wind up being used for the cover of an American album titled *Yesterday And Today*.

The early pictures were quite innocent. Paul was shot holding a large piece of cardboard with a question mark on it. This was quite appropriate as Whitaker's ideas for the photo session had remained a mystery to the Beatles. Whitaker also shot a series of photos of Paul and George interacting with a birdcage, which according to Whitaker symbolized that "these two guys had beautiful voices — they literally sang like canaries." It also implied that the Beatles were caged prisoners of their own success.

Another photo showed John unboxing Ringo to reveal the drummer's head and the number 2,000,000 written one of the box's flaps. In his book, *The Unseen Beatles*, Whitaker explained: "I wanted to illustrate the idea that, in a way, there was nothing more amazing about Ringo than anyone else on this earth. In this life he was just one of two million members of the human race. The idolization of fans reminded me of the story of the worship of the golden calf." He also took some pictures of George hammering nails into John's head to emphasize that the Beatles were not something to be worshiped, but were people as real and substantial as a piece of wood. They were flesh and blood like everyone else and could bleed.

From there, things got even weirder. John later explained that the photo session was a combination of Whitaker's desire to create surreal, Salvador Dali-like pictures and the group's "boredom and resentment at having to do another photo session and another Beatles thing." The umbrellas, brooms, baskets and springs of his earlier theme session were replaced with a birdcage, hammer and nails and a set of other strange props.

Whitaker obtained baby dolls and eyes from a doll factory in Barley Mow Passage and false teeth from an Australian dentist friend of his. He borrowed white butcher smocks, strings of sausages and raw slabs of beef and pork from an old school chum, Robert Sanford, who owned a butcher shop in the Stand On The Green region of Chiswick, West London. According to Whitaker: "[These props] were inspired by the German artist Hans Bellmer, who published a controversial book in the 1930s called *Die Puppe* [translated *The Doll*], which contained pictures of toy dolls with similarly dismembered arms and legs. That was my reference point." In his 1934 book, Bellmer's photographs of dolls in unconventional poses with mutilated joints were accompanied by prose poems by Paul Eluard. Bellmer constructed and photographed the dolls in their imperfect form as opposition to the Nazi Party's obsession with the perfect body. Prior to breaking out the meat, Whitaker and his assistant shot several color and black and white pictures of the Beatles sitting on the studio floor playing with dismembered baby dolls.

After completing the present day images of his Somnambulant Adventure, Whitaker was ready to turn to the meat of the session, which focused on the remaining themes of the past and mortality. This would be the life cycle of birth and death. For his image of birth, he photographed the group linked to a woman by a string of sausages. This symbolized the birth of the Beatles. According to Whitaker: "My own thought was how the hell do you show that they've been born out of a woman the same as anybody else? An umbilical cord was one way of doing it."

Somnambulant is defined as moving about in a trance-like state while asleep. By the time the photo session neared its climatic end, the Beatles must have felt like they were truly experiencing the Somnambulant Adventure envisioned by Whitaker. The final series of pictures have the Beatles wearing white butcher smocks with slabs of raw meat and baby doll parts. In the picture shown on the next page, the Beatles have their eyes closed, as if they are asleep.

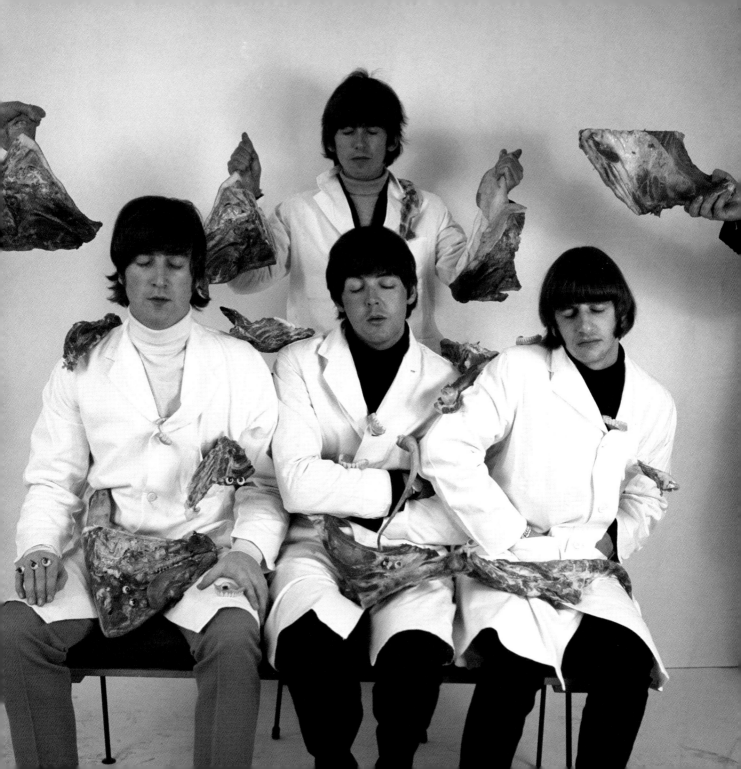

The butcher photos were taken with John, Paul and Ringo seated in chairs, with George standing behind them. In the initial pictures, the seated trio have raw meat slabs on their laps. They are also adorned with smaller pieces of meat, doll eyes and false teeth. The addition of decapitated and dismembered baby dolls brought the session to its grizzly end. Whitaker and his assistant each shot about a "butcher's dozen" photos of the Beatles in butcher smocks, both in color and in black and white. The only explanation Whitaker provided for the butcher pictures was the understatement that the photographs were way out of line with the group's public image.

While George and Ringo were apprehensive about participating in the final photos, Whitaker claimed that John loved the idea of posing with raw meat and baby dolls. "He and I used to paint together and he understood the whole thing." John's enthusiasm was confirmed by Beatles publicist Tony Barrow, who attended the photo session and recalled John showing gleeful delight in the proceedings while the others went along for the ride.

Barrow briefed Brian Epstein on the unconventional nature of most of the pictures taken by Whitaker. Other than the portraits shot at the beginning of the session, there was very little that could be utilized in promoting the band. Neither were concerned about the bizarre butcher photos as both were confident the pictures would never be used.

The trunk photo that ultimately graced the cover of the *Yesterday And Today* album was taken by Whitaker at Brian Epstein's NEMS Enterprises office at Sutherland House, 5-6 Argyll Street, London, W1, most likely on April 29, 1966. According to Barrow, the impromptu photo session was set up by Brian after he realized that the Beatles would be at his office for interviews on the same day Brian would be meeting with Whitaker. The scheduled interview was with Thomas Beyl, the chief reporter for Bravo, a popular teen magazine published in Germany. Although the Beatles would be interviewed by two other German magazines, Stern and Quick, on May 9, 1966, Bravo was given top priority as it was the sponsor of the Beatles German tour set to start on June 24, 1966, promoted as "Bravo-Beatles-Blitztournee." With the Beatles spending significant time at Abbey Road recording their next album, the group's hectic schedule left no room for extended time in a photo studio. Although the pictures taken at Brian's office that day by Whitaker were not for any particular intended use, there was always demand for fresh photos of the boys.

Due to the haste at which the session was arranged, there was no time to come up with clever props. Whitaker had to make due with what was available in the office—a blue steamer trunk. The above left photo, taken by Thomas Beyl, shows Whitaker behind the camera lining up a picture with Paul and John inside the open trunk with Ringo and George behind them. The picture was used on the cover of the French EP shown on the next page. After taking a few additional photos of the boys and the trunk, including the one used on the Capitol album, Whitaker showed the group some of the black and white pictures from their previous photo session as shown above right, with George holding a photo of the Beatles in butcher smocks. A doll's head and meat can be seen on Paul's lap.

the BEATLES

MEO 134

ODEON

EMI

LA PLUS GRANDE COMPAGNIE
MONDIALE DE DISQUES

STRAWBERRY FIELDS FOREVER

PENNY LANE

The above photo shows an animated Bob Whitaker describing his Somnambulant Adventure pictures to John, who appears quite pleased with the results. The butcher pictures were in sharp contrast to the framed image from the Beatles cartoon television show hanging on the wall behind them in Brian's office. And while the trunk pictures taken in Brian's office that day seemed rather pedestrian, Whitaker was proud of his work during the impromptu session. In correspondence with the author, Whitaker indicated that he viewed the trunk as being as important as the meat, dolls and false teeth used in his Somnambulant Adventure butcher session. When Capitol requested a picture of the Beatles for its upcoming summer album, Brian sent the company a color transparency of the trunk photo shown on the next page. It most likely arrived at the Capitol Tower on or shortly before May 11, 1966.

80

Upon receipt of the trunk image, Capitol's art department quickly came up with a cover design. Because the album was then titled *"Yesterday"...And Today* to emphasize that the hit single "Yesterday" was on the album, Capitol incorporated the color scheme from its "Yesterday" picture sleeve into the cover design. The top of the "Yesterday" sleeve has a royal blue horizontal rectangle with the group's name in white and the song titles in yellow. A photo of the group is at the bottom. The left side of the initial cover design for the album has a royal blue vertical rectangle with the group's name in white and the album and song titles in yellow. The trunk photo, cropped and flipped, is on the right side of the cover. The Capitol logo is in black in the upper right corner. The initial design mistakenly showed the album's name as *"Yesterday...And Today"* with the entire title in quotes. This was quickly modified to show the title as *"Yesterday"...And Today*. This design (shown on the following page) was approved by Capitol on or slightly before May 13, 1966, and, but for the intervention of Brian Epstein, would have been the album's cover.

Capitol's Ray Polley, who oversaw printing and manufacture of product, sent a memo to the company's Scranton and L.A. pressing plant managers on Friday, May 13, informing them that the new Beatles album was an extra special rush release. The forecast called for pressings of 800,000 albums by Scranton and 400,000 by L.A. The color litho films needed for printing the front cover slicks were to arrive at regional printers Queens Litho (New York) and Bert-Co (L.A.) on May 16. The back liners were set for mailing to the factories fabricating the album covers on May 17. Polley sent a copy of the memo to Barry Cohen of Queens Litho. In a hand-written note, Polley instructed Queens Litho to make the plates for the cover slicks, but not to print the slicks until talking with him on May 16. Polley explained, "We have a problem with Beatles manager that we do not want anyone to know of — including our plants."

The problem was that Brian Epstein had insisted on seeing the cover design before giving Capitol his approval. Due to the rush release of the album, a delay for the Beatles manager to review the cover design was clearly a problem. This was a change from the earlier protocol under which Capitol packaged its Beatles singles and albums in sleeves and jackets it deemed appropriate with minimal, if any, input from the Beatles camp. When Brian insisted on seeing the cover, Capitol arranged for a color proof to be sent to EMI for arrival in London by Monday, May 16. Much to Polley's dismay, Brian objected to the cover, perhaps disliking its colors.

"Yesterday"...and Today
THE BEATLES

YESTERDAY

DR. ROBERT

I'M ONLY SLEEPING

AND YOUR BIRD CAN SING

WE CAN WORK IT OUT

DAY TRIPPER

NOWHERE MAN

WHAT GOES ON?

DRIVE MY CAR

IF I NEEDED SOMEONE

ACT NATURALLY

Capitol
RECORDS

Capitol's art department was asked to come up with some alternate designs. Rather than wait for separation proofs, a simple cover mock-up was prepared and sent to Brian in hope of quickly gaining his blessings to get back on schedule. The mock-up overlaid a cut-out of the Beatles and the trunk against a white background. Polley sent a memo to Scranton with the following update: "Beatles cover has been held up again. We cannot print until we get OK from London. This might be on 5/19/66. We have notified Queens."

While Capitol was dealing with its cover crisis, the Beatles continued recording songs for their new album. On May 19, the group gathered at Abbey Road for the filming of promotional videos for their upcoming single, "Paperback Writer" and "Rain." By this time, they had seen the color transparencies of Whitaker's butcher session, as evidenced by Paul holding up and looking at the transparencies at the start of the "Paperback Writer" video. On the following day, the Beatles were at Chiswick House and Gardens in West London to film outdoor scenes for the videos. Brian brought the white background cover mock-up to Chiswick as evidenced by the picture shown right. This mundane trunk image was quite a contrast from the shocking color transparencies the group had seen the day before.

Although no confirming documentation exists, it was probably at this time that John, having just seen the butcher images and Trunk Cover mock-up, informed Brian that he wanted a butcher picture featured on the cover of the Capitol album. John later said, "I especially pushed for it to be an album cover, just to break the image." This horrified Brian as he hated the butcher photos and was rightfully concerned about the negative effect it would have on the band's image. But by 1966, the Beatles were in charge. Brian would have to sell Capitol on the cover he despised.

Back at the Tower, Capitol's art department came up with three alternate designs featuring the trunk photo (shown next page). The first design is a slight departure from the original cover, merely angling the photo and putting "THE BEATLES" in red in the same font used on *Beatles VI*. The second is a refined version of the mock-up, utilizing a cut-out of the Beatles and the trunk on a white background. The third is the strangest of the lot, having the same two images of the Beatles and the trunk, one straight and the other with the boys turned on their side. The back paper to the color separations for all of these designs is stamped "Ray Polley" and "Received May 27 1966."

84

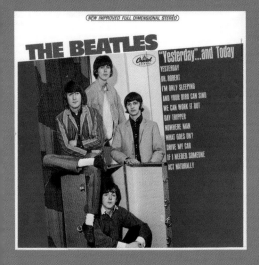

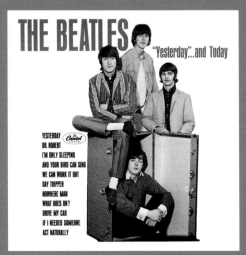

Shortly after John's decision to have a butcher photo serve as the cover to the Capitol album, Brian reluctantly sent a color transparency from the butcher session to the Capitol Tower with instructions that the image be featured on the cover of the *Yesterday And Today* album. The package most likely arrived on May 23 or 24. Although the butcher image raised a few eyebrows at the Tower, the head of Capitol's art department, George Osaki, loved the photo and thought it would make a great album cover, being "a departure from the usual four smiling heads." He did not find the photo offensive because "the Beatles weren't chopping things up."

Capitol sent the color transparency to Ted Staidle & Associates for production of a 20" x 16" color photographic proof. This proof was the starting point for Osaki's cover design. The picture was reprinted with a texture screen to create a fine-art appearance. Osaki cropped the bottom and right of the image to give it the proper dimensions. He added a gray banner along the top for the slick's stereo logo. Osaki's enthusiasm for the butcher photo inspired him to treat the cover as if it were a piece of art. To avoid a cluttered look, he left the space in the top left corner clear except for the Capitol logo. He was able to fit all of the text in the upper right corner by reducing the size of the song titles. Inspired by the new cover photo and remembering the attractive and innovative lettering used for *Rubber Soul*, Osaki selected a psychedelic-looking font for the group's name and the album title. All of the text and graphics were in black. An early butcher proof (shown next page) followed previous designs that had "Yesterday" in quotes. This surviving proof has red deletion marks and "OUT" written around and by the quotation marks, which were dropped before the final proof was run on or about May 26, 1966.

In addition to insisting on the butcher photograph, Brian demanded that the Butcher Cover be printed on the same paper stock used by Capitol for the covers of albums released on its Angel classical music label rather than the standard coated paper used on its pop albums. This "Angel-type" soft text paper, with its visible vertical ridges, gave covers a linen-like appearance similar to that of a fine work of art. The trade name for this paper is Kilmory Text. This paper was created by the Simpson Paper Company in Seattle, which applied for a trademark on the paper on July 2, 1964. Capitol reluctantly complied with this request, soaking up the increased cost to appease the manager of the label's most important recording artist.

While Capitol's art department was enthusiastic about the Butcher Cover, the sales force was deeply concerned. In his interview with the author, Capitol president Alan Livingston recalled: "The sales department came to me and said, 'Look at this album cover, how can we do this?' And I said, 'We can't put that out.' I called Brian in London and I said, 'Brian, I can't put this album out with this cover, I need another cover.' And he argued with me; he wouldn't listen." On May 25, a frustrated Livingston requested an estimate of the costs incurred by Capitol due to the delay occasioned by Brian Epstein and his approval requirement for the Beatles album. The following day Ray Polley provided a list of some of the costs, which included: expenses for color separations of the first design that were not used ($347); creating additional sets for Brian plus international shipping ($143); press plates made by Queens Litho and Bert-Co for the unused first design ($1,255); color separations for additional designs ($600); and the increased cost for using special cover paper ($11,380). The memo estimated costs of over $14,000. This would be a pittance compared to the costs Capitol would soon incur when the album was recalled.

Unbeknownst to Livingston, Brian shared the same concerns about the Butcher Cover. But the Beatles manager was in a no-win situation. Although he loathed the butcher picture and feared it would destroy the group's image, he was forced to demand that Capitol use the picture lest he face the wrath of John. And it was he who would take the heat from any negative fallout that the cover would cause. If the Butcher Cover created a storm of controversy, Capitol and the press would point to Brian as the one who insisted on the cover. As manager, he could not shift the blame to where it belonged. His job was to protect the image of the band, no matter what the personal cost.

Added to Brian's frustration was the realization that his own actions had led to the Butcher Cover. Capitol had initially prepared a simple non-controversial cover featuring his clean-cut boys posing with a steamer trunk. Had he allowed Capitol to proceed with the printing of the blue Trunk Cover sight unseen, he would not be this mess. He could have told the group that Capitol insisted that there was no time to review the cover if the album's release schedule was to be met. Had he approved the blue trunk design when it was sent to him, the covers would already be in production. By insisting that Capitol send him another design, Brian was caught holding a boring trunk mock-up shortly after John had feasted his eyes on the shocking butcher transparencies. Ironically, the Butcher Cover *was* Brian's fault.

Capitol was frantically trying to resolve the cover issue with Brian. The album's June 15 release date was in jeopardy if a decision was not soon reached. The printers (Queens Litho and Bert-Co), cover fabricators (Modern Album and Imperial) and pressing plants were all on stand-by and on hold. Everyone was waiting for Brian's approval. This was frustrating for Capitol because it was Brian who had sent them the photo for the cover that he was now objecting to.

On Friday, May 27, Polley sent a package for Saturday delivery to the home of Barry Cohen of Queens Litho containing the artwork and litho positives for the three new Trunk Cover designs (shown on page 85) and the Butcher Cover. Polley's accompanying letter asked Cohen to deliver the artwork of the four designs to Tom Morgan of Capitol's New York office at his home. Cohen was directed to take the litho positives to Queens Litho, with instructions that plates be made for the Butcher Cover slicks with a hold on the press run until the "printing OK" was given by Capitol. Polley indicated that he hoped to get Brian's approval for one of the four designs on May 30 or 31. Once approval was obtained, Queens Litho was to begin printing immediately.

Polley also sent a letter directly to Tom Morgan at Capitol's New York Executive Office at 1730 Broadway for Monday delivery, by which time Morgan would have received the artwork for the four cover designs from Cohen. Morgan was directed to meet with Brian, who was arriving in New York on May 30 to begin making arrangements for the Beatles 1966 North American tour. This gave Capitol the opportunity for a face-to-face meeting with the Beatles manager who had suddenly become such a problem. Morgan was to show Brian not only the cover featuring the butcher photo, but also the three redesigned Trunk Covers in hope that Brian would drop his insistence on issuing the album with a cover that Capitol had deep concerns about.

Morgan met with Brian on the morning of May 31. He recalled Brian calling London to discuss the cover designs (most likely with the Beatles) and confirming his insistence on the use of the butcher photo. Brian did, at least, approve of Capitol's design for the Butcher Cover. Morgan then called Polley, who informed the Scranton and Los Angeles plant managers that the cover had been approved and that Queens Litho and Bert-Co were printing the front cover slicks. He estimated that they would be finished on June 2.

As anticipated, the front cover slicks were sent to the album fabricators on June 2 and 3, with construction of the album covers taking place on June 2 through 5. The covers were then sent to Capitol's pressing plants. Original plans called for the records to be pressed solely by Capitol's Scranton and L.A. factories; however, the shortened production schedule caused by Brian prompted Capitol to also have albums manufactured by its year-old Jacksonville facility. The pressing of the records and their insertion into the Butcher Covers took place on June 4 through 7.

When Alan Livingston had earlier spoken with Brian about the cover, he told him that "We'll have some printed up and we'll put them out, send them to disc jockeys, our distributors and sales managers and see what happens." Although Livingston envisioned a limited run of a few hundred Butcher Covers to test industry reaction, Capitol's production department ignored his "suggestion." Because the company planned to issue the record in mid-June, there wasn't time to test market the cover. It was damn the torpedoes, full speed ahead.

Capitol documents indicate that 1,000,000 mono and 200,000 stereo covers were initially ordered. By June 7, Capitol had pressed, packaged and shipped 750,000 copies of the album to its distributors. Advance copies were sent to the Capitol Tower for forwarding to disc jockeys, newspaper and magazine record reviewers, and presidents of Beatles fan club chapters. Capitol salesmen showed the album to their accounts, which included independent distributors and radio stations. The response was immediate and uniformly negative. According to Livingston, the Tower was besieged with reports from its sales managers and distributors: "We got frantic phone calls. They said, 'We can't put this in the stores. The stores won't handle it.' They would not sell the album, and they wanted it badly."

Livingston called a high-level meeting to announce his decision to recall the album and reissue it with a new cover. Osaki vigorously defended the Butcher Cover, but to no avail. He was given the task to quickly come up with a suitable replacement cover. Because Osaki liked the stylized psychedelic font used on the Butcher Cover, he did not want to use any of the existing trunk designs. He took the image of the Beatles and the trunk from an earlier design and shifted it to the left to create a larger open space in the top right corner for the text. He then placed the black text overlay sheet from the Butcher Cover on his modified design. This concept is shown on the next page.

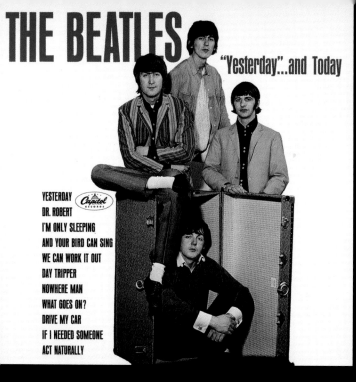

THE BEATLES

"Yesterday"...and Today

Capitol RECORDS

YESTERDAY
DR. ROBERT
I'M ONLY SLEEPING
AND YOUR BIRD CAN SING
WE CAN WORK IT OUT
DAY TRIPPER
NOWHERE MAN
WHAT GOES ON?
DRIVE MY CAR
IF I NEEDED SOMEONE
ACT NATURALLY

File Under: The Beatles   ST 2553

NEW IMPROVED *FULL DIMENSIONAL STEREO*

Capitol RECORDS

YESTERDAY · DR. ROBERT
I'M ONLY SLEEPING · AND YOUR BIRD CAN SING
WE CAN WORK IT OUT · DAY TRIPPER
NOWHERE MAN · WHAT GOES ON?
DRIVE MY CAR · IF I NEEDED SOMEONE
ACT NATURALLY

The Beatles Yesterday And Today

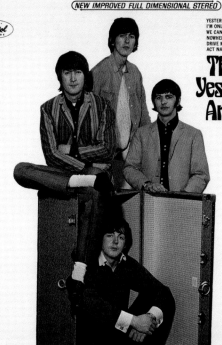

File Under: The Beatles   ST 2553

NEW IMPROVED FULL DIMENSIONAL STEREO

Capitol RECORDS

YESTERDAY · DR. ROBERT
I'M ONLY SLEEPING · AND YOUR BIRD CAN SING
WE CAN WORK IT OUT · DAY TRIPPER
NOWHERE MAN · WHAT GOES ON?
DRIVE MY CAR · IF I NEEDED SOMEONE
ACT NATURALLY

The Beatles Yesterday And Today

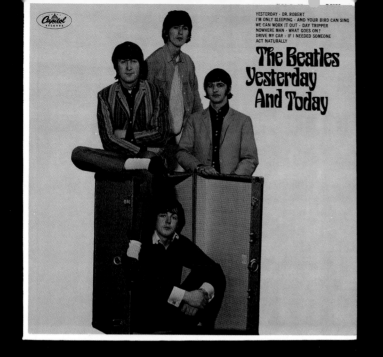

Although the final design chosen for the replacement cover has a white background, Capitol experimented with a silver background (shown above left). The only known printer's proof of this was trimmed for mono and pasted onto the front of an album jacket with the mono back liner for Nancy Wilson's *Tender Loving Care* LP (Capitol T 2555). To avoid further delays, Capitol chose not to update the album's title on the back cover and spine from *"Yesterday"... and Today* to *Yesterday And Today*. The back cover (shown above right) marked a return to Capitol's practice of placing a gallery of the covers to the company's previously-released Beatles albums, along with the song titles, in the lower part of the cover.

While the Butcher Cover was a drastic departure from the Beatles clean image, the trunk photo was reminiscent of the goofily-innocent pictures of bands and pop stars from the early to mid-sixties like the picture of the Beatles on the cover of the August 17, 1963 issue of Pop Weekly. The Trunk Cover was later misinterpreted as being one of the many clues supposedly proving Paul was dead. When the cover is turned sideways, Paul looks like he is lying in a coffin. Ringo, who is purportedly dressed as an undertaker on the cover of *Abbey Road*, appears to be closing the lid.

TWO PAGES
PHOTO-NEWS

SPECIAL BEATGROUP EDITION ★ GIANT PIC OF GERRY INSIDE

POP WEEKLY
PIN-UP

FULL PAGES OF BEATLES ★ SHADOWS ★ DREAMERS ★ DAKOTAS Etc.

POP WEEKLY

ONE
SHILLING

No. 51

Week Ending
17th August

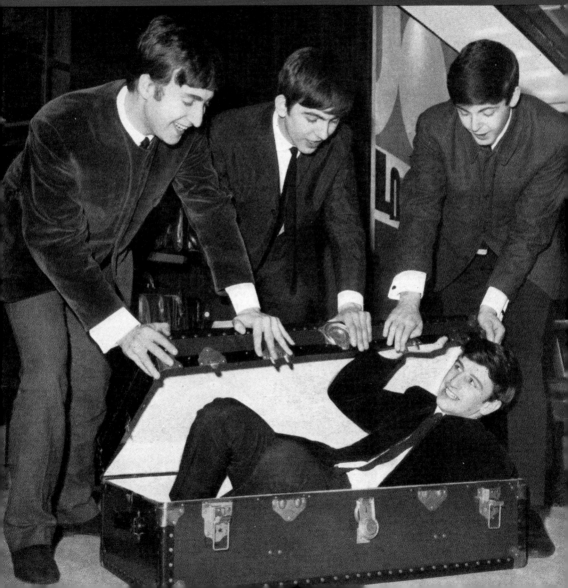

Capitol quickly formulated a massive recall plan, dubbed Operation Retrieve, that was set into motion on Friday, June 10. Capitol sales reps were sent telegrams directing them to ship all copies of the album back to the factories immediately. Failure to return all allotted albums would result in termination of employment. Boxes of albums were unloaded from trucks at the pressing plants to prevent additional shipments to distribution centers.

Capitol branch managers who had already received their initial allotment of *Yesterday And Today* were told that the records needed to be removed from the offensive covers so that they could later be repackaged in new covers. In New York, Capitol employees spent the weekend extracting 90,000 records from their covers. The tedious task involved cutting the shrink wrap, removing the records and inner sleeves from the jackets and placing them in stacks. The discs were then boxed up and sent back to the Scranton plant. This scene was repeated all weekend long at Capitol's other distribution centers that had received the new Beatles album as well as at its three factories.

The Butcher Cover fiasco had destroyed Capitol's best laid plans. According to Joe Sobeck, the manager for Capitol Records Distributing Corp.'s Boston office, the release of the album had been "shrouded in secrecy, primarily to prevent uneven distribution, which had plagued previous releases of Beatles product." The goal was to have ample copies of the album at every Capitol distribution center by the release date. But Operation Retrieve made that impossible. Capitol initially estimated the cost of replacing the covers at $200,000 to $250,000. The new covers, with replacement front cover slicks and reprinted back liners, would cost nearly 15 cents apiece. In addition, Capitol employees had to be paid overtime for their weekend warrior work of removing the records from the Butcher Covers. There would also be shipping charges and the cost of employees hand-placing the discs into the new covers.

The original orders given to Capitol's pressing plants and distribution centers included a directive to destroy all Butcher Covers. Factories were told a replacement cover was in the works and that mass quantities of the new album cover would be shipped to the pressing plants within a week. The Jacksonville plant manager took the lead in destroying the offensive covers. A Capitol employee recalls covers being cut up and dumped in an Illinois landfill. Boston's 50,700 covers were buried under two feet of dirt in a swampy part of the Needham Town Dump.

Before the other plant managers destroyed all of their Butcher Covers, someone came up with the cost-saving idea of reusing them. The plan was simple—paste a new front cover slick over the offensive Butcher Cover and trim the right side of the album jacket for a smooth opening edge. Employees would then place records in the recycled covers, saving Capitol approximately 10 cents per album. Although it was too late to save the Jacksonville covers, Capitol pasted over many of the covers returned to its Scranton and L.A. plants.

Capitol contacted Modern Album and Imperial to discuss the feasibility of pasting new trunk slicks over Butcher Covers. Babs Gates, who served as production manager for Imperial, warned Capitol that the trunk slicks would probably not adhere properly to the glossy paper unless a stronger glue was used. However, the stronger glue could soak through the cardboard and damage the records. Thus, Imperial declined to take part in Operation Paste Over.

Although Modern Album may have shared some of Imperial's concerns, the company agreed to paste over the Butcher Covers. Capitol's Scranton and Los Angeles plants sent surviving Butcher Covers to Modern Album factories in New York, Terre Haute and Burbank. Modern Album then had its machines paste the new trunk slicks (received from Queens Litho and Bert-Co) over the previously constructed Butcher Covers. The jackets were machine trimmed on the right to remove the overlapping portion of the slick. The paste-over covers were sent back to Capitol's pressing plants, where the previously pressed records (still in their orange inner sleeve dust jackets) were inserted by hand. The finished product was shrinkwrapped and boxed for shipment to distribution centers. Meanwhile, Imperial's newly constructed covers were also sent to Capitol factories where they were paired with the previously pressed records and sent to distribution centers. Thus, when *Yesterday And Today* began appearing in stores during the week of June 20, 1966, the album was being sold with both paste-over and newly-constructed trunk jackets.

While the decision to scrap the Butcher Cover was made by Capitol, the label reportedly sent Brian Epstein a telegram requesting permission to use an alternate cover. Livingston recalls telephoning Brian to explain Capitol's position: "So I called Epstein and I told him, 'We can't put it out. Here's what happened.' And he was very disappointed. And I said, 'Sorry, they won't sell the album. Our dealers won't take it and our sales managers won't handle it.'"

In addition to manufacturing replacement covers, Capitol was busy initiating its damage control program. An official statement was drafted and then approved by and attributed to Alan Livingston. Ron Tepper, manager of press and information services, was tasked with spreading the word through letters and press releases incorporating Livingston's comment on the controversial cover. This included a recall letter, dated June 14, 1966, that was sent to those who had received a review copy of the album, a letter to the Beatles Fan Club Chapter Presidents, and a consumer response letter (all shown on the next page). Reviewers were told that all consumer copies would be packaged in a new cover and that they would be sent a copy of the LP with the redesigned cover. They were asked to "disregard" the album or return it C.O.D. to Capitol. As expected, very few people sent the cover back to the Tower.

Livingston's statement from the letters, which also ran in magazines such as the June 25 Billboard and the July 9 Beat magazine, contained the following explanation: "The original cover, created in England, was intended as a 'pop art' satire. However, a sampling of public opinion in the United States indicates that the cover design is subject to misinterpretation. For this reason, and to avoid any possible controversy or undeserved harm to The Beatles' image or reputation, Capitol has chosen to withdraw the LP and substitute a more generally acceptable design."

This statement implies that while the cover was offensive to Americans, it was merely viewed as pop art satire in England. In other words, blame it on cultural differences. What the British recognized as black humor or thought provoking, Americans considered sick and cannibalistic. To understand the difference, one need only compare the cutting-edge humor of the late-sixties British TV show Monty Python's Flying Circus to the comedy of The Carol Burnett Show in the U.S. To the British, sick humor was acceptable as long as it was funny. For Americans in the sixties, sick humor was just sick. This type of comedy would not become acceptable in the U.S. until the seventies when Saturday Night Live flaunted the rules and pushed beyond what was previously considered in poor taste.

Although the cultural-difference explanation sounds plausible, it is not entirely accurate. When the butcher pictures were presented under different circumstances in England prior to the release of the Capitol album, reaction was mixed as detailed on pages 20 through 22.

CAPITOL RECORDS DISTRIBUTING CORP.

EXECUTIVE AND GENERAL OFFICES

HOLLYWOOD AND VINE • HOLLYWOOD, CALIFORNIA 90028 • TELEPHONE (213) 462-6252

Dear Beatles Chapter President:

In the past few days, you may have received
an advance promotional copy of The Beatles'
new album, "The Beatles Yesterday And Today."
In accordance with the following statement

CAPITOL RECORDS DISTRIBUTING CORP.

EXECUTIVE AND GENERAL OFFICES

HOLLYWOOD AND VINE • HOLLYWOOD, CALIFORNIA 90028 • TELEPHONE (213) 462-6252

Regarding your recent letter,
has withdrawn all copies of its ne
The Beatles' "Yesterday"...and Tod
order that new cover art may be s

The original cover, created
was intended as "pop art" satire.
a sampling of public opinion in
States indicates that the cover
subject to misinterpretation. F
reason and to avoid any possible
or undeserved harm to the Beatle
reputation, Capitol has chosen
the LP and substitute a more ge
able design.

Cordially,

Ron Tepper
Manager
Press and

RT/oa

CAPITOL RECORDS DISTRIBUTING CORP.

EXECUTIVE AND GENERAL OFFICES

HOLLYWOOD AND VINE • HOLLYWOOD, CALIFORNIA 90028 • TELEPHONE (213) 462-6252

June 14, 1966

Dear Reviewer:

In the past few days, you may have received an
advance promotional copy of The Beatles' new
album, "The Beatles Yesterday And Today." In
accordance with the following statement from
Alan W. Livingston, President, Capitol Records,
Inc., the original album cover is being discarded and a new jacket is being prepared:

> "The original cover, created in
> England, was intended as 'pop art'
> satire. However, a sampling of
> public opinion in the United States
> indicates that the cover design is
> subject to misinterpretation. For
> this reason, and to avoid any poss-
> ible controversy or undeserved harm
> to The Beatles' image or reputation,
> Capitol has chosen to withdraw the
> LP and substitute a more generally
> acceptable design."

All consumer copies of The Beatles' album will
be packaged in the new cover, which will be
available within the next week to 10 days. As
soon as they are, we will forward you a copy.
In the meantime, we would appreciate your dis-
regarding the promotional album and, if at all
possible, returning it, C.O.D., to Capitol
Records, 1750 N. Vine Street, Hollywood, Calif.
90028.

Thank you in advance for your cooperation.

Sincerely,

Ron Tepper
Manager
Press & Information Services.

RT:s

While the reaction in England may have been mixed, nearly all in America found the Beatles guilty of bad taste and worse. In the days before Alice Cooper's shock rock of the early seventies, dead babies and raw meat were taboo. Such a cover today might seem tame when compared to some of the more graphic album covers released in subsequent decades, but for America in the mid-sixties, it went way beyond acceptable standards.

The Butcher Cover was not what Bob Whitaker had in mind for his Somnambulant Adventure. In fact, he did not even know that the Beatles had sent his butcher transparencies to Capitol. Whitaker envisioned his photos as part of an elaborate gatefold cover. A butcher shot would serve as the front cover, but it would be altered to portray a "temple of bestiality" with all the gilt trappings associated with religious worship. According to Whitaker: "It was never meant to appear on a record sleeve in that unfinished state. The background to the picture would have been painted gold, and the whole image would have been quite small on the final cover, which would have been a gatefold. Around the Beatles heads would have gone silver halos—which represent canonization in Christianity— and into those halos would have been placed precious stones. The picture would have been crowned by bands of rainbow colours around its edges. And then you would have turned the page of the cover and come across other images in the series: of John, Paul, George and Ringo being unpacked. The hammer and nails which George knocked into John's head would have been covered in fur." In hindsight, Whitaker realized that his work could easily be misunderstood: "It would have been a very decorous piece, and unless you had the key to understanding it, the satire was wasted. People can read all sorts of rubbish into it. It's too complex."

The first media coverage of the incident appeared in an article by music critic Ralph Gleason of the San Francisco Chronicle. The front page of the newspaper's Monday, June 13, 1966, final edition ran a picture of the Butcher Cover in a news summary box below the headline "A Beatle Bobble." Gleason's article in his On the Town column was titled "A Capitol Stew Over Beatles." He reported that the latest Beatles album had been temporarily withdrawn due to adverse reaction from key record stores, disc jockeys and others who saw the cover in advance. The cover was described as showing the "four 'Liverpool minstrels'...in butchers' aprons with legs of meat on their laps and several decapitated Barbie dolls draped around them."

Gleason reported that Capitol was deluged with calls, both pro and con, after disc jockeys began talking about the ban on the air. Capitol's San Francisco office received a call from someone threatening, "I represent the young men of America and we are going to get you for this outrage." A Capitol spokesman divided the callers into two groups: the "Straight Arrows" who rejected with outrage the whole idea of the cover and "The Stoners" who thought it funny, an example of British sick humor and pop art. Industry historians believed it was the first time a record company had withdrawn an album cover due to public reaction viewing the cover as being in bad taste.

Gleason also commented on the cover's effect on the relationship between Capitol and the Beatles: "Under Capitol's contract with The Beatles, the singing group supplies the art work for the covers as well as the music for the album and must okay what goes on the album. It's understood that the 'butcher boys' cover was the subject of considerable hassle between Capitol and the Beatles management before the printing, with Capitol officials rejecting it and the Beatles insisting it be used. Finally a compromise was reached with the Beatles agreeing to the elimination of blood stains on the butchers' aprons."

After reporting on Capitol's unilateral decision to withdraw the album, Gleason observed: "This is especially interesting in view of the fact that Capitol's relationship with The Beatles, who re-signed for a reported $5 million less than a year ago, has been shaky for some time. 'This can cost Capitol The Beatles' one knowledgeable record industry spokesman said this weekend." A Capitol employee was quoted as saying: "It's kind of frightening that The Beatles can stir up such a storm. We were on the phone all day Friday to radio stations all over the country getting back the album and the heat was terrific."

Gleason closed his column on a serious note laced with political connotations of the anti-war movement that would soon gain support among the nation's youth: "Far from being offensive, the 'butcher boys' cover strikes me as a subtle protest against war, as well as an example of 'black humor.' Isn't there something paradoxical about the shrill reaction of disc jockeys and program directors to this cover at a time when the heads are being blown off real children and their bodies seared by American napalm in Vietnam?"

Billboard reported the flack over the cover in its June 25 issue in a story titled "Beatles' LP Makes Cap. Run for Cover." Although the magazine described the cover as showing the Beatles surrounded by dismembered baby dolls and butcher shop cuts of meat, it did not run a picture of the cover.

The June 21 New York Post ran a story on the incident, complete with picture, titled "Mop Heads—or Lop Heads? Beatles Had the Wrong Groove." Capitol's recall of the album was described as "costly and embarrassing." A Capitol spokesman estimated that the recall, repackaging and redistribution of the album would cost $250,000, turning a good money-maker into a break even item.

The Associated Press wire service reported that: "The high-riding Beatles may have had a close call with economic disaster...the loss of popularity in the United States, where they make most of their money. Not because of their vocal talents...which is another question...but because of their sad taste in album jacket art." The article described the cover as bizarre, grisly and grotesque. According to the AP, Capitol's recall effort corrected "what could have been a bad Beatlemania blooper." The WNS wire service started its article with: "Even that fantastically successful, multi-million-dollar entity known as The Beatles and its entourage of advisers can goof. They just did—to the tune of $250,000." The article stated that the controversial cover had brought a mountain of protest and was considered cannibalistic by some of the individuals who had received advance copies of the album. The cover was described as showing the "four British mop-heads surrounded by decapitated, naked baby dolls, and raw loins of beef."

The July 2 Beat magazine ran an article on the banned cover, calling it the "most nauseating album cover ever seen in the U.S." After describing the picture, the article states that although someone had the brains to ban the cover, the damage was already done by people having seen it. The magazine then asked, "Why would a group who will obviously sell a million copies of the album no matter what they put on it stoop to posing and giving their blessing to such a ridiculous attempt at humor, or shock, or whatever it is meant to evoke?" The article then provided comments from people connected to the music business. None who saw the cover liked it or found it even slightly amusing. "They felt it was the most sickening spectacle they'd ever seen." Many thought it was done for shock value.

Others said it was John's idea, with one saying "Only he could think of something as morbid as that." Gary Lewis, who was on the charts again with "Green Grass," didn't get it: "What does it mean? I hate that." Others speculated that the Beatles were trying to tell us something, perhaps their end. They were becoming so weird that "they don't even know what their public wants anymore." The article ended with the magazine asking for reader's comments. "Do you think it was done for shock value, that they were trying to tell us something, or that it means nothing?"

Readers began responding the following week in the July 9 Beat. Sue Herbert wrote that she had gotten a sneak peak at the cover and had never been more shocked. She commented that "Only the Beatles would have the nerve to think they could get away with something like that" and that the group thought "people will go for anything they do...no matter how degrading or unpleasant." She found it fortunate that the cover was banned before too many people saw it for "it would even make Beatle fans a little sick." Others saw it differently. Rod Sanger thought the cover was "groovy!" and really said something. While admitting it was a little gory, he still dug it and thought others would have too if not banned "just because a few old ladies were complaining." He hoped the cover would clear the way for more original and wild covers. Mike Gorham couldn't help but laugh at how upset people got when they talked about the cover. "They just can't believe their darling Beatles would stoop to something so 'nauseating' and 'unprofessional.'" To him, the concept was "nothing new" as babies were "starving all over the world" and the U.S. military did much worse with napalm bombs in Vietnam. He wasn't disappointed when the Beatles put the album cover out; he was disappointed when "they lost their nerve and withdrew it at the last minute."

The following week more fans came to the group's defense. Joni Sawnier didn't understand the protests. She had seen the cover in the San Francisco newspaper and felt it was clever and very original. She lamented that "lately the Beatles can't do one darn thing without being criticized." Kathy Sedwick also couldn't understand all the fuss. She dug the humor of the pose and asked, "Has it ever occurred to any of you that the Beatles just liked the idea of posing that way and decided to do it?" While others saw it as nauseating, she saw its amusing side. She thought the Beatles were courageous to expose themselves to the "witch-hunting" pursued against them for the cover. Elise Kurutz thought they did the cover because they thought it was funny.

While Randi Vreeland admitted the Beatles could have found a better cover, she wasn't gonna crucify them over it. She understood that some might find it in poor taste, but thought it was ridiculous to call it "revolting and nauseating" as there were worse paintings in art museums and galleries. Thomas Ganiats asked "Why is the sight of a few decapitated Barbie Dolls and freshly butchered sides of beef more sickening than the lurid daily photographs of the effectiveness of our bombing and napalming in Viet Nam?" A reader named Sue found the uproar over the album cover to be ridiculous, saying the cover "looked no more nauseating than four little boys who had frolicked through the refrigerator steaks and then the toy box." She agreed it was not in the best taste and was not very artistic, but found the "halfwitted" reactions to be amusing it itself, which might have been what the Beatles intended.

The July 23 Beat published additional letters about the cover. One reader didn't find it "so shocking or gruesome," but rather more like a picture you laugh about. Sherry Matthews said it might represent "human carnage," but still thought it was great. Lisa Mason commented that if done to shock, "Since when have the Beatles needed shocks to sell an album?" While Linda Wheeler admitted it wasn't the most desirable cover to look at, she asked, "Did any one of you ever stop to think that they may have been referring to war and how ugly and distasteful that is?"

In the KRLA edition of the July 9 Beat, disc jockey Dave Hull described the Butcher Cover as horrible and extremely distasteful. Hull said that he had showed the cover to several kids hanging out at the station and they didn't like it either. In the July 16 KRLA Beat, the magazine reported Capitol's claim that recalling the cover would cost $250,000, which "wipes out the profit." While intended as pop art, the cover was "vehemently rejected and some even charged it was cannibalistic." The KYA (San Francisco) edition of the July 9 Beat ran an article titled "'Hello Dolly' Flops as Pop Art—Beatles Yank 'Sick' Album Cover." Although a picture of the cover appeared above the article on page 9, KYA Beat decided against putting the butcher picture on its cover. Instead, the newspaper's front cover consisted of a red background box with "The S(l)ick Humor of The Beatles" printed in large black letters. After reporting that most of the copies of the albums were returned to Capitol, the KYA Beat article stated: "The questionable covers are now expected to bring astronomical prices as rare collectors' items." This prediction came true as Butcher Covers are among the most sought after and valuable Beatles collectibles.

Shortly after the album's release in its newly pasted over Trunk Cover, some people noticed there was something under the white background front cover slick. Those with sharp eyes detected the exposed portion of Ringo's black shirt that was not covered over by his white butcher smock. This image appears as a downward-pointing black triangle located approximately 1¼" to the right of the top corner of the trunk's open lid (as shown enhanced above left). In addition, the knees of Ringo's black pants are faintly visible in the lower right corner and his hair can sometimes be seen below the word "Today." Some jackets have trunk slicks that do not completely cover the butcher slick, revealing a thin gray or black strip running along one or two of the trunk slick edges.

Beatles fans who were aware of the controversial original cover correctly surmised that the Butcher Cover was hiding behind the Trunk Cover slick. The adventurous and curious attempted to expose the forbidden treasure by steaming and peeling off the trunk slick. Those who were careful and lucky were able to resurrect the Butcher Cover in all its gory glory. Many others damaged the butcher slick and ended up with a "Botched Butcher" (as tragically shown above right). Many people peeled back a corner of the trunk slick only to find disappointment and cardboard.

Dealers and collectors have developed special terminology to describe Butcher Covers. A "First State Butcher" is a cover that was never pasted over with a trunk slick. It features the Butcher Cover in its pure, unaltered form. This is the most sought after and valuable variation. A "Second State Butcher" or "Paste-Over Butcher" is a cover with a trunk slick pasted over the original butcher slick. These covers are becoming increasingly scarce as people continue to have trunk slicks peeled off to reveal hidden butcher slicks. A "Third State Butcher" or "Butcher Peel" is a cover that has had its trunk slick removed to expose the Butcher Cover. Although not as rare as a First or Second State Butcher, these covers are still very much in demand as a more affordable alternative to the First State Butcher. Many collectors prefer a Third State Butcher over the rarer Second State Butcher because the Butcher Peel shows the controversial cover whereas the Paste-Over Butcher does not.

Out of the initial 750,000 run of the album, mono copies were pressed at a ratio of approximately 5:1 over stereo. Thus, a stereo Second or Third State Butcher should be at least five times scarcer than a mono Butcher. For First State Butchers, the disparity between stereo and mono is much greater. Most surviving First State Butchers were albums either sent to reviewers or given to Capitol sales reps for distribution to radio stations and accounts as promotional copies. Nearly all albums used for promotional purposes were mono. Other surviving jackets originate from Capitol employees who risked termination by pulling Butcher Covers from boxes either before or after shipment back to the factories. Although most of these albums are mono, some stereo albums escaped destruction this way. While it is not possible to determine exactly how many stereo First State Butchers survived, it is clear that they are significantly rarer than the mono version.

The money paid for Butcher Covers is worth noting. Mono First State Butchers in near mint condition have recently sold in the range of $12,500 to $14,500. Stereo First State Butchers in near mint condition have sold for between $17,500 and $27,500. Mono Second State Butchers in near mint condition have gone for between $2,000 and $3,500. Stereo Second State Butchers in near mint condition have sold for $4,000 to $6,000. Mono Third State Butchers in otherwise mint condition that are expertly peeled have sold in the range of $2,500 to $4,000. Stereo Third State Butchers in otherwise mint condition that are expertly peeled have sold in the range of $4,500 to $6,500.

Sealed copies of the Butcher Cover in the original shrink wrap command a hefty premium. A sealed stereo Butcher sold at auction in 2022 for $112,500. But the most sought after and valuable Butcher Covers are those known as "Livingston Butchers." As Operation Retrieve was winding down, a Capitol employee dropped by Alan Livingston's office with a box containing approximately 20 mono and four stereo copies of the album. The employee told Livingston he should take the albums home and save them. By this time, the last thing in the world Livingston ever wanted to see again was a Butcher Cover, so he had to be persuaded to bring them home. He put the box of sealed Butcher Cover albums in a closet in his Beverly Hills home where they remained for over 20 years.

In November 1986, Livingston gave several of the albums to his son, Peter, "to dispose of as he wishes." Peter took two stereo and two mono copies to the November 1986 Beatlefest convention at the Bonaventure Hotel in Los Angeles. Although most dealers were initially skeptical of Peter's claim that he was the son of the former president of Capitol Records, Perry Cox purchased one of the stereo albums for the asking price of $2,500. The two mono copies were sold to collectors for $1,000 each. Peter decided not to sell the other stereo copy. During the next several months, Peter sold most of the remaining copies at much higher prices (up to $3,000 for mono and $10,000 for stereo). To confirm the authenticity and origin of the albums, each was issued with a notarized letter from Alan Livingston stating: "Please be assured that any album that Peter shows you is from my private collection, and is in its original shrink wrapped condition. You should, therefore, feel absolutely confident of its authenticity. I am confident that these albums are among the few, if not the only, genuine remaining editions in mint condition, and hope that you will treat and respect them accordingly." These Livingston Butchers are considered pedigree copies, noted for their mint condition and for being from the collection of the president of Capitol Records. Although these albums are rarely sold, when they are they fetch a significant premium over other sealed albums. Mono Livingston Butchers have sold for as much as $60,000. A stereo Livingston Butcher could bring between $125,000 to $150,000 or more.

Collectors must be careful not to mistakenly purchase a Butcher Peel for the price of a rarer unaltered original. Buyers also need to beware of counterfeits. Those purchasing a Butcher Cover from someone other than a reputable dealer or collector should have the jacket inspected by an experienced and trustworthy dealer or collector.

Although Capitol made every effort to reel in all copies of the album, the label was not entirely successful. While most disc jockeys and reviewers found the Butcher Cover offensive, only a few returned their copies. Despite threats of termination if they could not account for all copies of the album sent to them, several Capitol employees risked the consequences and kept copies for themselves and friends. Other employees were bold enough to pull copies from distribution centers, factories and trucks. At the time, Capitol insisted that no copies of the album with the offensive cover were sold to the public. While Capitol's distribution centers got the word not to ship the album, some rack jobbers were unaware of the recall and placed copies of the album in department stores (such as Sears) and other outlets. There are reports that Wallichs' Music City, which was owned by Capitol co-founder Glen Wallichs, was given preferential treatment and was selling the album prior to its scheduled release. Thus, a limited number of Butcher Covers were sold in stores before the recall.

It is not known how many of the 750,000 albums prepared with the Butcher Cover were destroyed, survived intact or were pasted over, or how many paste-over covers have been peeled. What is known is that demand for Butcher Covers continues to grow. While First State covers, particularly stereo, are truly rare, the economics of supply and demand have created a market in which the Butcher Peel is best described as "the world's most common rare record."

Capitol prepared promotional posters which also had to be recalled. Judging by the small number of genuine Butcher Cover posters that have survived, the vast majority of the posters were destroyed prior to being distributed to record stores. The 18" x 22" white background poster features the cover of the album with the Capitol logo centered below and the word "INCREDIBLE!" in tall red letters at the top.

What seems incredible today is that Capitol ever agreed to release the cover in the first place. When asked by the author why he went against his better judgment and gave in to the group's cover selection, Livingston explained: "Because of our relationship with the Beatles—they were terribly important to us—I wasn't about to fight with them or tell them they were crazy. In this case, I was willing to take the chance that we could get by with it."

INCREDIBLE!

YESTERDAY · DR. ROBERT
I'M ONLY SLEEPING · AND YOUR BIRD CAN SING
WE CAN WORK IT OUT · DAY TRIPPER
NOWHERE MAN · WHAT GOES ON?
DRIVE MY CAR · IF I NEEDED SOMEONE
ACT NATURALLY

The Beatles Yesterday And Today

Livingston's recollections are consistent with an explanation offered by a Capitol spokesman in a newspaper article published shortly after the fiasco. "Epstein doesn't have the final say on The Beatles covers, but The Beatles are an important property to Capitol and so they—or Epstein—usually get what they want." And, in this case, the Beatles wanted the butcher photograph to adorn Capitol's latest "specially created for the American market" album. But, to get to the meat of the matter, were the Beatles really telling us that "Capitol butchers the Beatles"?

When asked whether the butcher picture was motivated by the Beatles resentment of how Capitol reconfigured their albums, photographer Bob Whitaker replied, "Rubbish, absolute nonsense." After all, the picture was his idea, not that of the Beatles. When asked about the controversy in the June 25, 1966 Melody Maker, Paul said: "We were asked to do the picture with some meat and a broken doll. It was just a picture. It didn't mean anything." John added, "it's as valid as Vietnam!" During his discussions with Brian Epstein regarding the group's insistence of using the butcher picture for the cover, a perplexed Alan Livingston asked Brian what the cover meant. Epstein responded, "It's their comment on war. That's what it means to them." John was later asked about the controversial cover during the Beatles 1966 summer tour of America. In a then-rare political statement by a rock star, Lennon replied, "It's as relevant as Vietnam. If the public can accept something as cruel as the war, they can accept this cover." But in 1966, most Americans could accept the war, but not the cover, so Capitol was forced to initiate Operation Retrieve.

In addition to being one of the most collectible items of Beatles memorabilia, the Butcher Cover became a topic of discussion over the years in several interviews with members of the group. The *Anthology* book provides insight into how the group viewed the incident with the passage of time. George said he personally did not like the infamous photo session at the time. "I thought it was gross, and I also thought it was stupid. Sometimes we did stupid things, thinking it was cool or hip when it was naive and dumb; and that was one of them. But again, it was a case of being put in a situation where one is obliged, as part of a unit, to co-operate. So we put on those butchers' uniforms for that picture. In the photograph we're going, 'Ugh!' That's what I'm doing, isn't it? I'm disgusted, and especially so by the baby dolls with their heads off. What the bloody hell was that about? Quite rightly somebody took a look at it and said, 'Do you think you really need this as an album cover?'"

Ringo emphasized that the group was oblivious to the affair. "I don't know how it came about. I don't know how we ended up sitting in butchers' coats with meat all over us. If you look at our eyes, you realize none of us really knew what we were doing. It was just one of those things that happened as life went on."

Paul explained that the photographer would normally have an idea for the session and the group would comply. He gave the example of Dezo Hoffmann having the group wear eyeglasses in some pictures so that he could sell the photos to eyeglass magazines throughout the world. "We were used to photographers giving us bizarre ideas." As for Whitaker, Paul stated: "We'd done a few sessions with Bob before this, and he knew our personalities; he knew we liked black humour and sick jokes. It was very prevalent at that time. And he said, 'I've had an idea—stick these white lab coats on.' It didn't seem too offensive to us. It was just dolls and a lot of meat. I don't know really what he was trying to say, but it seemed a little more original than the things the rest of the people were getting us to do—eyeglasses! We thought it was stunning and shocking, but we didn't see all the connotations."

John observed that photo sessions had become an ordeal, so he really got into it when Whitaker, who he described as a bit of a surrealist, livened things up with "all these babies and pieces of meat and doctors' coats." John admitted, "I don't like being locked into one game all the time, and there we were supposed to be angels. I wanted to show that we were aware of life, and I was really pushing for that album cover. I would say I was a lot of the force behind it getting out and trying to keep it out." (In a 2002 interview with Mojo, Alan Livingston confused his butcher conversations with Brian as being with Paul, leading him to falsely state that Paul pushed for the Butcher Cover.) Lennon later joked: "My original idea for the cover was better—decapitate Paul—but he wouldn't go along with it."

As for Brian Epstein, the Butcher Cover fiasco left him drained. Against his wishes and judgment, he publicly backed the group's decision to use the butcher photo and battled Capitol over its use. When Capitol recalled the album, he had mixed emotions. He was worried about how the group would react to his failure to get Capitol to issue the album with the cover, but was relieved the matter was over. Tony Barrow recalled Brian burning his copies of the butcher transparencies with his cigarette lighter, perhaps wondering if the Beatles image was also going up in smoke.

Rubber Soul through *Revolver* in Canada

by Piers Hemmingsen

For many Canadian Beatles fans, the run of Beatles recordings released between December 1965 and August 1966 represented the Beatles at the very peak of their powers. It was a magical musical record ride that proved that the Beatles were in fact the best group in the world at that time.

Capitol of Canada's Paul White broke the news of upcoming Beatles releases in the November 19, 1965 edition of The Sizzle Sheet. White assured disc jockeys that they would have an "active Christmas" with a brand new album from the Beatles titled *Rubber Soul* (adding "yes auntie that is the title!") and a single featuring two songs, "We Can Work It Out" and "Day Tripper," not on the album. He predicted, "When your listeners get an earful of the selections you'll be working like crazy to programme the LP continually." As for the single, Beatles A&R man George Martin claimed the A-side was "the most interesting the boys have ever done- parts are in WALTZ yet!!" Both were set for December 6 release. The following week White described the album's cover as the "greatest yet" and the single as an "absolute gas," adding that both would be rushed to his readers the next week. The December 10 edition of The Sizzle Sheet described the reaction to *Rubber Soul* as "WOW!" White reported that the LP had dominated the sales picture, with teenagers swarming into record stores to pick up the new album. Early reports indicated that "In My Life" and "Michelle" were the most popular cuts. Both sides of the single were getting equal play across Canada.

Billboard's listing of the top ten records in Canada (compiled by Billboard Canadian reporter Kit Morgan) showed "Day Tripper" debuting at number 3 in its December 25, 1965 issue. The following week Billboard listed the single, now described as "Day Tripper"/"We Can Work It Out," at number one, where it remained for five straight weeks before dropping down to two and then four in its last two of eight weeks on the chart.

DAY TRIPPER
(John Lennon–Paul McCartney)

Maclen Music, Inc.
BMI–2:47

5555
(45–X45378)

THE BEATLES

WE CAN WORK IT OUT
(John Lennon–Paul McCartney)

Maclen Music, Inc.
BMI–2:10

5555
(45–X45377)

THE BEATLES

RUBBER SOUL
JOHN LENNON, PAUL McCARTNEY,
GEORGE HARRISON and RINGO STARR

MONAURAL   T–2442
(T–X–1–2442)

1. I'VE JUST SEEN A FACE (BMI)
(John Lennon–Paul McCartney)
2. NORWEGIAN WOOD (This Bird Has Flown)
(BMI–2:00)(John Lennon–Paul McCartney)
3. YOU WON'T SEE ME (BMI)
(John Lennon–Paul McCartney)
4. THINK FOR YOURSELF (BMI–2:16)
(George Harrison)
5. THE WORD (BMI)
(John Lennon–Paul McCartney)
6. MICHELLE (BMI–2:42)
(John Lennon–Paul McCartney)

THE **SIZZLE** SHEET

FAST TALK ABOUT HOT CAPITOL RECORDS

Dateline: Week Ending November 19/65   No: 159/60   From the Desk of *Paul White*
* *

NEW ALBUM BY BEATLES ... NEW SINGLE TOO!

Want an active Christmas -- then we'll give you one . . . "RUBBER SOUL" . . . a brand
new album from The Beatles. When your listeners get an earful of the selections you'll
be working like crazy to programme the LP continually. In addition to the new LP – due
for release on December 6 – we will be releasing a single featuring two new titles not
contained on the "Rubber Soul" album (yes auntie that is the title!) The singles were
written by John and Paul and are titled – "We Can Work It Out" and "Day Tripper". George
Martin – the Beatles' A & R man claims the top side is the most interesting the boys have
done – parts are in WALTZ time yet!! Now – here are the twelve titles from the great
new package....   (S)T 2442 –   RUBBER SOUL

I've Just Seen A Face	It's Only Love
Norwegian Wood (This Bird Has Flown)	Girl
You Won't See Me	I'm Looking Through You
Think For Yourself	In My Life
The Word	Wait
Michelle	Run For Your Life

HOLLIES ARE ON THE B I G CHARTS
Talk about a sleeper! . . . "Look Through Any Window" by The Hollies was almost ready to
be buried when – WHAM! – Chicago – and other major U.S. cities climbed aboard the deck –
the result – great sales and now the side is on the Billboard and Cash Box Top–100 chart.
Top–40 stations in Canada – please note!

ALSO BUILDING UP . . . .
"Baby What You Do To Me"– Ernie Lyons. This talent from Saskatoon has a winner first time
out for us! The side was picked by CHUM–Toronto as their Canadian Spotlight Disc of the
week and sales reaction has been good. We are taking Ernie on a jaunt to Ontario radio
stations next week to further promote his new deck.

"Walk Hand In Hand"– Gerry And The Pacemakers – do it again. . . . "Pick Of The Week" in
both Billboard and Cash Box and a nod from Gavin.

"Spanish Eyes" crashes onto the Cash Box survey next week. Al Martino will probably have
his biggest hit with this one. It is already an out and out SMASH in Montreal where the
guys have been programming the song from Al's "My Cherie" album (S)T 2362.

AND THEN THERE'S . . .

THE CARNIVAL IS OVER – THE SEEKERS	I'M A MAN – THE YARDBIRDS
OVER AND OVER – THE DAVE CLARK FIVE	DON'T PITY ME – PETER & GORDON

Four sides with POWER! The Clark side is moving faster up the charts than any previous
hit by the group!

re announcing their
UK poll is that
chard was replaced
l British Male
Outstanding World
utstanding
her winners:–

Stones

rporated

Ontario and very
into the tongue
stardom.

RACE MARBLES MARCHES ON !

Rapidly building up a buying public in the States – Race has been willing to join any
"ANTI" group down there – almost goofed this week when asked to join the "Anti Dribblin'
Frams Society" –– Race was pulled back just in time – bird slightly damaged! There is
no truth to the rumour that we were sending Race on a tour of Vietnam . . . we may, however
trundle out the company bicycle and send him off on a publicity tour to the Northwestern
Territories! Seriously (?) though LIKE A DRIBBLIN FRAM" is turning out to be a HIT!

BEATLES ALBUM . . . WOW!. . .

"RUBBER SOUL" dominated the sales picture this week. Teenagers swarmed to the record bars
to pick up their copies of the brand new album . . . early reports indicate "In My Life"
and "Michelle" as the most popular cuts. Meanwhile their double–sided smash single
continues to race its way to No.1 spot in the country – "We Can Work It Out" and "Day
Tripper" are getting equal play across the nation.

–MORE–

Canada's RPM Weekly listed "We Can Work It Out" for six weeks on its RPM Top 40 Play Sheet, including one week at number one. RPM added a "(f/s)" designation indicating the record's flip side was also getting air play. Toronto's CHUM listed the single as "Day Tripper"/"We Can Work It Out" during the disc's 15 weeks on the charts, which included six weeks at number one. Vancouver's CFUN listed the single as a "Twin Pick Hit" on its December 1 chart, initially listing "Day Tripper" first before reversing the order by the time the single hit number one. The station took the unusual step of listing two tracks from *Rubber Soul*, "Michelle" and "Norwegian Wood," at number 30 on its January 15, 1966 singles chart. Montreal's CFCF debuted "Day Tripper" at seven on its December 10 survey. The next week the disc topped the chart as "We Can Work It Out." CFCF reported the single for 11 weeks, including three at number one. The single sold about 150,000 copies as did *Rubber Soul*, which CHUM charted in its Top 5 Albums listing for 19 weeks, including eight at the top. Looking back years later, acclaimed Canadian journalist Robert Fulford recalled that "'Michelle' was the song everyone was singing everywhere from night clubs to nursery schools."

The popularity of "Michelle" and its inclusion of a few lines in French made the song a natural to be reworked with French lyrics. Les Atomes, a French-speaking Canadian band from Saint-Jérôme, Québec, released their version of the song with French lyrics written by Canadian songwriter Lucien Brien on a Capitol single issued in February 1966. The April 20 Québec chart Palmarès Disc-O-Logue listed "Michelle" by Les Atomes at number 11. Some listeners initially thought the song was re-recorded by the Beatles "en Francais" for the French-speaking Canadian market.

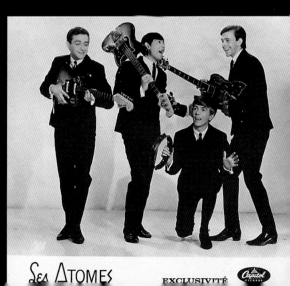

Although "Day Tripper" and "We Can Work It Out" were still receiving significant air play throughout January 1966, disc jockeys learned from the January 21 Sizzle Sheet that Capitol was planning to release a new Beatles single pairing "Nowhere Man" and "What Goes On" on February 7. The following week White announced that the release date had been pushed back a week until February 14. Most Canadians were not aware that these songs were on the British version of *Rubber Soul*. "Nowhere Man" debuted at number 3 in the March 19 Canadian Top Ten published by Billboard before topping the charts the following two weeks and then dropping to two and then three before Billboard temporarily stopped printing a Canadian chart. RPM charted the single for nine weeks on its newly-expanded RPM 100 chart with a peak at number one on March 28. Toronto's CHUM charted "Nowhere Man" for 13 weeks, including three weeks at the top. The station's April 18 chart features a cubist drawing of a face and a request for listeners to send in their own version of the Nowhere Man (see page 117). Vancouver's CFUN charted the single as "Nowhere Man"/"What Goes On," indicating that the B-side also received air play. The disc topped the CFUN survey for two weeks in early March. Ottawa's CFRA reported "Nowhere Man" at number one for two weeks on its Swing Set Survey. Small market station CFJR in Brockville, Ontario distributed a music survey called The Disc Count, which listed "Nowhere Man" at number one for two weeks. The single sold over 85,000 copies.

Paul White used the May 27 Sizzle Sheet to inform readers that two great new Lennon-McCartney songs, "Paperback Writer" and "Rain," had been shipped and that teenagers were "already applauding this latest triumph as a fab disc to dance to." Stations were told: "Keep that No. 1 spot ready...The Beatles are headed for it!" True to form, "Paperback Writer" held down the number one spot in the Billboard Canadian top 10 for four of its seven weeks on the charts. It also topped the RPM 100 chart on July 11 during its seven-week run. Toronto's CHUM listed the disc as "Paperback Writer"/"Rain" during its ten weeks on the charts, including two at the top in late June. Vancouver's CFUN charted both songs as a single entry for seven weeks, including two at number one. Montreal's CFCF charted the single for nine weeks. It was listed solely as "Paperback Writer" up through its fourth week, June 24, when the song tied with Frank Sinatra's "Strangers In The Night" for the number one spot. The following week the single took sole possession of the top as "Paperback Writer"/"Rain." Brockville's CFJR was a few weeks behind the major markets, reporting the single at number one for two weeks in July. "Paperback Writer" sold just under 100,000 units.

Shortly after the release of "Paperback Writer" Paul White issued a news flash in the June 3 Sizzle Sheet that Capitol would be issuing a new Beatles album titled *Yesterday And Today* on June 20. The new disc featured six hit singles and five songs new to Canada. White arranged for the manufacture of about 50,000 (mostly mono) albums. Parr's Print & Litho, located in Toronto, received the color separations for the front slicks for the album cover from Capitol during the week of June 6. The front cover featured the same picture of the Beatles wearing butcher smocks and covered with raw meat and baby doll parts as the U.S. version. The printed slicks were then trucked across town to Modern Album for the manufacture of the album jackets, which were sent to Compo's pressing plant in Cornwall. White received two sample mono covers and a stereo slick from Parrs so he could check for color match and errors. Capitol's sales reps were given "sales slicks" of the cover to show to customers. These slicks were three-hole punched on the right side to fit into a binder with other sales slicks and pages of information about Capitol releases.

It is not known how many records were packaged in Butcher Covers before White received a telephone call from Alan Livingston, President of Capitol Records in Hollywood, informing him that the Butcher Cover was "kaput!" as per directive from EMI Chairman Sir Joseph Lockwood. White immediately halted production and arranged for the destruction of all Butcher Covers and sales slicks. Compo employees spent an entire evening removing records from covers. Unlike America, where thousands of copies were sent to reviewers, salesmen and even a few stores before the recall order was issued, only a handful of Canadian Butcher Covers survived. The front cover slicks for the covers are distinguishable from their American counterparts by the LITHO IN CANADA ▣ marking with the Parrs logo on the lower right edge of the cover. In addition, the Canadian Butcher slicks are laminated, whereas the U.S. slicks are not.

White's mono Butcher Cover (shown right) and stereo slick are now owned by Bruce Spizer. The other mono jacket and a few sales slicks are in the hands of collectors. There are also a few production copies that have survived, including one owned by Bob Purvis' family. Purvis worked as a truck driver who picked up boxes of records at Capitol's Toronto office for delivery to distributors. He was occasionally given albums by Capitol's shipping department in gratitude for his work. In June 1966 he received a shrinkwrapped mono copy of *Yesterday And Today* with the Butcher Cover, thus establishing that some boxes of manufactured albums with Butcher Covers were sent to Capitol by Compo.

IS THIS ALBUM COVER SICK? See Page 6

NEW
STEREO

Capitol RECORDS

YESTERDAY · DR. ROBERT
I'M ONLY SLEEPING · AND YOUR BIRD CAN SING
WE CAN WORK IT OUT · DAY TRIPPER
NOWHERE MAN · WHAT GOES ON?
DRIVE MY CAR · IF I NEEDED SOMEONE
ACT NATURALLY

The Beatles
Yesterday
And Today

File Under: The Beatles

T 2553

Although Capitol Records was unable to keep the Butcher Cover controversy contained in America, most Canadians only saw the album's replacement cover featuring the lads hanging around a steamer trunk and were totally unaware of the incident. An exception was those who read the "after FOUR" pull-out section for teens in the June 23, 1966 Toronto Telegram, which featured an untrimmed stereo/mono slick of the Canadian butcher cover on its front page with the banner "Is this album cover sick?" (see previous page). The inside article was full of errors, including attributing the idea for the cover to the Beatles manager, but it did contain some practical insights. "The Beatles have bungled. A little joke thought up by manager Brian Epstein has showered down charges of infanticide, cannibalism and sadism on the shaggy heads, bruising their image like hellstones. It all began when Epstein developed a taste for pop art and sick humor. For the newest Beatle LP, Today And Tomorrow, he decided on an unusual cover. The Beatles, each with a happy, if not mad grin on their faces, are sitting nonchalantly in white butcher coats. Dismembered baby dolls, their heads removed and legs and arms off, are perched on Beatles' shoulders and knees. Gory red slabs of raw meat are intermingled with dolls' heads and bodies, hanging out of Beatles' pockets and draped over their shoulders. Sick? Capitol Records thought so from the first. And they refused the picture. Finally Epstein and his charges made threats like 'We won't make records for you anymore,' until Capitol finally gave in." After stating that Capitol recalled the cover after a sampling of public opinion showed the portrait, intended as pop art satire, was misinterpreted, the article stated: "This is a mild description. What parents were asking was why the Beatles were promoting infanticide. Did the Beatles want their 13- and 14-year-old fans killing off their baby brothers and sisters?"

When *Yesterday And Today* went on sale in mid-June, it underperformed compared to other Beatles albums, selling just over 50,000 copies. CHUM charted the LP for ten weeks, including four weeks at number one. Sales of *Yesterday And Today* were most likely affected by the disc having only five new songs and the subsequent release of a new Beatles album less than two months after it went on sale. Paul White alerted disc jockeys to the new disc in the August 5 Sizzle Sheet: "Next week probably the greatest Beatles album ever...'Revolver'...hits the market featuring a whole batch of new songs." White's praise of the LP, which was issued on August 8, was spot on. *Revolver* sold about 80,000 units and held down the number one spot in CHUM's album listings for eight of its eleven weeks on the chart. One of disc's tracks, "Good Day Sunshine," got extensive air play on Ottawa's CFRA despite not being a single.

"Yellow Submarine" and "Eleanor Rigby" were pulled from *Revolver* for single release. The disc topped the Billboard Canadian top ten listing for two weeks. The single also topped the RPM 100 chart on September 19 during its ten-week appearance. Vancouver's CFUN debuted "Yellow Submarine"/"Eleanor Rigby" in its August 6 survey at number one, where it remained for three weeks. Toronto's CHUM charted each side separately, tracking "Eleanor Rigby" for 12 weeks and "Yellow Submarine" for 11, with both hitting number one. Montreal's CJMS also listed the songs separately, but only "Yellow Submarine" surfaced to the top. Montreal's other pop powerhouse, CFCF, featured a cartoon of the Beatles aboard a Yellow Submarine on the cover of its September 2 survey, which listed the song at number one. Ottawa's CFRA also charted "Yellow Submarine" at one. The single sold about 105,000 copies and provided a wonderful end to one of the Beatles most creative periods.

The Beatles Rendezvous with Greatness (As 1965 Spins into 1966)

by Al Sussman

December 1965 was a remarkable month for the Beatles and the National Aeronautics and Space Administration ("NASA"), giving both the confidence to reach for greater heights in the upcoming year. For NASA, 1966 would bring the final five Gemini manned space missions, the first test launch of the Saturn 1B rocket and the Block I Apollo spacecraft, the first U.S. soft landing on the moon and the first U.S. lunar orbit. As for the Beatles, they would shoot for new sounds during their *Revolver* recording sessions, embark on world and North American tours and begin work on what would be their landmark album, *Sgt. Pepper's Lonely Hearts Club Band*. But 1966 would also bring missteps, drama and near and real catastrophes for not only the Beatles and NASA, but for the world at large.

On December 4, Gemini VII blasted off for a 14-day endurance flight aimed at determining if man could survive and function in space for two weeks, more than enough time to complete a manned moon mission. Commander Frank Borman and pilot James Lovell tested new lightweight spacesuits and performed 20 experiments. As Borman and Lovell orbited the earth, the Beatles released their fabulous new single, "We Can Work It Out" and "Day Tripper," and long player, *Rubber Soul*, a remarkable collection of songs that showed the Beatles were evolving as a band, experimenting with new sounds and different instruments. Meanwhile, NASA was preparing Gemini VI and its crew, commander Walter Schirra and pilot Thomas Stafford, to join Gemini VII in space. Gemini VI had been scheduled for liftoff on October 24, with the goal of rendezvousing in orbit and docking with an unmanned Agena target vehicle, but when the Agena broke apart shortly after separation from its Atlas rocket, the mission was delayed. NASA came up with an alternate plan under which Gemini VI would be launched days after Gemini VII and then rendezvous with Gemini VII. Liftoff was set for December 12, but 1.2 seconds after the Titan booster's engines ignited, they shut down, with Schirra calmly deciding not to eject. Three days later, Gemini VI finally lifted off and rendezvoused with Gemini VII before returning to earth the next day. Gemini VII completed its mission, landing on December 18.

Newsweek

DECEMBER 27, 1965   35c

Rendezvous in Space

THIRTY-FIVE CENTS

DECEMBER 24, 1965

TIME
THE WEEKLY NEWSMAGAZINE

Rendezvous on the Road to the Moon

APOGEES

TRANSFER ORBIT

Gemini 7
187 mi.
16 mi.
Gemini 6
170 mi.
161 mi.

8 RENDEZVOUS A final forward burn matches Gemini 7's velocity.

Gemini 7
120 ft.
Gemini 6

3 At 2nd apogee a forward burn raises perigee 40 mi.

6 At 3rd apogee a forward burn circularizes orbit.

Gemini 7
Approach lights

Gemini 6's radar tracks Gemini 7 from 30 mi.

Gemini 6

9 Approach to less than 10 ft.

4 A burn to match Gemini 7's orbital plane

NIGHT SIDE

1 LIFT-OFF 8:37 a.m. Dec. 15

7 Rendezvous starts with a forward burn to transfer to Gemini 7's orbit.

2 At perigee a forward burn to raise apogee 9 mi.

Gemini 6's initial orbits (Elliptical)

100 mi.

5 Tweak burn raises apogee ½ mi.

Gemini 7

140 mi.

Gemini 6's first catch-up orbit (Elliptical)

12 Gemini 6 descends to lower orbit and splash-down.

PERIGEES
165 mi.

Gemini 6's second catch-up orbit (Circular)

10 FLY-AROUND Gemini 6 circles around Gemini 7 at 40 to 60 ft.

183 mi.

Gemini 7's circular rendezvous orbit

11 FORMATION FLYING Spacecraft stay together for 5¼ hrs.

R.M. Chapin, Jr.

VOL. 86 NO. 26
(REG. U.S. PAT. OFF.)

Just as the Beatles new single and LP arrived in record stores on December 3, the band began what would be their final U.K. tour, with 18 shows at nine venues in nine days. Unlike their final American tour in 1966, when they didn't perform any songs from their just-released *Revolver* LP, the group played two songs from *Rubber Soul*, "If I Needed Someone" and "Nowhere Man," and their new single "Day Tripper" and "We Can Work It Out" (with John on organ).

Meanwhile, on December 9, CBS-TV debuted a new animated Christmas special featuring the popular characters from the Charles Schultz comic strip *Peanuts* with a wonderful musical score by jazz pianist Vince Guaraldi. *A Charlie Brown Christmas* was an instant hit that would go on to become a beloved holiday perennial for decades to come.

1966 began with the start of a 12-day transit strike in New York City on John Lindsay's first day as mayor of what he would later dub "Fun City." A week later and 3,000 miles away, author Ken Kesey and his Merry Pranksters held the first truly high-profile Acid Test at San Francisco's Fillmore Auditorium, with music by a group called the Warlocks, who would soon change its name to the Grateful Dead. Acid Tests were parties centered around LSD, which was still legal in California at the time but not all that familiar to the general public. Later in the year, disc jockey Tom Donahue led the Bay Area's pioneering underground FM radio station KSAN, which gave early exposure to the Grateful Dead and the other members of the emerging San Francisco music scene, which owed a great deal to the atmosphere created at the Acid Tests. The Bay Area music scene and LSD really wouldn't achieve widespread awareness until the following year, but Newsweek magazine ran a cover feature on LSD in its May 9 issue, albeit in its Medicine section. It described the differences between LSD and other hallucinogens and the up-and-down effects of amphetamines and barbiturates. It introduced the public to the high priest of the "psychedelic experience," 45-year-old former Harvard psychologist Dr. Timothy Leary, who declared in 1966 that "the psychedelic battle is won…His next piece of advice: turn on parents and teachers by the messages you have learned."

On Wednesday, January 12, a mid-season replacement for ABC's canceled rock showcase Shindig debuted. It was an instant sensation. The show was a campy version of the DC Comics fixture Batman starring Adam West as the deadpan Caped Crusader and Burt Ward as his crime-fighting, holy pun-making partner, Robin.

LIFE

MAD NEW WORLD
of Batman, Superman
and the Marquis de Sade

MARCH 11 · 1966 · 35¢

Newsweek

MAY 9, 1966   40c

LSD
and the Mind Drugs

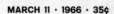

The initial Batman episode ended on a cliffhanger with Robin trapped by the villainous Riddler. The show's narrator ominously intoned "The worst is yet to come!" An hour later, President Lyndon Johnson delivered his third State of the Union address, in which he asked the 89th Congress for more funding for the war in Vietnam. He pledged that the U.S. would remain until Communist aggression was defeated. At that time, the vast majority of the country agreed with LBJ's position on the war. America's patriotic sentiment was confirmed in February when a song called "The Ballad Of The Green Berets" by SSgt. Barry Sadler took just five weeks to become the No. 1 single in the U.S. and spent five straight weeks at the top.

The day after his State of the Union, LBJ announced the appointment of Robert C. Weaver as Secretary of the new Department of Housing and Urban Development (HUD). Weaver was the first African-American cabinet-level appointee. Six days later, on January 19, Indira Gandhi, daughter of India's first prime minister, Jawaharlal Nehru, took office as that nation's first female prime minister.

Also in mid-January, Truman Capote's *In Cold Blood* went on sale. The non-fiction crime novel explored the 1959 quadruple murders of the Clutter family in the small farm town of Holcomb, Kansas, from the perspectives of the killers, the victims and members of the rural community. Capote detailed the background and mental characteristics of the murderers, Richard Hickock and Perry Smith, who were captured six weeks after the crime and subsequently executed. The book quickly became the top-selling true crime book of all time, a title it held until 1974, when its sales were exceeded by Vincent Bugliosi's book on the Charles Manson murders, *Helter Skelter*. The heinous crime depicted in Capote's *In Cold Blood* would sadly be surpassed by the hideous murders of eight student nurses later in the year.

On January 29, the Broadway show *Sweet Charity*, starring Gwen Verdon and directed by Bob Fosse with music by Cy Coleman, lyrics by Dorothy Fields and book by Neil Simon, debuted at New York's Palace Theatre. On February 10, Jacqueline Susann's potboiler novel, *Valley Of The Dolls*, was published and would become the biggest-selling novel of 1966 with a feature film based on the novel two years later.

Newsweek

APRIL 4, 1966   40c

Prime Minister
INDIRA GANDHI

Newsweek

JANUARY 24, 1966   35c

'IN COLD BLOOD'
Truman Capote's Hot Book

The space race between the U.S. and the U.S.S.R. was one of the year's ongoing major stories. On February 3, the unmanned Russian spacecraft Luna 9 became the first space vehicle to achieve a soft landing on the moon. On the last day of the month, a NASA Northrop T-38 Talon jet crashed at Lambert Field in St. Louis, claiming the lives of the planned crew for the Gemini IX mission, Charles Bassett and Eliot See. The aircraft, piloted by See, struck the roof of the McDonnell factory building containing the Gemini IX spacecraft and simulator.

One and a half months after the tragic deaths of astronauts Bassett and See, Gemini VIII lifted off from Cape Kennedy on March 16 with a crew of first-time astronauts Neil Armstrong and David Scott. The planned three-day mission was to include the first rendezvous and docking in space and a two-hour space walk by Scott. Less than seven hours into the mission, the Gemini capsule successfully docked with an Agena target vehicle. Shortly thereafter, during a radio blackout, the Gemini spacecraft suddenly went into a roll. Thinking the problem was with the Agena, Armstrong separated the capsule from the target vehicle, but that only made things worse, with the roll rate approaching one revolution per second. By firing the reentry thrusters, Armstrong steadied the spacecraft moments before he and Scott would have lost consciousness, saving their lives and possibly the space program as well. Having recently lost two astronauts in a plane crash, losing two more in space might have pushed Congress to stop funding the manned space program. The fuel depletion caused by the faulty thruster responsible for the near-deadly roll necessitated the immediate termination of the mission. After only six orbits in space, Gemini VIII safely splashed down in the western Pacific Ocean. Armstrong's coolness in dealing with the sudden emergency on his first spaceflight was not lost on the brass at NASA. He would later become the first man to walk on the moon. On March 31, the Soviets launched the unmanned Luna 10, which went into lunar orbit on April 3, where it remained until May 30.

Back on earth, George Harrison married Pattie Boyd on January 21. Liverpool's Cavern Club closed on February 28, only to reopen on July 23. On March 4, the London Evening Standard ran a John Lennon article as part of a series of interviews with each Beatle conducted by Maureen Cleave. In a wide-ranging conversation, John gave his views on a number of subjects, including Christianity. While the U.K. reaction was rather muted (a raised eyebrow here, a sigh there and perhaps "That cheeky Lennon!"), it would cause quite a different reaction in America a few months later.

Although the majority of Americans supported the country's involvement in Vietnam, the anti-war movement was gaining momentum. One of the first multi-city demonstrations was held on March 25-26 in eight U.S. cities (the New York protest attracted over 20,000 demonstrators) and six foreign locations around the world. Undeterred, the U.S. government increased troop levels from 215,000 in early March to 250,000 by the end of April. Another major protest on May 15 brought an estimated 10,000 to Washington, D.C. The next day, Rev. Dr. Martin Luther King, Jr., the civil rights movement's apostle of non-violence, publicly announced his opposition to the war.

On May 1, the Beatles headlined the annual New Musical Express Poll Winners Concert with a short set that would be their last performance before a concert audience in England. The Rolling Stones, second on the bill, released their most musically-adventurous single, "Paint It Black," the following week. That month also saw the release of the Beach Boys' masterpiece album, *Pet Sounds*. Brian Wilson's greatest work would be judged as such in later years, but its influence would be felt right away via the next two Beatles albums.

The space race continued onward. On June 2, the unmanned Surveyor 1 made the U.S.'s first soft landing on the moon. Until its shutdown on January 7, 1967, the lunar lander transmitted data and over 11,000 photographs that would be used in the Apollo moon program. The day after Surveyor 1's landing, Gemini IX, with its new crew of Tom Stafford and Gene Cernan, took off from Cape Kennedy for a three-day mission. Although the spacecraft successfully rendezvoused with its target vehicle, it could not dock because the target's nose cone failed to separate, giving the appearance of an "angry alligator." The crew achieved its primary objective, a spacewalk by Cernan that proved hot, difficult and tiring. Gemini IX's return to earth on June 5 set the stage for a hot, difficult and, at times, tiring summer.

The White House held a Civil Rights Conference on June 1 and 2 in follow up to the 1964 Civil Rights Bill and the 1965 Voting Rights Act. It was hoped that this would help prevent a repeat of the "long hot summers" of urban riots of the last two years. Nearly all of the major civil rights groups were represented, although it was boycotted by the increasingly-radicalized Student Nonviolent Coordinating Committee led by Stokely Carmichael, who would soon be exhorting its followers to embrace the philosophy of "Black Power."

Three days after the conference's end, James Meredith, the first black student to attend the University of Mississippi four years earlier, embarked on a low-key civil rights march from Memphis to Jackson, Mississippi. On June 6 Meredith was shot in the leg by a white sniper and was hospitalized. Many of the organizations who had attended the White House Conference now took up Meredith's cause. By June 26, some 15,000 marchers completed his intended journey to the Mississippi capital. Less than a month later, though, five days of racial disturbances in Cleveland's Hough district resulted in the deaths of four people and some 275 arrests.

Change was very much the order of the day that summer. On June 13, the Supreme Court ruled in *Miranda v. Arizona* that an arrestee had to be read his or her "Miranda" rights: "You have the right to remain silent. Anything you say can and will be used against you in a court of law. You have the right to talk to an attorney...." On July 1, Medicare, which passed the year before after furious congressional debate, officially took effect. On the Fourth of July, President Johnson signed the Freedom of Information Act, which would be a thorn in the side of LBJ and succeeding presidents since it required the partial or complete release of federal documents upon request. And on June 30, a group of women, led by *Feminine Mystique* author Betty Friedan, founded the National Organization for Women (NOW). Its founding conference would take place that October, ushering in the modern feminist movement.

The hot summer also produced three of the most heinous crimes of the '60s. On the night of July 13, eight student nurses from South Chicago Community Hospital were tortured and murdered by a career criminal and drifter named Richard Speck. He was apprehended within a couple of days after trying to commit suicide at a seedy Chicago hotel. Then, on August 1, a court-martialed Marine sharpshooter and former University of Texas student named Charles Whitman killed his wife and mother and drove to the UT Austin tower. He killed three people at the tower and then went on a shooting rampage from the top of the tower, killing 11 more and wounding 31 before being killed by Austin police. At the time it was the deadliest mass shooting by a lone gunman in U.S. history. And, on September 18, 21-year-old Valerie Jean Percy, daughter of Chicago business executive and Republican candidate for the U.S. Senate from Illinois Charles Percy, was bludgeoned and stabbed to death in her bedroom in the Percy mansion in Kenilworth, Illinois. The case has never been solved.

Newsweek

JUNE 20, 1966

THE
MEREDITH
MARCH

Martin Luther King

LIFE

THE
TEXAS
SNIPER

Store window
shattered by
bullets fired from
tower in background
by Charles Whitman

AUGUST 12 · 1966 · 35¢

In stark contrast to these crimes, Project Gemini was literally reaching new heights. On July 18, Gemini X lifted off from Cape Kennedy's Pad 19 with a crew of Gemini III veteran John Young and first-timer Michael Collins. Once again, the objective was to rendezvous and dock with an Agena tracking vehicle, but this time it would be a double rendezvous. The first rendezvous and docking was in low orbit with an Agena booster that was launched into space 100 minutes prior to the Titan rocket lifting the Gemini capsule into orbit. While docked, the crew ignited the Agena's rocket engine, climbing to a then-record height of 474 miles above the earth. The Agena's rocket was also used to bring the spacecraft down to a lower orbit. During this time, Collins opened his hatch, stood up and took pictures of the southern Milky Way. After 39 hours joined together, the Gemini capsule separated from its Agena and then headed for a rendezvous with the Agena from the aborted Gemini VIII mission. Collins made his second EVA (Extra Vehicular Activity), this time outside the capsule and tethered with a 50-foot umbilical cord. After removing a science pack from the nearby Agena, he returned to the capsule. This spacewalk took place on July 20, exactly three years before the first lunar landing would take place, with Collins orbiting the moon in the Apollo 11 command module. Gemini X splashed down on July 21 after an action-packed three-day mission.

Next up was Gemini XI, a three-day flight from September 12-15 with a crew of Gemini veteran Pete Conrad and first-timer Richard Gordon. The main objective this time was a direct-ascent rendezvous with an Agena, simulating a lunar module's rendezvous and docking with an Apollo command/service module after taking off from the moon. This was achieved without any problems. The crew also practiced docking and un-docking maneuvers, and Gordon took two difficult spacewalks. The Agena was used to push the capsule to a record height of 852 miles.

The final Gemini flight, Gemini XII, lifted off on November 11. The crew consisted of Gemini VII veteran Jim Lovell and Edwin "Buzz" Aldrin. The main objective of the mission was to see how well astronauts could work outside of the spacecraft. Aldrin had three EVAs, the longest lasting nearly 2½ hours. Unlike the spacewalkers of the previous three missions, Aldrin had only minimal difficulties and was not exhausted by the experience. A 2008 documentary, *When We Left Earth*, credited Aldrin's underwater training and other innovations of his with making his EVAs much easier. He was the first human to take a "selfie" in space and would later be the second man to walk on the moon.

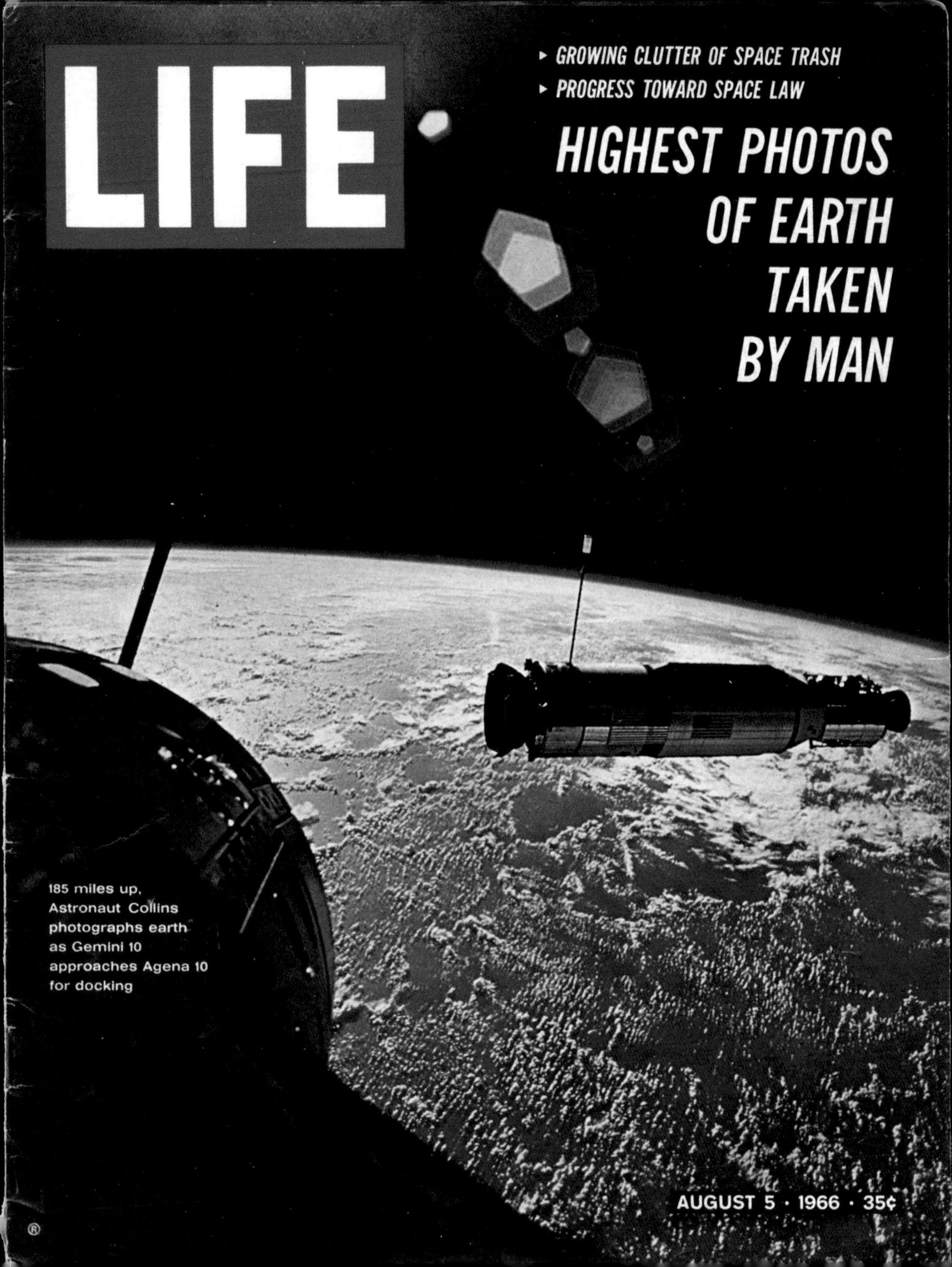

LIFE

▸ GROWING CLUTTER OF SPACE TRASH
▸ PROGRESS TOWARD SPACE LAW

HIGHEST PHOTOS OF EARTH TAKEN BY MAN

185 miles up,
Astronaut Collins
photographs earth
as Gemini 10
approaches Agena 10
for docking

AUGUST 5 · 1966 · 35¢

Bob Dylan closed his 1966 world tour with a concert at the Royal Albert Hall in London on May 27. John Lennon and George Harrison were in attendance. For the tour, Dylan opened up with a seven-song acoustic set followed by an eight-song electric set in which he was backed by the Hawks (soon to become The Band). During the electric part of the show Dylan was often heckled and ridiculed by folk music purists, with some walking out. He released his most elaborate album, the double-disc *Blonde On Blonde*, on June 20. Then, on July 29, Dylan had a mysterious motorcycle accident that would keep him professionally sidelined for nearly a year and a half. The next day, before a huge crowd of nearly 97,000 at Wembley Stadium, England's national football (soccer) team defeated West Germany, 4-2 in extra time to win its first and, to date, only World Cup. Three days later, on August 3, groundbreaking topical comic Lenny Bruce died at his home in the Hollywood Hills from a morphine overdose. Less than three weeks later, Simon and Garfunkel recorded a piano-backed version of "Silent Night" counterbalanced with a faux August 3 radio newscast in the background, effectively increasing in volume as the recording progresses. The newscaster covers the Civil Rights Bill, the death of Lenny Bruce, a planned open housing march through Cicero, Illinois led by Martin Luther King, Jr., Richard Speck being indicted for the murder of eight student nurses and the war in Vietnam. "Silent Night/Seven O'Clock News" would be released on the duo's *Parsley, Sage, Rosemary And Thyme* LP on October 10.

While all this was going on, the Beatles were living through their own tumultuous summer roiled by heat and controversy. After taking much of the spring to record their next LP, which would later be titled *Revolver*, the group embarked in late June on a quick world tour that would take them from Germany to the Far East and finally to North America. It should have been a relatively easy trek, but there was great controversy in Japan over the decision to stage the Beatles Tokyo concerts at the hallowed Budokan Hall martial arts venue. After the concerts were held without serious incident, it was on to the Philippines, where the group immediately came under the heavy-handed tactics of the newly-elected administration of Ferdinand and Imelda Marcos. The Beatles fall from grace was due to their "no-show" for a state luncheon for which Brian Epstein had already turned down the supposed "invitation" that was in reality a command to appear. The group was roughed up as they tried to leave the country and extorted by Philippine authorities of their fee for their concert in Manila before their plane could take off. It was the first time the Beatles had encountered an adversarial reception in 3½ years of touring.

Meanwhile, in America, just as the Beatles latest single "Paperback Writer" was getting its initial spins on the radio, the group was involved in a relatively minor controversy that got more national press in England than in the United States. The June 4 Melody Maker reported that the Beatles had "stirred up a heated controversy in America's midwest" after a "Pittsburgh disc-jockey broadcast an alleged telephone interview last week in which the Beatles put down the Barry Sadler recording 'The Ballad Of The Green Berets' as 'rubbish.'" Apparently this was viewed as an attack on the elite special operations force of the U.S. Army in Vietnam rather than their dislike of a particular song that had outperformed their U.S. single "Nowhere Man" and the Rolling Stones' "19th Nervous Breakdown" in the Billboard Hot 100 a few months earlier. This led to a "wave of anti-protest" with "several major disc retailers reported to have contacted Capitol Records and asked them to 'have the Beatles cool it with this kind of talk.'" The magazine added that some "retailers reported that fans have threatened to boycott the stores unless Beatles discs were removed from the racks." Although this mini-controversy escaped the attention of the American music trade magazines, it was an omen of things to come.

Capitol quickly faced a much more intense barrage of anti-Beatles fervor when it sent out advance copies of the Beatles LP *Yesterday And Today* during the second week of June. The response to album's cover, featuring the Beatles dressed in butcher smocks and covered with decapitated baby doll parts and slabs of raw meat, was so negative that Capitol was forced to immediately recall the album and reissue it with a mundane photo of the boys hanging around a steamer trunk. The epic story of the Butcher Cover controversy is told in an earlier chapter beginning on page 64. Despite the disruptions caused by the album's recall, *Yesterday And Today* raced to the top of the album charts published by Billboard, Cash Box and Record World by the end of July, just in time for the main event of the group's "summer in hell."

On Sunday, July 3, while the Beatles were arriving in the Philippines, the New York Times Magazine ran the four individual interviews that the group had given to Maureen Cleave four months earlier. Once again, there was virtually no reaction. But Beatles press officer Tony Barrow had also offered the interviews to Datebook, an American teen magazine.

Datebook ran the Lennon and McCartney interviews in its September 1966 issue, which reached newsstands at the end of July. The magazine's cover features a close-up of Paul in concert and a series of controversial quotes under the banner "SHOUT-OUT ISSUE." Paul is quoted on the cover as saying, "It's a lousy country where anyone black is a dirty nigger!" Inside the magazine, we learn that Paul's actual statement was edited down for effect and that he wasn't saying all blacks are dirty or condemning the U.S. as a lousy racist country, but rather commenting on a picture he saw that disturbed him (a statue lying in the gutter of "a good Negro doffing his hat and being polite"). Although Paul's use of "the N word" would have caused more trouble today, it was the following remarks by John that came back to haunt John and the Beatles: "Christianity will go. It will vanish and shrink. I needn't argue about that; I'm right and I will be proved right. We're more popular than Jesus now; I don't know which will go first, rock and roll or Christianity. Jesus was all right, but his disciples were thick and ordinary. It's them twisting it that ruins it for me."

Datebook's editor, Ari Unger, sent copies of the issue to American radio stations, including those in the Deep South. Disc jockey Tommy Charles at WAQY in Birmingham, Alabama was offended and seized on the opportunity for piety and publicity. He turned Lennon's out-of-context comments about the Church of England, particularly "We're more popular than Jesus now," into a "Ban the Beatles" campaign. It spread nationally, especially in the South among Christian Fundamentalists, when the UPI wire service ran an article on the controversy written by the manager of its Birmingham office, Al Benn. The New York Times ran a story on the hot topic on August 5, the same day as the U.K. release of the Beatles *Revolver* LP. Charles organized a mass destruction of Beatles records and memorabilia while other radio stations in the South organized bonfires. Even some Northern stations that had been very pro-Beatles stopped playing their records for a week or so before realizing that failure to play the Beatles was ratings suicide.

On August 6, as *Revolver* and the "Yellow Submarine"/"Eleanor Rigby" single were released in America, Beatles manager Brian Epstein, rising from a sickbed, flew to New York to hold a press conference explaining Lennon's five-month-old comments and trying to head off cancellation of the Beatles North American tour, now less than a week away. On August 11, the group landed in Chicago, where the tour would begin the next night. Lennon made a non-apology apology (since he really had nothing to apologize for) during a tension-filled press conference.

Youngsters and adults attend a "Beatles Burning" organized by radio station WAYX-AM in Waycross, Georgia to protest John Lennon's comment that the Beatles were more popular than Jesus. Former fans tossed Beatles memorabilia and record jackets into a bonfire to burn their "Beatles trash." Because the burning of vinyl records gave off noxious fumes, record albums and singles were often stomped on instead. The press conference with John's "apology" was recorded by Ken Douglas and released by Chicago Tribune photographers Bill Bender and Barney Sterling as a mail order album titled *I Apologize.*

Lennon's "apology" seemed to placate the media and most radio stations, but the controversy hovered over the tour. The Ku Klux Klan picketed their Washington, D.C. concert. The scariest moment occurred during the tour's only Southern concert in Memphis, where a cherry bomb firecracker went off, causing the Beatles and many in the audience to think it was a gunshot. Attendance was down for several shows, perhaps because of the controversy, perhaps because the group's fandom was growing older and no longer enjoyed the screamathon concerts. And, in the midst of the decade's hottest summer in North America, several shows were threatened by heavy thunderstorms. Their Cincinnati concert was postponed until the next afternoon, forcing the Beatles to play that show in oppressive afternoon heat and then fly to St. Louis for another thunderstorm-marred show that evening. Lennon created additional controversy with comments opposing the war in Vietnam at a press conferences in Toronto and New York. The tour lasted just two weeks, but must have seemed like two years to the Beatles. It finally ended on a windy, chilly Monday night, August 29, at San Francisco's Candlestick Park. The group had already decided that this would be their last concert for at least some time so Paul McCartney asked Tony Barrow to record the show on his cassette tape recorder. Paul pulled out their long-time show stopper "Long Tall Sally" to end the show and the tour.

Despite all the controversy and the fact that the Beatles performed nothing from *Revolver* on the tour, the album reached the top of Billboard's LP chart the week of September 10 and remained there for six weeks. "Yellow Submarine" got extensive airplay, but was denied the top spot in Billboard by the Supremes' "You Can't Hurry Love."

September brought a new TV season in which NBC premiered two significant, if not highly-rated, shows. On Thursday, September 8, debuting in the slot formerly occupied by the western Laredo was sort of an outer space western called Star Trek, starring veteran actor William Shatner and a diverse, talented supporting cast that included Leonard Nimoy, DeForest Kelley, Nichelle Nichols, Majel Barrett, George Takei, Walter Koenig and James Doohan. The following Monday evening, September 12, NBC's pop/rock showcase Hullabaloo was replaced by a show about a fictional rock group called The Monkees, starring actor/singers Micky Dolenz and Davy Jones and singer/songwriters Michael Nesmith ("Wool Hat") and Peter Tork. The October 24 Newsweek called the group the "direct videological descendants of the Beatles" and described the show as a "calculatingly manufactured a product as a TV Dinner."

Monday

September 12, 1966

Evening

Swanson is traveling west to meet her fiancé—with her $1000 dowry sewn in her hat. Huldah: Anna-Lisa. Jack Desmond: Carl Reindel. George Bennett: Tris Coffin. Whitney Phillips: Laurence Haddon.

6 BUDDY STARCHER—Music
8 MARSHAL DILLON—Western
13 McHALE'S NAVY—Comedy
15 MOVIE—Drama

"Backfire." (1950) A war veteran tries to find his missing buddy to clear him of a murder charge. Virginia Mayo, Gordon MacRae, Edmond O'Brien, Dane Clark. (One hour, 45 min.)

NEW SHOWS

For information about the new series on Monday night, see pages 23-28.

7:30 4 8 GILLIGAN'S ISLAND

COLOR The show begins a third season in this new time spot. Tonight, Gilligan is bitten by a bat—and the horror-stricken castaway is certain he will turn into a blood-thirsty vampire. Gilligan: Bob Den-

ver. Skipper: Alan Hale. Howell: Jim Backus. Ginger: Tina Louise. Professor: Russell Johnson. Mary Ann: Dawn Wells. Mrs. Howell: Natalie Schafer.

6 MONKEES—Comedy

DEBUT COLOR The Monkees are hip to a plot endangering the life of Princess Bettina of Harmonica. Songs: "Take a Giant Step," "This Just Doesn't Seem To Be My Day." Davy: David Jones. Micky: Micky Dolenz. Wool Hat: Mike Nesmith. Peter: Peter Tork.

Guest Cast

Otto .... Theo Marcuse
Sigmund .... Vincent Beck
Princess Bettina .... Katherine Walsh
Chambermaid .... Ceil Cabot
Vendor .... Dick Wilson

13 IRON HORSE—Western

DEBUT COLOR "Joy Unconfined." After winning a railroad in a poker game, Ben Calhoun faces his first problem: Ben's former partner Luke Joy claims the line is rightfully his. Ben: Dale Robertson. Dave Tarrant: Gary Collins. Bar-

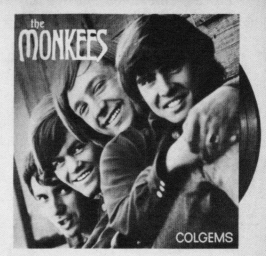

Reminder: See TV Guide listings for exact times in your area.

In the months before The Monkees premiered on television, the show's producers decided that a lot of good money could be made by having the "group" make records. In recording sessions mainly held that July and overseen by Don Kirshner, the Monkees, backed by top-notch session musicians, recorded two albums' worth of material. Their first single, "Last Train To Clarksville," written by Tommy Boyce and Bobby Hart, the duo who produced the single and much of the early Monkees material, was released in mid-August, right in the middle of the controversy-ridden final Beatles tour. The song conveniently debuted on the Billboard Hot 100 the week before the TV show's premier, reaching the top on November 5. The disc was certified gold on October 27, 1966, signifying sales of one million units. The first Monkees LP did even better. It was released on October 10 and began its run of 13 straight weeks at the top on November 12, being replaced on February 11, 1967, by *More Of The Monkees*. It sold five million copies.

By 1966, television had replaced the newspaper as the number one source for news, with 58% of the American public getting most of its news from the tube. The most prestigious program was the CBS Evening News, led by anchor and managing editor Walter Cronkite, viewed by many as "the most trusted man in America." In a cover story in Time magazine dated October 14, Cronkite was the centerpiece, labeled "the single most convincing and authoritative figure in TV news." He ended each broadcast with "And that's the way it is," and viewers believed it. Figures like "Uncle Walter" and NBC's team of Chet Huntley and David Brinkley were highly influential and delivered the news with straight-down-the-middle objectivity, save for Cronkite's obvious enthusiasm for the space program.

And there was "The Bobby Phenomenon," profiled in a cover story in Newsweek the week of October 24. The junior senator from New York, Robert F. Kennedy, had been out campaigning for Democratic candidates in the upcoming elections, but was often greeted with Beatlemania-type scenes that overshadowed the candidates actually up for election. Though the younger brother of President Kennedy was still four years away from running for re-election to his Senate seat and, presumably, six years away from a possible presidential run, liberals unhappy with LBJ's Vietnam policies were already heavily lobbying Bobby to take on Johnson in 1968. There were certainly indications that there was no love lost between LBJ and RFK, but we wouldn't find out the extent of their enmity until many years later. But Bobby was still being the good Dem soldier while keeping a higher profile in the Senate than younger brother Ted.

Newsweek

OCTOBER 24, 1966 40c

The Bobby
Phenomenon

All year long, Americans wondered how big the war in Vietnam would grow. In late October, President Johnson visited the troops in Cam Ranh Bay. The mid-term national elections, held on November 8, were the first referendum of sorts on LBJ's Vietnam war policies. The Democrats held on to their majorities in the House of Representatives and the Senate for the 90th Congress, a benefit of the Johnson/Democrat landslide two years before, but lost 47 House seats and three in the Senate. Edward Brooke (D-Mass.) became the first popularly-elected black U.S. senator since the end of the Reconstruction era in 1877. The Republicans gained seven new governorships, with the highlight being the victory of actor Ronald Reagan in California. Reagan's tight-fisted policies as governor would soon make him the darling of conservatives still smarting from Barry Goldwater's big loss in 1964. Richard Nixon, while not running for office, was already setting himself up as the man to beat for the G.O.P. Presidential nomination in 1968.

Perhaps fittingly, another new animated Christmas classic, Dr. Seuss' *How The Grinch Stole Christmas*, debuted on CBS-TV on December 18. And the U.S. Northeast had a very white Christmas, with a blizzard moving up the Atlantic Coast on Christmas Eve, dumping anywhere from 10 to 20 inches of snow in its wake.

Following the frenzy of the summer, the Beatles went their separate ways after returning from America. Ringo spent time at home with wife Maureen and year-old son Zak. George and wife Pattie journeyed to India for sitar instruction with Ravi Shankar and, for Pattie, the discovery of transcendental meditation. Paul, with some help from George Martin, composed the score for a new Hayley Mills film, *The Family Way*, and became immersed in the London underground scene. John went to Spain for his first solo acting role as Musketeer Gripweed in the Richard Lester-directed *How I Won The War*. When he returned to London in November, Beatles breakup rumors were breaking out in America, the Beach Boys' "Good Vibrations" was the hot record of the moment in England, there was a rumor in London of a McCartney car crash, and Lennon had his first encounter with a Japanese avant-garde artist named Yoko Ono. On November 24, the Beatles reconvened at EMI Studios on Abbey Road and began work on a new Lennon song called "Strawberry Fields Forever." Now that they had stopped touring, the Beatles could fully concentrate on their music. A new chapter had begun. On June 1, 1967, when the songs recorded during the sessions went on sale as *Sgt. Pepper's Lonely Hearts Club Band*, the Beatles would once again rendezvous with greatness.

138

Newsweek

LBJ IN VIETNAM

NOVEMBER 7, 1966 40c

Newsweek

HOW BIG THE WAR?

FEBRUARY 14, 1966 35c

VIETNAM:
The Bombers
Go North

A Song For Every Purpose Under Heaven

by Al Sussman

The release in early December 1965 of the Beatles double-sided hit single, "We Can Work It Out"/"Day Tripper," and trailblazing album, *Rubber Soul*, symbolically climaxed what many consider rock 'n' roll's greatest year. 1965 was the year of high tide for the British Invasion, the birth of folk-rock and...Herb Alpert and the Tijuana Brass.

For all of December, two of the top five albums in the U.S. were by an L.A.-based faux-mariachi band, led by trumpeter Herb Alpert (also a record producer and co-owner of A&M Records). The group spent November and the first half of December in the singles Top 10 with its version of "A Taste Of Honey," a show tune that the Beatles recorded for their first album in 1963. The Tijuana Brass version was on their album *Whipped Cream & Other Delights*, the cover of which features a photograph of a naked model, Dolores Erickson, covered in chiffon and shaving cream (whipped cream would have melted under the studio lights). Two songs from the album, "Whipped Cream" and "Lollipops And Roses," plus "Spanish Flea" from the group's *Going Places* LP, were heard weekdays starting in December 1965 on the popular ABC-TV game show The Dating Game, which was added to ABC's Saturday night lineup in 1966. In March of 1966, "A Taste Of Honey" won Record of the Year for 1965 at the annual Grammy Awards ceremony. The group's *Going Places* and *What Now My Love* LPs would dominate the top of the album chart into the summer.

The Byrds essentially invented 1965's new musical trend dubbed folk-rock. They had the number one single in the U.S. for three weeks in December with their version of Pete Seeger's adaptation from the book of Ecclesiastes, "Turn! Turn! Turn!," a song that felt perfectly appropriate at the mid-way point in a rapidly-evolving decade. The group performed the song with its "time for every purpose under heaven" message on the December 12 Ed Sullivan Show. The following May the Byrds flew up the charts to number 14 with "Eight Miles High," considered to be the first psychedelic rock song. The Beatles and the Byrds had mutual admiration for each other. George Harrison admitted he nicked a couple of Byrd leader Jim McGuinn's guitar figures for his "If I Needed Someone" on *Rubber Soul*.

140

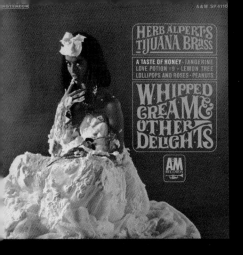  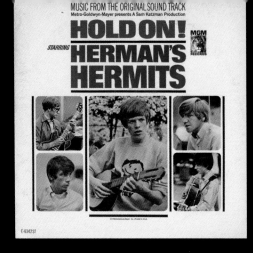

1965's final number one single was the first and only American chart-topper for the Dave Clark Five, a band that, nearly two years earlier, had been hyped as the first serious challenger to the Beatles. Early in 1964, the DC5's first major hit, "Glad All Over," had broken the hammerlock "I Want To Hold Your Hand" had on the top of the British charts. Two years later, they had racked up six U.S. Top 10 singles before snagging their first U.S. chart-topper with a cover of Bobby Day's "Over And Over." During the mid-sixties the DC5 appeared on The Ed Sullivan Show 18 times. But the group that had boasted "Catch Us If You Can" in the summer of 1965 soon found out that their failure to evolve musically left them lagging behind groups that experimented with new sounds. The DC5 would have only one more U.S. Top 10 hit for the rest of the decade, a cover of Marv Johnson's 1959 hit "You Got What It Takes." Many other British bands who followed the Beatles to America in 1964 would suffer a similar or worse fate, including the Searchers, Gerry and the Pacemakers, Billy J. Kramer with the Dakotas, Freddie and the Dreamers, the Swinging Blue Jeans and the Honeycombs.

There were, of course, exceptions, such as the Rolling Stones. But they were not alone. Herman's Hermits (fronted by teen idol Peter Noone) continued their American chart success in 1966 with "A Must To Avoid" (#8), "Listen People" (#3), "Leaning On A Lamp Post" (#9), "This Door Swings Both Ways" (#12) and "Dandy" (written by Ray Davies of the Kinks) (#5). They also starred in the film *Hold On* with Shelley Fabares. The Animals scored big with "Don't Bring Me Down" (#12) and "See See Rider" (#10). Peter and Gordon remained on the charts with "Woman" (written by Paul McCartney under the pseudonym Bernard Webb) (#14) and "Lady Godiva" (#6).

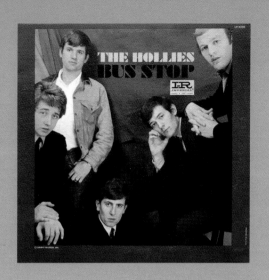  

The Kinks, after two riff-driven Top 10 singles in the second half of 1964, developed a more versatile sound, largely through the diverse work of the Davies brothers, Ray and Dave, and a devoted cult following. They found success in 1966 with "A Well Respected Man" (#13), "Dedicated Follower Of Fashion" (#36; #4 U.K.) and "Sunny Afternoon" (#14; #1 U.K.). Dusty Springfield returned to the charts in 1966 with "You Don't Have To Say You Love Me" (#4).

Although the Hollies had success in England dating back to 1963 covering American R&B songs such as "(Ain't That) Just Like Me" and "Searchin'" by the Coasters, "Stay" by Maurice Williams and the Zodiacs, and "Just One Look" by Doris Troy, the band did not have any success in America until 1966 when it reached the charts four times with two minor hits "Look Through Any Window" (#32) and "I Can't Let Go" (#42) and the Top 10 smashes "Bus Stop" (#5) and "Stop Stop Stop" (#7).

A second, harder-edged wave of British bands that gained popularity in 1965 had a greater impact in 1966 and beyond. The blues-based Yardbirds broke through in 1965 with "For Your Love" (#6) and "Heart Full Of Soul" (#9), but the band's more adventurous singles would come in 1966 with "Shapes Of Things" (#11), "Over Under Sideways Down" (#13) and "Happenings Ten Years Ago" (#30). During this period, the band had three different lead guitarists: Eric Clapton, Jeff Beck and Jimmy Page. The literally-explosive Who, owners of six U.K. Top 10 singles over 1965-66, developed an American cult following through TV appearances on shows like Shindig. But the group's U.S. breakthrough would not happen until 1967. The band's 1966 classic "My Generation" stalled at 74 in the charts.

  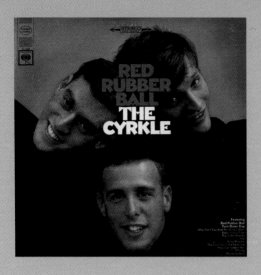

The first American number one single of 1966 had a history going back to March 1964. That month, singer/songwriter Paul Simon and his occasional musical partner Art Garfunkel recorded their first LP, *Wednesday Morning, 3 AM*, a folk music album that included a Simon original called "The Sound Of Silence." The LP was released that October on Columbia Records and disappeared among the wave of new folk albums released in the wake of the success of the Kingston Trio and Peter, Paul & Mary. The following year, with folk rock on the rise and "The Sound Of Silence" getting some college radio airplay, Tom Wilson, who had produced the original recording, added electric instrumentation and released it as a single, now called "The Sounds Of Silence," in September 1965. Simon, performing solo in England, and Garfunkel, attending Columbia University in New York, knew nothing of this until the single took off in December, reaching number one on January 1 and trading places with "We Can Work It Out" throughout January. A hastily-recorded and rather inconsistent new Simon & Garfunkel LP, dubbed *Sounds Of Silence*, just missed reaching the album Top 20 in the spring of 1966 but, after Paul and Art notched two more Top 5 singles in the first half of 1966 with "Homeward Bound" and "I Am A Rock," their new album, the much-loved follow-up that fall, *Parsley, Sage, Rosemary And Thyme*, would be a Top 5 LP. Their late 1966 single "A Hazy Shade Of Winter" peaked at 13.

Simon had another big hit that summer when his song "Red Rubber Ball" became a million-selling number two smash when released as a single by the Cyrkle, a Pennsylvania group managed by Brian Epstein and named by John Lennon. The group scored a number 16 hit with its follow-up single, "Turn-Down Day," that featured sitar. The Cyrkle was one of the opening acts for the Beatles 1966 North American tour.

In the face of Beatlemania and the British Invasion in 1964, one American record company more than held its own. Motown and its family of labels (including Tamla, Gordy and Soul) had been steadily growing through the early 1960s. But, with the emergence of hitmakers such as the Temptations, the Four Tops and especially the Supremes and the Holland-Dozier-Holland songwriting/production team, Motown came very close to fulfilling its corporate motto and becoming "The Sound of Young America." By mid-February 1966, three Motown singles were in the U.S. Top 10 — Stevie Wonder's second major hit "Uptight (Everything's Alright)," the Marvelettes' "Don't Mess With Bill" and the Supremes' seventh Top 5 single in less than two years (albeit the first not to top the charts), "My World Is Empty Without You." By late February, charter Motown composer/producer/performer Smokey Robinson and the Miracles had a Top 15 single and Top 10 album with "Going To A Go-Go." By that November, *The Supremes A' Go-Go* LP would break the Beatles near-summer-long lock on the top of the album chart. Holland-Dozier-Holland would notch three more writer/producer number one singles with the Four Tops' "Reach Out I'll Be There" and the Supremes' "You Can't Hurry Love" and "You Keep Me Hangin' On." The Temptations had a string of hits in 1966 with "Get Ready" (#29), "Ain't Too Proud To Beg" (#13), "Beauty Is Only Skin Deep" (#3) and "(I Know) I'm Losing You" (#8).

1966 was the year that rock and R&B LPs began to have a more significant presence in the upper reaches of the charts. Until then, the most successful albums were movie soundtracks, Broadway cast albums, comedy albums and LPs by pop singers and folk artists. The Beatles, of course, were the exception, selling millions of albums starting in January 1964. But in 1966, other teen-oriented artists began racking up impressive album sales.

144

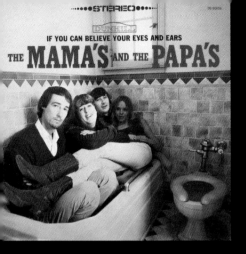

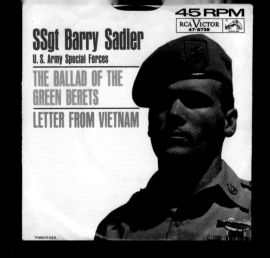

The Mamas & the Papas were one of the first acts to emerge from the Laurel Canyon music scene and one of the few groups of the time with unique personalities and a trademark sound. Their debut album, *If You Can Believe Your Eyes And Ears*, included their first two Top 5 singles, "California Dreamin'" (#4) and the chart-topper "Monday Monday," as well as Cass Elliot's arguably definitive cover of the Beatles "I Call Your Name." Their eponymous second album, released that September, would yield two number five hits, "I Saw Her Again" and "Words Of Love."

Cass and Denny Doherty of the Mamas & the Papas had worked with John Sebastian and Zal Yanovsky back in their folk club days in Greenwich Village (as chronicled by John Phillips in the Mamas & the Papas' 1967 single "Creeque Alley"). Sebastian and Yanovsky then formed the Lovin' Spoonful. Their first single of 1966, "Daydream," greatly influenced Paul McCartney's "Good Day Sunshine" and was a number two hit, as was the next disc, "Did You Ever Have To Make Up Your Mind?" The Spoonful topped the charts for three weeks in August with "Summer In The City" and followed it with "Rain On The Roof" (#10). Their December single "Nashville Cats" peaked at eight in 1967.

SSgt. Barry Sadler was a Special Forces medic in Pleiku before suffering a knee injury in May 1965. Back in the States, he collaborated with writer Robin Moore, author of the novel *The Green Berets*, on a song paying tribute to the Special Forces unit. "The Ballad Of The Green Berets" was released in January 1966 just prior to Sadler's appearance on The Ed Sullivan Show. The song topped the U.S. singles chart for five weeks beginning in early March and Sadler's very unmemorable album held down the number one spot for five weeks on the Top LP's chart.

"The Ballad Of The Green Berets" not only kept the Beatles North American single "Nowhere Man" from reaching number one, but also stopped the Rolling Stones "19th Nervous Breakdown" from being their third U.S. chart-topper in less than a year. After establishing themselves in 1965 as the number two band in the world behind the Beatles, the Stones issued a string of outstanding singles in 1966. The group's out-of-character ballad "As Tears Go By" peaked at number six in late January. And while "19th Nervous Breakdown" stalled at number two in March, the group's next single, "Paint It Black" (with Brian Jones on sitar) topped the charts for two weeks in June before being displaced by the Beatles "Paperback Writer." The Stones' "Mother's Little Helper" (with its lovely baroque B-side "Lady Jane") stalled at number eight in August, but should have done better, and the underrated "Have You Seen Your Mother, Baby, Standing In The Shadow?" squeaked into the Top 10 at number nine in late October. On the album front, their U.S. album *December's Children (And Everybody's)* was issued in early December 1965 and peaked at number four in January. The compilation LP *Big Hits (High Tide And Green Grass)* was released in late March and peaked at number three. The group's musically-adventurous *Aftermath* LP, the first with all songs credited to Mick Jagger and Keith Richards, was released on April 15 in the U.K. and on July 2 in the U.S. (with a slightly different lineup). The album topped the U.K. charts and peaked at number two in the U.S. The Stones ended the year by releasing a poorly-recorded live album in America, *Got Live If You Want It*.

Little Steven Van Zandt of Bruce Springsteen's E Street Band has noted that the Stones were the biggest influence on garage bands that were springing up all over America in the mid-sixties. One of the first to attain commercial success

was the Rascals, who Stevie would induct into the Rock and Roll Hall of Fame in 2010. The Rascals were made up of three former members of the Starliters, Twist-era star Joey Dee's backing band, plus flashy jazz drummer Dino Danelli. They made their debut in February of '65 at a Garfield, New Jersey, dive called the Choo-Choo Club, near the home of percussionist/singer Eddie Brigati, and soon moved up to the Phone Booth in Manhattan and the trendy Long Island club The Barge. It was during their stint at The Barge that the Rascals came to the attention of promoter Sid Bernstein. Sid became their manager and, as promoter of the huge first Beatles concert at Shea Stadium, put a "The Rascals Are Coming!" message on the scoreboard, much to the annoyance of Brian Epstein. They quickly got a contract with Atlantic Records, the first rock band signed to the already-legendary R&B label. But when Johnny Puleo's Harmonica Rascals objected to the band being called the Rascals, they were forced to change their name. With the Little Rascals taken for the TV version of the Hal Roach *Our Gang* films, Bernstein renamed the band the Young Rascals. Their first single, "I Ain't Gonna Eat Out My Heart Anymore," peaked just short of the Billboard Top 50 in early 1966. With the R&B keyboardist Felix Cavaliere taking over the primary lead vocal spot, their second single, a cover of the Olympics' "Good Lovin'" (with a great B-side cover of Wilson Pickett's "Mustang Sally"), produced by Atlantic's Arif Mardin and Tom Dowd, was released late in February and reached the top of the charts by the end of April. Their debut LP, *The Young Rascals*, was released in late March, and reached number 15. Highlights included a cover of Pickett's 1965 hit "In The Midnight Hour." "You Better Run," the followup single, reached number 20. All this set the stage for greater successes in 1967 and 1968. The pop/R&B-flavored material on the first two Rascals LPs provided plenty of cover material for young bands who would be emerging over the next couple of years.

147

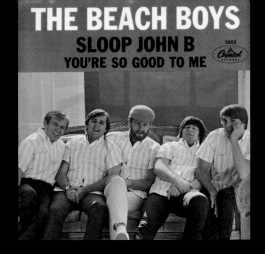

Meanwhile, on the other side of the country, as the Beach Boys' "Barbara Ann" was racing up the charts, the group's guiding musical genius, Brian Wilson, was working on a project he had been hinting at since he stopped touring with the band in early 1965. Portions of that year's *The Beach Boys Today* and *Summer Days (And Summer Nights)* LPs were filled with songs that strayed from the surfing/cars/chasing girls formula of most previous Beach Boys albums. These were songs about relationships and growing through adolescence in the turbulent mid-sixties. With the band on tour in early 1966, using the Wrecking Crew of ace session players and production techniques inspired by Phil Spector, Brian created his ultimate collection of these more personal songs, plus a Beach Boys cover of the folk song "Sloop John B" that reached number three on the singles chart just before the release of the new album, *Pet Sounds*. Despite the album's excellence and the Top 10 success of the beautiful followup single, "Wouldn't It Be Nice"/"God Only Knows," *Pet Sounds* peaked at number ten, the lowest for a new Beach Boys LP since their second album, *Surfin' U.S.A.*, three years earlier. Capitol Records considered *Pet Sounds* a failure and, within weeks, issued *Best Of The Beach Boys*, which did slightly better with a peak at number eight. In England, though, with the help of Derek Taylor's promotion of the album among his friends in the British pop world, *Pet Sounds* spent six months in the album Top 10, setting up the spectacular success that fall of Brian's next masterwork, the single "Good Vibrations," which topped the charts on both sides of the Atlantic and was the Beach Boys' first million-seller in the U.K.

The same week in May in which "Sloop John B" reached its peak on the singles chart, Bob Dylan reached the Top 10 with "Rainy Day Women #12 & 35," which most people remember for its "Everybody must get stoned" refrain.

The song was the lead single from Dylan's double LP *Blonde On Blonde*, the climax of his trilogy of classic albums, starting with 1965's *Bringing It All Back Home* and *Highway 61 Revisited*. These albums marked Dylan's transition from unpredictable folk stylist to his full embrace of rock, while retaining a connection to his folk roots, which *Blonde On Blonde* did spectacularly. But Dylan's tour of England that spring, in which he was backed by a group that would soon become The Band, starkly showed the ideological split between Dylan's core audience of folkies (one who famously yelled "Judas") and the young fans making Dylan the pop idol of the moment in the U.K. Not long after returning from the U.K. tour, Dylan would have a still-mysterious motorcycle accident that put the brakes on his out-of-control career momentum and would result in a radical musical about-face for Bob over the next several years.

On the heels of the success of the Rascals' "Good Lovin'," a number of young bands from both America and the U.K. had hit singles that created the genres of garage band rock and the first iteration of punk rock. There was the Shadows of Knight's cover of the Irish band Them's "Gloria," the Syndicate of Sound's "Little Girl," Question Mark and the Mysterians' "96 Tears" and Count Five's "Psychotic Reaction." There was an obscure two-year-old record by a group called the Shondells (and their singer, Tommy James), "Hanky Panky," that took off during the summer following airplay on Pittsburgh Top 40 radio, knocking the Beatles "Paperback Writer" from the top of the charts in mid-July. And another of that summer's biggest hits was a cover of a failed 1965 U.S. single composed by Chip Taylor and recorded by the New York band the Wild Ones. An English band called the Troggs recorded it the following year, and their version of "Wild Thing" topped the American charts and nearly did so in England that summer.

Then there was the saga of Napoleon XIV and "They're Coming To Take Me Away, Ha-Haaa!" Jerry Samuels was a songwriter who had written, among others, "The Shelter Of Your Arms," a Top 20 hit for Sammy Davis, Jr. in early 1964. Two years later, Samuels took on the persona of Napoleon XIV for this novelty record about a guy who had been driven crazy by his girlfriend. As often happens with novelties, this one took off for no logical reason. By mid-August, "They're Coming To Take Me Away, Ha-Haaa!" had reached number three in the Billboard Hot 100 singles chart and had topped Cash Box's chart. It even was a Top 5 single in the U.K. But then, mental health organizations began to protest the record. Top 40 radio, just coming off the John Lennon "We're more popular than Jesus now" controversy, quickly dropped Napoleon XIV from their playlists. That fall, a pair of novelties, the New Vaudeville Band's "Winchester Cathedral" and Sopwith Camel's "Hello Hello," launched a vogue of recordings with a 1920s/'30s flavor that Paul McCartney would take advantage of over the next couple of years.

Two solo artists of the British Invasion's second wave had great success in 1966. Petula Clark, the most successful of the British female vocalists, knocked the Beatles "We Can Work It Out" from the top of the charts in February with "My Love," just missed the Top 10 in April with "A Sign Of The Times," and reached the Top 10 in August with one of her finest records, the Tony Hatch-written/produced "I Couldn't Live Without Your Love." Donovan, who emerged in 1965 as a Dylan clone, took on a new producer, Mickie Most, and a new, more mainstream image. He had a number one single in September with "Sunshine Superman" and nearly another in December with "Mellow Yellow" (with Paul McCartney participating in the background revelry), but was blocked from the top by "Winchester Cathedral."

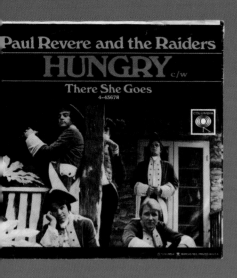  

Paul Revere and the Raiders, who gained national recognition with numerous appearances on the ABC-TV week-day teen show Where The Action Is, just missed the Top 10 with "Just Like Me" in January 1966. Their next single, "Kicks," with its anti-drug message, peaked at number four in May. They continued their assault on the charts with "Hungry" (#4) and "The Great Airplane Strike" (#20), before ending the year with "Good Thing," which peaked at four in 1967. The Knickerbockers, from New Jersey, scored a Top 20 hit with "Lies," a rocker that some mistook for the Beatles. The Standells sang of "muggers, lovers and thieves" in the garage band classic "Dirty Water" (#11 in July). Although lead singer/drummer Dick Dodd snarled "Boston, you're my home," the group was from L.A. The Bobby Fuller Four fought their way into the Top 10 in March with "I Fought The Law." That July in L.A., Fuller was found dead of asphyxiation in his mother's car. One of the finest American groups of their time, the Association, had their first hits in the second half of 1966, including "Along Comes Mary" (#7) and "Cherish" (#1 for thee weeks).

Although he grew up in Baton Rouge, Louisiana, Johnny Rivers became part of the Los Angeles scene with a regular gig at the Whisky a Go Go on Sunset Strip. He had two big hits in 1966 with "Secret Agent Man" (#3) and "Poor Side Of Town" (#1). Lou Christie struck gold with the chart-topper "Lightnin' Strikes," but some program directors balked at his "Rhapsody In The Rain" with its theme of making love in a car, causing the song to stop at 16. Frank Sinatra remained a force with "Strangers In The Night," a number one million seller and Grammy Record of the Year, and "That's Life" (#4). Sinatra's daughter Nancy made it big with "These Boots Are Made For Walkin'" (#1 million seller), "How Does That Grab You Darlin'?" (#7) and "Sugar Town" (#5 and a million seller).

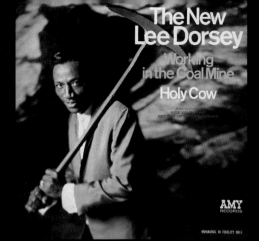
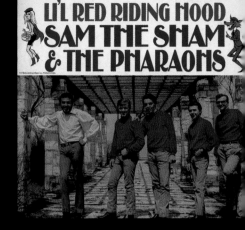

On the R&B front, Percy Sledge topped the charts with his million seller "When A Man Loves A Woman." Although

Sam & Dave's "Hold On! I'm Comin'" only got to number 21 in the Billboard Hot 100, the song topped the R&B charts

and sold a million copies. Bobby Hebb scored a number two hit with "Sunny," which led to his being an opening act

on the Beatles 1966 North American Tour. Billy Stewart had a Top 10 hit with his wild rendition of "Summertime," a

George Gershwin-penned aria from the opera *Porgy And Bess*. Eddie Floyd gave Stax Records in Memphis a million

seller with "Knock On Wood," which stalled at 28 in the Billboard Hot 100, but was a number one R&B single.

Down the Mississippi River in New Orleans, songwriter/producer Allen Toussaint's continued collaboration with

Lee Dorsey led to the hits "Get Out My Life Woman" (#44), "Working In The Coal Mine" (#8) and "Holy Cow" (#23).

Robert Parker danced his way up the charts with his self-penned tune "Barefootin'" (#7). As 1966 came to a close,

Aaron Neville was gaining national attention with "Tell It Like It Is," which peaked at number two in January 1967.

There were several other notable songs in 1966, including the Left Banke's baroque pop classic "Walk Away

Renée," which peaked at number five, and "Five O'Clock World" by the Vogues, a number four hit. The Righteous

Brothers showed they could survive without producer Phil Spector with their number one hit "(You're My) Soul And

Inspiration." A pair of somewhat goofy songs hit number two, "Snoopy Vs. The Red Baron" by the Royal Guardsmen

and "Lil' Red Riding Hood" by Sam the Sham & the Pharaohs. The Statler Brothers' "Flowers On The Wall" peaked at

number four. Tommy Roe, who was on the bill for the Beatles February 1964 concert at the Washington Coliseum,

had two Top 10 pop hits, "Sweet Pea" (#8) and "Hooray For Hazel" (#6).

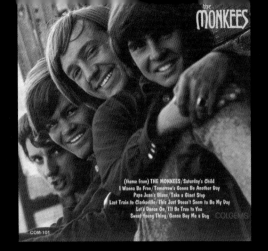
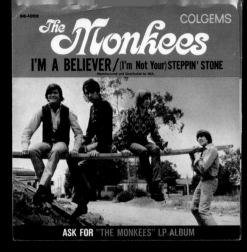

Neil Diamond, a Brill Building songwriter who would later become a superstar performer, had his first hits as a recording artist in 1966 with "Solitary Man" (#55), "Cherry, Cherry" (#6) and "I Got The Feelin' (Oh No No)" (#16). But his biggest success that year would be as a songwriter for the biggest musical story of the last months of 1966.

The Monkees, a TV comedy about a young rock band, was heavily influenced by the Beatles films *A Hard Day's Night* and *Help!* The band was made up of a former child actor turned musician (Micky Dolenz), a former jockey turned actor/singer (Davy Jones) and two singer/songwriters (Peter Tork and Mike Nesmith). Originally, the four were just going to be sitcom actors, but it was decided early on that a lot of money could be made by having the Monkees make records. Don Kirshner was brought in as music supervisor, along with his stable of Brill Building songwriters. Tommy Boyce and Bobby Hart were given production duties. They lined up top session musicians to provide instrumental backings for the Monkees' vocals. The first Monkees release, a single of Boyce-Hart's "Last Train To Clarksville," was released on August 16 and topped the Billboard Hot 100 for one week in early November. The Monkees' first LP was released on October 10 and reached the top of album charts a month later, remaining there until February 1967, when it was replaced by the group's second album, *More Of The Monkees*. At Kirshner's request, Neil Diamond provided "I'm A Believer" for the Monkees' second single, which hit the top of the Hot 100 on December 31, 1966, remaining there for seven weeks and becoming 1967's biggest-selling single. Diamond also penned the group's third single, "A Little Bit Me, A Little Bit You." The Monkees' third album, *Headquarters*, topped the charts for one week on June 24, 1967, before giving way to *Sgt. Pepper's Lonely Hearts Club Band*.

A Funny Thing Happened in 1966 in Film & Comics

by Frank Daniels

While Beatles fans and music lovers were listening to the landmark albums *Rubber Soul* and *Revolver*, their associated singles and all the other great music of that era, the world was busy entertaining itself in ways that were not always directly associated with music. The time from December 1965 through 1966 was a period during which a fair number of outstanding and memorable movies, television shows and literary forms came out for the people to enjoy.

Dramatic movies of the period were led by *Dr. Zhivago*, which was released on December 22, 1965. Based on Boris Pasternak's novel about the Russian Civil War (1917-22), the movie is not an historical drama but is instead a love story – one that was banned in the U.S.S.R. at the time of its release. Critics panned the length of the film, but it garnered 20 awards internationally, including five Academy Awards. The American Film Institute rates the film among the 50 best movies. *Dr. Zhivago* contains outstanding performances by Omar Sharif (Zhivago), Julie Christie, Rod Steiger and Alec Guinness. The soundtrack LP, scored by Maurice Jarre and including the motif "Lara's Theme" in multiple passages, topped the Billboard Top LP's chart for one week in March 1966 during its 157 weeks on the charts.

Another popular dramatic love story was the July 1966 French film *A Man And A Woman* starring Anouk Aimée and Jean-Louis Trintignant. The movie won several honors, including two Academy Awards (Best Foreign Language Film and Best Original Screenplay), two Golden Globe Awards (Best Foreign Language Film and Best Actress- Drama) and the Palme d'Or (highest prize awarded) at the 1966 Cannes Film Festival. The soundtrack album, featuring Francis Lai's score, peaked a number ten during its 93 weeks on the charts. Another dramatic film worthy of viewing is *A Patch Of Blue*, about a black, educated office-worker in his late 30s (Sidney Poitier) and an 18-year-old white, blind woman (Elizabeth Hartman). Poitier's performance is touching, and the ending proves to be a bit unexpected – both romantic and tragic at the same time. The film, scored by Jerry Goldsmith, was released a few days after *Rubber Soul*.

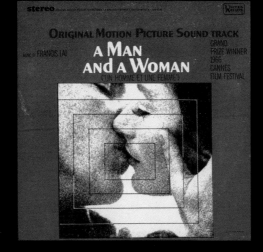

Alfie is a British romantic comedy-drama starring Michael Caine in the title role as a narcissistic womanizing chauffeur living in 1960s Swinging London. The film's jazz soundtrack is performed by saxophonist Sonny Rollins. Its title song, written by Burt Bacharach and Hal David, was a hit in the U.S. for Cher (heard over the film's closing credits in America; peaking at #32 in August 1966) and Dionne Warwick (#15 in July 1967); and in the U.K. for Cilla Black (produced by George Martin at Abbey Road with Bacharach on piano and conducting the 48-piece orchestra; #9 in May 1966). Another British comedy-drama starred Lynn Redgrave as *Georgy Girl*. The title song was a hit for the Australian group the Seekers (#2 in the U.S. and #3 in the U.K.). Other dramas included *The Sand Pebbles*, starring Steve McQueen as a machinist's mate aboard the gunboat USS San Pablo on Yangtze River Patrol in China in the 1920s, and *Who's Afraid Of Virginia Wolf?* with Richard Burton and Elizabeth Taylor as a bitter middle-aged couple.

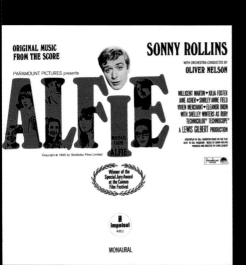

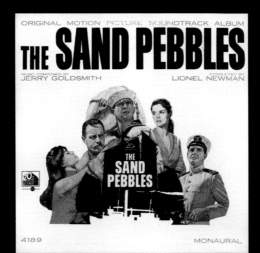

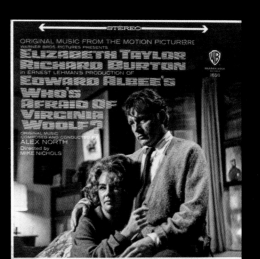

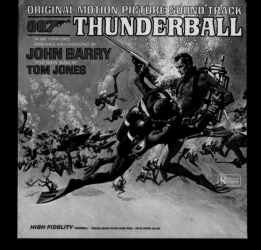  

One of the biggest film trends of late 1965 through 1966 was the "spy movie," which also lent itself to spy parodies. Taking the genre seriously was the king of espionage films, James Bond. *Thunderball* was scheduled to be the first film featuring the British agent with a license to kill, but shortly after the novel's release in 1961, two former collaborators of author Ian Fleming claimed that he had stolen elements of the plot from a screenplay that they had all written together. The matter was settled out of court, and by 1964, the producers determined that it was logical to release a *Thunderball* film with the approval of all of the involved parties rather than face the possibility of the collaborating authors releasing their own movie. Sean Connery continues to dominate the screen as Bond, establishing him as the leader in the genre. The film's soundtrack by John Barry features the title song "Thunderball" (lyrics by Don Black) sung by Tom Jones, who had recently scored with "It's Not Unusual" and "What's New, Pussycat." The single charted at #25 in the U.S. and #35 in the U.K. Also released in December 1965 was the film adaptation of John le Carré's Cold War suspense novel, *The Spy Who Came In From The Cold*, starring Richard Burton.

The year 1966 saw the release of *Our Man Flint*, the first of two light comedic spy films starring James Coburn. Dean Martin appeared on the screen for the first time as Matt Helm in *The Silencers*, a comedy adaptation of two books in the Helm series. The Man From U.N.C.L.E. made it to the big screen with a double-bill of two expanded episodes from the TV series, *To Trap A Spy* and *The Spy With My Face*. Hanna-Barbera brought its Stone Age sitcom TV cartoon series The Flintstones to theaters with an animated spy parody film called *The Man Called Flintstone*. The movie was bittersweet for fans of the TV show, which ended its six-year prime time run before the release of the film.

The world of comedy in late 1965-1966 moved from ridiculous to more ridiculous. *That Darn Cat* and *The Ghost And Mr. Chicken* were typical comedic fare. The former is a Walt Disney production about a rambunctious Siamese cat who assists the FBI in bringing a pair of kidnappers to justice. The film stars Hayley Mills, Dean Jones, Dorothy Provine, Roddy McDowell, Frank Gorshin and Neville Brand. Gorshin, an impressionist and comedian, would soon move on from his film role of the incompetent bank robber/kidnapper Iggy to the criminal mastermind The Riddler on the Batman TV series, which would spin-off a feature film in the summer of 1966 in which the Caped Crusader has to save the equivalent of the UN Security Council while fighting four villains. The feline film's theme song was sung by pop singer Bobby Darin. *The Ghost And Mr. Chicken* is both a mystery and horror film, in addition to a crazy comedy, featuring Don Knotts in one of his most memorable roles. *Munster, Go Home!* is a color adaptation of the black and white TV sitcom *The Munsters*, which had just completed its two-year run on the small screen.

The Russians Are Coming, The Russians Are Coming is a comedy about the chaos that erupts after a Russian submarine accidentally runs aground off the coast of New England. The film stars Carl Reiner, Eva Marie Saint, Alan Arkin, Jonathan Winters and Tessie O'Shea (who, like Frank Gorshin, was on the February 9, 1964 Ed Sullivan Show with the Beatles). On the Roman side, *A Funny Thing Happened On The Way To The Forum* is a farce based on a play based on a farce. Zero Mostel is hilarious as Pseudolus, the lying slave, and Buster Keaton appears here in his last movie role. Jon Pertwee, later to become the third Doctor Who, is featured in *Forum* as Crassus. The incidental music for the film was created by Ken Thorne, who had performed a similar task for the Beatles *Help!* in 1965.

Swinging London is also the setting for *Blow-Up* (also written as *Blowup*), a movie about the adventures encountered by a fashion photographer (played by David Hemings) as he goes about his work. The mystery-thriller also stars Vanessa Redgrave and Sarah Miles, and was directed by Michelangelo Antonioni. With the film featuring sex, drugs and even death, the critics praised the work as a "mod masterpiece." The movie's score is by jazz pianist Herbie Hancock. Also included is a scene in which the Yardbirds (then featuring Jimmy Page and Jeff Beck on guitars) perform a version of Tiny Bradshaw's "The Train Kept A-Rollin,'" which they label as "Stroll On." According to actor Ronan O'Casey (who played an uncredited role in the film), the movie was unfinished – therefore failing to solve the murder that occurs in it, but the final cut gives the events an air of mystery.

This period saw the release of the second and third installments of director Sergio Leone's Spaghetti Western trilogy starring Clint Eastwood, *For A Few Dollars More* and *The Good, The Bad And The Ugly*. Ennio Morricone scored the films, with the title track from the latter film becoming a number two hit in 1968 when covered by Hugo Montenegro. Younger audiences went for an astonishing Biker flick, *The Wild Angels*, starring Peter Fonda, Nancy Sinatra, Bruce Dern and Diane Ladd. Elvis delivered two films, *Frankie And Johnny* and *Paradise, Hawaiian Style*.

One of the highlights of 1966 was the science fiction drama *Fahrenheit 451*, a dystopian movie about information control based on the novel by Ray Bradbury and directed by François Truffaut. The government has determined that information that contradicts its narrative must be stamped out due to its belief that critical thinking and reasoning

are threats to society. As a consequence, many books are banned. The government punishes the possession of books, sending firemen out to burn the offending literature. The plot follows fireman Guy Montag through an odyssey of discovery.

With so much going on in the cinemas, one might wonder if there was any room for other entertainment. Indeed there was. The season of 1965-66 saw the big transition on the small screen from black-and-white to color television. The most popular programs included: Bonanza; Gomer Pyle, U.S.M.C.; The Lucy Show; The Red Skelton Hour; Batman; The Andy Griffith Show; Bewitched; The Beverly Hillbillies; Hogan's Heroes; Green Acres; and Get Smart.

In comics, Marvel's Fantastic Four #48 was the first installment of the Galactus Trilogy, which also introduced the Silver Surfer. Four months later, Black Panther was introduced in issue #52 of the magazine. Amazing Spider-Man #38 became Marvel's first appearance in the Top Twenty comic book sales for the year and marked a transition towards Marvel dominance in comics. Life With Archie #42 and the issues that followed showed Archie developing super powers – an indicator that the Silver Age of Comics was in full swing and that superheroes were "in." Meanwhile, Batman #183 made a tie-in between the television show and the comic book that had spawned it.

Wherever people looked and listened, there was exciting and adventurous entertainment in late 1965-1966. While these were not as important as *Rubber Soul* or *Revolver*, they were delightful in their media and in their own ways.

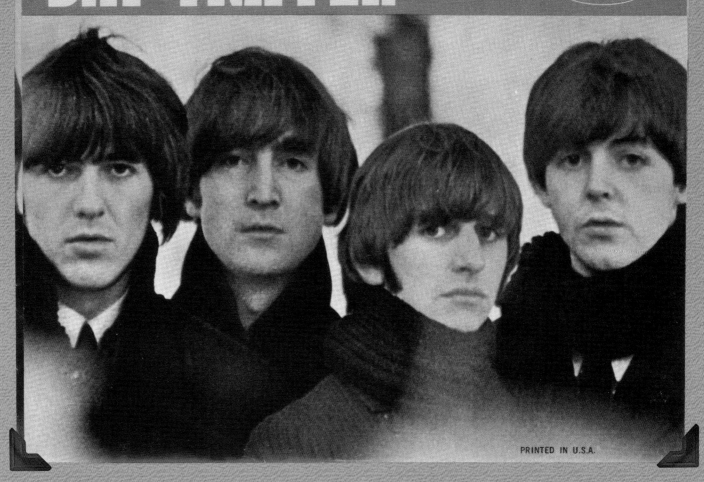

THE BEATLES

WE CAN WORK IT OUT
DAY TRIPPER

5555   Capitol RECORDS

PRINTED IN U.S.A.

160

THE BEATLES
NOWHERE MAN
WHAT GOES ON

5587

Capitol
RECORDS

161

THE BEATLES
PAPERBACK WRITER
RAIN

5651

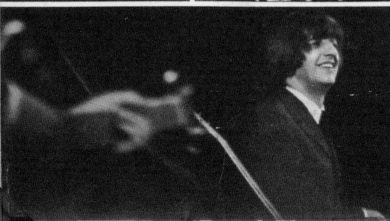

FAN RECOLLECTIONS

Back in the sixties, we didn't have a lot of access to cameras like everyone does now with cellphones. But I found this picture taken at my mom's house on my birthday in 1966. It shows me with my Regina High School (all girls Catholic school!) classmates, posing with some of our favorite recent albums, including *The Beach Boys Concert*, *Command Performance Jan & Dean/Live In Person*, *Go Away From My World* by Marianne Faithful, and of course, the Beatles! That's me wearing the "mod" hat and sitting on the floor with my two little sisters, Kelly and Susie. That's Susie pointing to a picture of George and holding *Rubber Soul*, which was and still is, one of my favorite Beatles albums.

When *Rubber Soul* came out, we were blown away

by the unique sound of it, so different from the previous albums which had more of a "rock" feel. The harmonies throughout were so beautifully sung, and all of the songs on it were written by the group, with no cover versions included. As you can tell by the framed photo of George and his poster on the wall in my photo, he was my favorite! I loved hearing him sing "Think for Yourself." It was also exciting to hear him play sitar in "Norwegian Wood," our first exposure to the Indian sound in western music! It was cool to hear Paul sing in French in "Michelle," and I loved the sound of the guitars in "It's Only Love." John's incredible lyrics to "In My Life" still move me to this day.

And of course, there was the album cover! So different, and showing them maturing into men from those "young Fabs!" Definitely one of my favorites!

Kristen Tash

I was born in St. Louis in 1956. My teenage uncle would bring his Elvis records over, indoctrinating me in my crib! Later I loved the Beatles on Ed Sullivan, but was still collecting Elvis records. Christmas 1965 was a magic day! My brother Paul received the "Day Tripper"/"We Can Work It Out" single. I got a Sonny and Cher 45! I guess Santa couldn't find any new Elvis. But my memories are clear, all day, on our Jr. Juke record player, both sides of Paul's gift were played over and over. Now, we had faithfully watched Beatles cartoons and listened to Beatles at our cousins, but this was the first beautiful Capital label to grace our record player. It changed my life! Eventually, Paul and I played music together, him on drums and vocals, and I writing songs, playing guitar, keys, and singing. I've made a living playing live and running my recording studio near Tulsa. Everything I've learned was from taking Beatle songs apart in the headphones and seeing how the best band of the 20th century achieved immortality!

Hank Charles Hanewinkel Jr.

A month after *Rubber Soul* was released, I turned 15. My parents surprised me with the LP for my birthday. I have countless memories associated with most of my Beatles albums, but I credit *Rubber Soul* for being the reason I learned to play guitar. It may seem strange, but of all the tunes I could have been inspired by, the song "I've Just Seen A Face" was the song that finally motivated me to stop wishing I could play the guitar to actually learning how to play the instrument.

It took a while to save up enough money, but I was able to purchase a used Sears Silvertone acoustic as well as a "how to" book of guitar chords. I was determined to teach myself to play. Immediately, I set to work practicing. At the time my goal was to be able to play "I've Just Seen A Face." I didn't care if I learned to play another song, I was going to learn that one. Each day after school I would rush home, head to my bedroom, close the door and practice!

Finally, one afternoon through persistence and some very sore fingertips, it all came together. I could sing and play, and it actually sounded like a song! My family got a free one song concert later that evening. Decades and hundreds of songs later, I'm still playing thanks to *Rubber Soul*. It is just one of the countless gifts and memories the Beatles unknowingly gave to me and I'm sure to countless others throughout the years.

Gene Flanagan

In 1965 at the age of six, I was infected (for life) by my older brother's Beatlemania due to his constant playing of the *Rubber Soul* LP he received for Christmas. This was the Capitol stereo release. Thus, for me, the real *Rubber Soul* will always be a 12-track folk-rock album leading off with "I've Just Seen A Face" and featuring those brilliant false starts in "I'm Looking Through You."

Brian Burhans

In the fall of 1965, I was a 14-year-old 9th grader living in Williamsport, Pennsylvania, who (like many of my friends) was a huge Beatles fan since first seeing them on The Ed Sullivan Show in 1964. From that time forward, I bought all Beatles 45s and LPs with money from grass mowing, snow shoveling, birthday gifts and allowances. I purchased mono versions of *Meet The Beatles!* through *Help!* to play on my mono "bedroom" record player.

I lobbied my Dad to get a stereo console for our family room so that he could listen to the music that my Mom and he enjoyed on stereo FM radio. I convinced him that he could also start buying LPs of his favorite singers and instrumentalists. (Then of course I could start buying stereo Beatles LPs!) It worked! My Dad purchased a Wurlitzer stereo console with stereo FM tuner, Garrard turntable and stereo 3-way speakers.

The first stereo LP I bought was *Rubber Soul*, which came out in early December 1965. I still remember being blown away listening to the first cut, "I've Just Seen A Face." I laid down on our green shag carpet with my head positioned between the speakers for an incredibly unforgettable experience listening to the rest of the LP (getting up only to flip the disc to Side 2). With the superior stereo separation and sound quality (that shamed my poor bedroom record player), it almost seemed like I was in the studio with the Beatles. Not only was the sound amazing beyond belief, but also *Rubber Soul* contained all new songs (none were contained on any previous 45 releases in the U.S. as was usually the case). After the last track, "Run for Your Life," played, I just had to flip it over and listen to the entire album again. Breaking in the Wurlitzer with *Rubber Soul* was a lasting experience that causes me to rank *Rubber Soul* near the top of my favorite Beatles albums. To this day, I still get goose-bumps every time I hear the album.

Rob Foust

For me *Rubber Soul* is the first, the beginning, the soul of the Beatles, my most favorite album. Why? Imagine in the U.S.S.R. a 7-year-old kid sees the Beatles faces for the first time ever after only listening to several songs here and there. On September 17, 1989, the Soviet newspaper Komsomolskaia Pravda announced the first ever legal public broadcast of a Beatles full album, *Rubber Soul*. They even encouraged people to record the songs on a tape recorder directly from the radio. This was in a form of a cut-out double-sided cassette inlay for the album *Rubber Soul*, with several Beatles pictures (mostly John), the news of release of the first ever Beatles biography book and, most important, a list of Beatles U.K. album discography. We cut it out. I still keep it in my collection. From this inlay we found out that the Soviet record company Melodya had already released two albums, *A Hard Day's Night* and *A Taste Of Honey*, which my mother bought for us shortly afterwards.

The album *Rubber Soul* marked, for us Soviet kids, a real start of freedom—no more undercover bootlegs and distorted radio-recorded bits of the songs. No, no, the album in its entirely in best quality possible, and this, my friends, was a start of a life changing journey.

Yaakov Edisherashvili

I was about to turn 11 when *Rubber Soul* came out in December 1965. That January a friend loaned me his copy, which I listened to incessantly for days and days while I wrote a fifth grade report on the early history of baseball. I listened to that album nonstop while I read about and perused pictures of players from the turn of the century through the 30s and 40s. For years after the music on the U.S. version of *Rubber Soul* evoked for me an era that had passed decades before the making of the music. I guess that's timeless!

John Place

I was 14 years old and a lifelong Beatles fan when *Rubber Soul* was released in December 1965. However, I was only familiar with their hit singles and a few other tunes that were played constantly on WMCA-AM in New York on my transistor radio. When *Rubber Soul* came out it became the very first LP I ever bought. I just had to hear the other songs not played on the radio. I must have listened to it on my small record player every day. The songs of *Rubber Soul* became embedded in my consciousness.

On a family car trip about two weeks later, all the melodies kept jumping around in my head. I was hopelessly ear-wormed! And one other thing, my cousin was about to have her second child, a girl, and they were thinking about a name that started with the letter M. Of course, I suggested "Michelle." My cousin Michelle is now 56! Nothing but fond memories for this album, which I still have. It is my favorite all time Beatles LP!

Garry Wilbur

The first album I ever bought was the Capitol Records version of *Rubber Soul*. It was August 1966, nearly a year after the album's initial release, but I knew it was the one I wanted to buy to start my Beatles album collection. It cost $2.49 at Alexander's Department Store on Fordham Road in The Bronx. I remember being so captivated by the cover as well as all the cool photos on the back.

But it was the music. The album's music just hooked me from the start. I actually thought that the false start in "I'm Looking Through You" was meant to be there and thought they were so ingenuous by doing that! I came to love this version of the album, and continue to do so more than 55 years later—so much so that it's actually hard for me to listen to the Parlophone version.

Steven Springer

When *Rubber Soul* came out, I was only eight years old. Since I grew up in Zurich, Switzerland, I was securely hidden away from this crazy new music coming from Britain. At the time, I was only listening to Swiss Folk Music or German Hits, just like my parents.

When I became a teenager five years later, a schoolmate bought the British version LP *Rubber Soul*, which we listened to together. I was immediately smitten by the opening track, "Drive My Car." The track "The Word" seemed strange, but I liked the closing track from Side One, "Michelle." Flipping the LP to Side Two, the opening track, the country-ish "What Goes On," was again my favorite. I liked "Girl" and "In My Life," while the closing track "Run For Your Life" sounded pretty weird.

Five years later, I had the chance to visit my relatives in Long Island, New York. This was my first time in the States. I subsequently noticed that earlier-released Beatles albums were quite different than their British counterparts. In the nearby Sam Goody store, I bought all the Beatles U.S. releases I could find, which I would be adding to my Beatles collection when I arrived back home in Zurich.

Marcel Reichmuth

I first purchased a copy of *Rubber Soul* in the summer of 1977. My sister and I went to a record store in our local mall where she purchased a 45, and I the album. I discovered upon listening that it has some incredible music, especially "Drive My Car," "Think For Yourself," "Michelle," "You Won't See Me," "Nowhere Man" and "The Word." I listened to it religiously that whole summer and fall, occasionally for years after. Now every early December, on its anniversary, I think back to the day I bought it and am so glad I did. It is probably the best thing I ever bought.

Jason J. Young

I was 10 years old in 1965. The two songs I loved hearing on the radio during the summer holidays were "Pretty Woman" by Roy Orbison and "I Feel Fine" by the Beatles. I was French-speaking from Montreal, Canada, but knew, thanks to my English lessons at school, what John Lennon meant, and the song made me feel happy. Later that year I often heard "Yesterday," but I found the song too quiet. I had a hard time recognizing the Beatles. In early 1966 I was listening less to the Beatles music and enjoyed much more the rhythmic songs of groups from Quebec without actually knowing that most of the songs were French covers of English or American hits. For a while, I was a 45-rpm fan, and I used to listen to those on my blue Shine ED100 mono record player.

In the summer of 1966, while I was listening to the album *Les Sultans* (on my father's Zenith console stereo cabinet), my 14-year-old brother arrived home with his friend and a Beatles LP. They wanted to listen to the entire disc, and I was lucky to get my mom's permission to join them! When I heard the guitars and the melody of the first song, "I've Just Seen A Face," I was flabbergasted. It didn't sound anything like the songs I heard on the radio. Paul McCartney was singing very fast, and I couldn't understand a word of what he was saying, but it was a no-brainer: I liked it immediately. Even though I was young, it felt like love at first sight! However, it was with the next song that I got my real crush. "Norwegian Wood" had an instrument that really impressed me, yet I didn't know what it was. My brother's friend showed me the cover (what an extraordinary photo!). The back text said that George Harrison played sitar on this song. It was beautiful and music to my ears. And what can I say about the fuzz sound in "Think For Yourself," which reminded me of the fuzz in the Rolling Stones song, "Satisfaction." It was really exciting! I was learning lots of things. All the songs on the LP blew me away. I remember my mother asking us twice to lower the volume of our music and to finally ask us to stop everything because my father was coming home from work. It was with *Rubber Soul* that the Beatles would stay anchored in my head forever, that LPs would definitely overthrow 45 rpm and, bonus, that those new songs would definitely improve my English.

Normand Tremblay

In December 1965 my older brother, who played in a rock band called The Vons, brought home a package saying it was my Christmas present. I could tell by its shape that it was an album. I was very excited as my record collection at the time consisted of *Meet the Beatles!*, *Chet Atkins Picks On The Beatles* and a few 45s. "She Loves You" on Swan was my best. All my other music beamed magically in on the AM dial via WQXI, Quixie in Dixie.

My present was a mono copy of the Beatles album *Rubber Soul*. The coolest picture I had ever seen quickly told me that the Beatles were in a much different place. On Christmas my cousin Janie and I held a 'tete a tete' on "THE" new album. We agreed that John's "Girl" and "Norwegian Wood" were the best songs, though we sang and hummed Paul's beautiful love song to Michelle.

The gift of *Rubber Soul* began my 55-year love affair with collecting Beatles songs. *Rubber Soul* remains my favorite Beatles album and thus my favorite album of all time. Now as I am getting older, people sometimes will say "Watch your step," and I say, "Don't worry, I am wearing my rubber souls."

Tommy Archibald

The first time I heard "Nowhere Man" was on the compilation LP *Yesterday And Today*. Sadly, it is no longer in my possession. This was about 1966. It was a very upbeat song, but was sad at the same time.

Jim Possee

The truth is, I didn't buy "Paperback Writer" when it was first released. In fact, I didn't buy any Beatles singles until later on. I didn't own a record player until my 13th birthday in September 1966. Plus I felt no need to buy singles when I could tape them off the radio. My dad had a big Gramophone record player, a massive thing that he still played his 78s on, and a Grundig TK20 reel-to-reel tape recorder, which I used every Sunday afternoon to tape Pick Of The Pops on the BBC Light Programme. The Light Programme also regularly played songs from the Top Ten, so I could listen to pop music in general.

I probably recorded "Paperback Writer" on Sunday, 12th June 1966, two days after its release. I had already heard the track on Top Of The Pops the week before on Thursday 2nd June. Before anyone says anything, of course it was in black and white. The first color program in the U.K. was a year away when BBC2 broadcast the 1967 Wimbledon tennis championships in color to those few homes with color TVs. I had no idea that the Beatles were not live, as I was only 12!

I remember the "granny glasses" and their hair being longer. I took photos of them on our Rediffusion rental TV, a primitive cable-TV, from Top Of The Pops. Today I still have those photographs, though they show nothing on the screen because of the camera flash reflecting off the glass!

The following week Top Of The Pops had the Beatles singing "Rain." I thought it was a terrific song. I loved the weird ending on it, not realizing what was actually going on. (Again I must point out I was only 12 years old.) "Rain" didn't get much air play at the time, not even on Radio Luxembourg.

I thought "Paperback Writer" was a great song, as did my school friends, especially Chris Seaton, with whom I'd wander around the school playground singing it with. We were astonished to hear that our French Teacher, Mr.

Cyples, liked it too, and it was he who pointed out that they were singing "Frère Jacques" on it, much to our amazement. It was also interesting that the Beatles were singing about "a man named Lear," as we were doing Shakespeare then, even though the song had nothing to do with that.

Garry Marsh

I was home from my freshman year at Adelphi University when I first heard the Beatles new single, "Paperback Writer"/"Rain" on New York's WABC-AM. Because it was the Beatles, the station played both sides in heavy rotation. It was a refreshing release, like nothing we had heard before. It was a little more adventurous, more sophisticated (a Paperback Writer, hmmm) and a lot more experimental (backwards loop in "Rain"). Something was different with this release.

I immediately drove to my local Sam Goody Record store to buy my copy, which came in a great picture sleeve. I went home and proceeded to play it over and over again. As an 18-year-old, I wasn't a so-called deep thinker where I could say, "Hey, look at the way they're progressing." There wasn't anything I could wrap my head around. And I, like most listeners, had no idea that John and George were singing "Frère Jacques" behind Paul's lead vocal. It would be decades before this was "discovered." The Beatles introduced video clips of the two new songs on The Ed Sullivan Show with Ringo doing the honors. I remember scenes from a nice garden with their hair at a great length. They looked very fab. Although "Paperback Writer" would top the national charts, it stalled at number two in New York, blocked by Sinatra's "Strangers In The Night." The Beatles were leading the way in ways we couldn't understand yet. But our common love for them kept on growing.

Mark Lapidos, Promoter of the Fest for Beatles Fans

I bought the mono *Yesterday And Today* album at the end of June 1966 about two weeks after it was issued. I was nearly twelve years old and was not aware of the controversy over the previous Butcher Cover. I was not aware that I had a paste-over cover until 1977 when I happened to catch a glimpse of Ringo's dark shirt (appearing V-shaped) under his smock through the Trunk Cover. That was exciting, as by then, I was quite aware of the controversy.

I decided to peel the cover in 1977 in a very un-professional manner using small bits of water. I sprayed a clear lacquer coating onto the result to help seal and preserve the Butcher photo. I left a small piece of the previous paste over cover in the upper left.

Of course, now I wish I had not peeled it, as it would be more valuable. I didn't know any better. But then I still possess an original peeled Butcher Cover!

Jon Roe

I bought my first stereo copy of *Yesterday And Today* the first day it was available in my local store in June 1966. While I was listening to the new album and memorizing everything on the cover, I realized that the cover had been pasted over another one. I put on a pot of water to boil and steamed the front cover off. Of course, in my haste, it wasn't a perfect job. I knew I could do better so I promptly bought another one and took my time with an almost perfect peel job. When I showed this one to my friends, they all wanted one and I ended up peeling about six copies for them. Who would have known that I was "GIVING AWAY" such valuable items. I wish I would have taken photos of them all, but we were young and just loved the Beatles music!

Stephen M. Spence

I was lucky enough to go to Disc Records on Public Square in Cleveland, Ohio on the day that the *Yesterday And Today album* came out. The Butcher Cover LP was on sale for $5.98. Had I known that it was going to be withdrawn, I would have purchased another copy of the album.

Ed Fagan

Spring 1968 my 19-year-old brother and I (15) were driving to Lou's Record Paradise in Hollywood to check out the latest English import albums for $8. Later, we decided to walk across the street to Phil Harris Records and see if we could find any cut out bargains. While looking through the cut out section, a distributor from Capitol Records arrived with boxes of mono punched records. We got first look, and to our amazement, we found 3 sealed Trunk covers. We went home and peeled them. My copy came out beautifully, and I still have it in my collection. Total cost for the 3 records was $3 plus tax.

Rick Hilliard

Los Angeles KRLA had announced that the Beatles *Yesterday And Today* would launch on June 5, 1966. On that day, I visited my local record store in Westwood Village and found it mobbed with teenagers like myself. By the time I could get to the album rack, *Yesterday And Today* was gone. Disappointed, I approached the store owner, whom I knew, and asked him when he'd be getting more copies in. He assured me in a few days time.

I returned a few days later only to discover two burly gentlemen pulling every copy of *Yesterday And Today* off the rack and stacking them on a two-wheeled hand truck. When I asked one of them for a copy, one barked, "No!" After they left, the store owner again apologized and said that the two men were from Capital Records. There had been quite a stink about the album's gruesome cover.

I went back four days later and much to my delight, there was the LP now donning a completely different cover. I quickly grabbed a copy and asked the store owner what happened to the original cover. He pointed to the album. "It's underneath that one," he said. "But how do I get to it?" "Just soak it in hot water," he said.

At home, I filled up the tub with scalding hot water and soaked the entire cover for 30 minutes. The jacket was completely destroyed except for the artwork. I hung the covers over the shower curtain rod to dry. After I carefully ironed the heavily wrinkled covers, I proudly and carefully taped them to my bedroom wall side by side. My mother took one look at the butcher cover and deemed it obscene. One day while I was at school she removed it from my wall. When I confronted her, she said it was in very poor taste and threw it away. I scoured the trash to no avail. I never saw it again.

In 1988, while I was going through my mother's office desk after she retired, I found a torn fragment of the Butcher Cover. On the reverse side was a grocery list.

W.R. Wilkerson III

July 3, 1966

Put the Kettle On

Beatle fans are steaming over the new Beatle album cover. In fact, they are so steamed-up that they're spending as much as three hours over boiling hot water so they can peel off the new album picture and get down to the old one.

The old one being the photo that Capitol Records recalled because they felt the picture of the Beatles dressed as butcher boys with hatchets and dismembered dolls all about might offend public taste. But

two local Beatle fans, Chris Ryan, 19, left, and Jody Campbell, 18, fired up by Capitol's slap at the Beatles' taste, set the kettle to boiling and by patient scrapping they steamed off the new and rubbed in the old.

In 1966, a friend told me his mom watched a talk show where the host held the *Yesterday And Today* album over boiling water and the cover peeled off. I tried it and saved the album cover. Also, the "Nowhere Man" 45 was the first record I ever bought without hearing it —just because it was the Beatles.

Larry Miller

In the summer of 1966 I was 14 years old growing up in a suburb of Chicago. As a Beatlemaniac since February 1964, I always stayed on top of the Beatles latest news. While waiting for the release of *Yesterday And Today* that June, I read an article in Chicago's American Newspaper reporting that the release was delayed due to a controversial "gruesome" cover. I finally bought the album with the replacement cover at Goldblatt's Department Store.

Later that summer I learned that the replacement cover had been pasted over the original to speed up the release. I lifted a corner and could see the original beneath the outer cover! How could I get this off? I didn't think of steaming it. Instead, I used wet facial tissue to rub away the "trunk" cover. I spent a couple of hours sitting on my bed, meticulously removing a little at a time. As you can see in the photo above, I did a pretty decent job. I still have it and it is one of my favorite Beatle treasures!

Bob Schuller, Frankfort, IL

I don't recall how I learned about the Butcher Cover. I was 12, and rode my bike to every department store in San Diego's East County to find one. No success until the last store – Unimart in La Mesa. I saw a shadow underneath and knew I had found one. Because it was in stereo, it cost $1.00 more than I had with me. I placed it in the Country & Western section and left. The next day, I collected every pop bottle I could find, cashed them in at the neighborhood market, and rode back to Unimart. It was still there!

I slid the shrinkwrap off and started peeling one corner using a steam kettle. I'd stop every couple of inches, pat the moisture off the cover, and then continue. It was tedious, but I was able to peel the top cover off, with a great-looking butcher cover underneath. I slid the shrinkwrap back over the jacket to protect it, and was able to paste the intact Trunk Cover slick onto a white LP sleeve. I now had a stereo butcher cover and a new cover as well. The record was carefully played on my parent's stereo console.

Larry Clark

In 1968 I was 8 years old. My family was visiting my Aunt and Uncle's house in Massillon, Ohio. I had an older cousin named Tim who played guitar. I remember hearing this guitar riff coming from his room. I thought it was the greatest sound I had ever heard. I came running into his room and asked him what he was playing. He told me it was "Day Tripper" by the Beatles. After that I couldn't get the song out my head. That Christmas I received the album *Yesterday And Today*. Thus began my lifelong love of the Beatles and their music. I played that album back to back to back to back so many times I wore it out and had to buy another copy! To this day it is my favorite Beatles album. (You never forget your first.)

Brett Evans

In 1967, something had spilled on my *Yesterday And Today* album cover, leading me to notice an image showing through. I had heard that there had been a banned cover, and that some early releases had been covered over with a Capitol U.S.-friendly version. I didn't think to steam it off; what I did was soak in hot water in the bathtub. As you can see, there was damage in doing so. That didn't stop me, though; it just made me more careful. In rough a shape as it is, it is still one of my treasures.

Bill Badon

I found out about the Butcher Cover in the mid-70s and became obsessed. I fantasized about traveling back in time to June 15, 1966, and buying two or three "Butchers." I made my own copy by snipping the image out of an INCREDIBLE poster and gluing it over a Trunk Cover. It's all about the artwork and I'm quite happy with it.

Farrell McNulty

Purists may argue that any of the reconfigured Capitol albums are not the original British albums that were made the way the Beatles intended. But those Capitol albums are the way that we in America heard the Beatles records for the first time. And although I came to appreciate the original British albums, those Capitol albums are still very nostalgic for me. And *Yesterday And Today* is one of my favorite Capitol Beatles albums.

At first I thought it was a nice collection of some of my favorite Beatles songs that I had already heard. And when I first listened to the album, I found that the songs I was unfamiliar with were also good. It contained both the A and B sides of three of their American singles from the previous year. The remainder of the album has some of the best songs from the British versions of *Rubber Soul* and *Revolver*. And the album is unique as one of only two Beatles albums with two lead vocals by Ringo. It's also interesting that the album's songs from *Revolver* were released in America ahead of their British release.

Michael Rinella

I remember going on a date with Beth to a New Orleans Saints football game at Tulane Stadium. She let me drive her car, a big Continental. With the Bless You Boys already behind by three touchdowns shortly after the half, Beth and I left early like many of us did back then. When we got to Beth's car, it was very tightly sandwiched between two other cars, meaning we might have to wait a long time. After listening to many sixties hits on WTIX and probably enjoying the "submarine races," as we used to say back then about smooching, I must've pulled her car back and forth at least 100 times, gently bumping the surrounding cars, before I was able to get out. It was so cool to then hear the Beatles singing "Baby you can drive my car" as we drove off down South Claiborne Avenue.

Keith John Paul Horcasitas

on the Beatles titled "The Beatles in Retrospect." A publicity photo was taken of me holding my copy of the cover, and it was used to promote the course. Needless to say, the cover solicited a wide variety of reactions from the students. My stereo copy of the Butcher cover still holds a place of pride in my Beatles collection to this very day!

John Bezzini

I was 11 when I was introduced to the Beatles when my mom called me into the kitchen to hear what she called "that new band the Beatles." WHYN AM radio in Springfield, Mass. was playing "She Loves You," and I was forever hooked. Like any Beatles fan, I bought (well, my parents bought for me at that age) all their singles and albums leading up to *Yesterday And Today*. We were on a trip to Miami when the album came out, and I remember making my parents go to some store so I could buy the new album. I looked through all the albums in the rack hoping to find a Butcher Cover or at least one that you could see bleeding through the new Trunk Cover, but to no avail. I was young and read all the teen magazines, so I knew about the controversial cover.

After my father died in 1968, my mom brought me record shopping in New York City. At House of Oldies, high on a shelf out of the reach of anybody, was a Butcher Cover still shrink-wrapped for $250. I would have bought it in a minute if I had my own money, but for my mother to pay was too much money after losing my father.

As for the music itself, I was again mesmerized by the songs sounding so different. The album had "Drive My Car," "And Your Bird Can Sing" and three of my all-time faves, "Nowhere Man," "We Can Work It Out" and "Day Tripper." It was only soon after that when I learned we were being cheated and were not getting their records as originally released in England.

Keith O'Connor

Rubber Soul and *Revolver* marked the transition years of the Beatles. They were growing up and maturing like their audience, and the subject matter of their songs reflected that. During that time, I became aware of the fabled Butcher photo taken by Robert Whitaker that appeared on the cover to *Yesterday And Today*. With its depiction of raw meat and assorted pieces of dolls with the Beatles in butcher smocks, the album was quickly withdrawn from the market. The Butcher Cover soon became one of the Beatles ultimate collectibles.

I could not locate one for my collection until the very first Beatles convention run by Joe Pope in the 1970s. I bought a copy from the then-king of the Butcher Cover dealers, Wayne Rogers. In 1984, I taught a college course

My first encounter with *Revolver* did not take place until late spring of 1967, several months after its release. By then, most of my friends and I had kinda moved on from the white hot days of Beatlemania. Although *Rubber Soul* was only a year or so old then, to a ten-year-old kid, that seemed like ages! The Beatles were no longer on the forefront of our minds. We had moved on to so many other bands and brands of music, British and otherwise.

I was spending the night at a friend's house close to my home in west Phoenix. His family was to be out for a while, so we planned a "Whatever we want to do night," be it watching TV or listening to any albums we wanted to sneak out of his older brother's collection!

We pulled out the Beatles *Revolver* album and gave it a spin on the family stereo. It caught us by surprise. I thought, "Whatever happened to simple themed songs like "A Hard Day's Night" and "Can't Buy Me Love"? Songs we embraced so much for so long! Being too young to appreciate the evolution and musical progression the album represented, we were left bewildered, although there were some great sounds we instantly liked.

Of course we had already heard "Yellow Submarine" numerous times on the radio. It's a classic tune children loved then and now. But for me, the song that blew me back in a positive way was "Eleanor Rigby," an incredible song that had instant amazing sound appeal. My own children reacted the same way to that one! I also loved "For No One." Although the disc had other catchy tunes, I and my young ears did not embrace the songs as much as the earlier material. "Tomorrow Never Knows" was just plain weird sounding, but today, I think it's a great tune of wonderful creativity and innovation.

Looking back, you can see the LP had less than a bubbly atmosphere. More cynicism, like love gone bad, complaining about taxes, etc. Cool today, but not back then. We were simply too young to grasp it all.

After that night, my friend and I were awakened to the fact the Beatles had dramatically changed. We didn't really see it as evolving (which it clearly was). To us at that time, we didn't receive it so positively in it's entirety. We simply weren't ready to let go of the lovable mop-top images burned so firmly into our heads and hearts.

Reflecting back, we never had to "let them go," but we certainly had to "let them grow." And grow they did. *Revolver* is now one of my favorite Beatles albums. It is another landmark building block in the creation of the greatest band of all time. The LP could have just as aptly been titled "Evolver," for it truly was evolutionary in every way compared to the earlier material and no less great.

Perry Cox

In 1987 I was only a very casual Beatles fan with only one compilation album in my collection, and I knew only an overview of their story. The 25th anniversary of *Sgt Pepper* prompted me to read Philip Norman's *Shout*, which triggered my interest. What were their other albums like?

The first LP I got from the local library was *Revolver* and it blew me away. As only "Yellow Submarine" and "Eleanor Rigby" were familiar to me, the album surprised me with songs I had never heard before that created a varied but somehow still cohesive entity. The flow from "Taxman" to "Eleanor Rigby," "I'm Only Sleeping" to "Love You To" and "Got To Get You Into My Life" to "Tomorrow Never Knows" was magical. I eventually listened to the rest of their catalogue, but *Revolver* has remained my favorite of their work ever since. The same year, a local department store chain here in Finland imported the Canadian pressings of the Beatles albums, so the Capital version was my first experience of *Rubber Soul*. I still prefer it to the original one.

Mikko Suhonen, Nurmijärvi, Finland

The Beatles changed the world in 1964 with a new musical explosion, and that was the best I had ever heard when *Rubber Soul* came out. I listened to it over and over. What great lyrics and music. I said "they've done it again."

When *Revolver* came out I again listened over and over, but this time I listened much closer. I thought the music world as we knew it was about to explode into a new style of music, especially listening to "Tomorrow Never Knows." It was a refreshing, eerie song. It was obvious that the Beatles had changed the direction of rock as we knew it again.

Mark Woodward

Whenever I hear the song "Eleanor Rigby" I think of riding in a car with my younger sister in Cleveland, Ohio to attend the Beatles concert on August 14, 1966, at the Cleveland Municipal Stadium. I was a Junior in high school and this was my very first concert. As I stared out the back window of the car looking up at the Cleveland skyline, "Eleanor Rigby" was playing on the car radio by station WIXY, the local AM radio station promoting the concert.

I'll never forget the concert. My sister and I jumped from our seats onto the field and ran towards the stage with thousands of other fans as the Beatles started to play "Day Tripper." We got very close to the front of the stage before the Beatles were taken off and the concert stopped. When we tried to turn around, I remember everybody pushing and crowding to the point where you physically couldn't move. How my sister and I eventually got back to our original seats is still a mystery to me. It was the greatest concert of my life and something I'll never forget. The song "Eleanor Rigby" always takes me back to that day.

Jeffrey Pillot

When people ask me which Beatles album is my favorite, I do not hesitate when I say *Revolver*. Although I was "in-utero" when the album was originally released, my favoritism first sparked when I heard what became my favorite Beatles song, "And Your Bird Can Sing," which was played during the opening sequence of the syndicated Beatles cartoon show I watched on television as a child.

I literally begged my Grandma in 1979 to buy me the Uruguay Odeon-labeled *Revolver* release in a strange plastic-bagged cover, only because it had more songs on it than the U.S. version. The variety of the album amazed me. I recognized "Got to Get You Into My Life" as a song from our family jukebox and realized only then it wasn't actually a Wings song!

When I later went to Beatleweek in Liverpool, I was all smiles hearing *Revolver* played live by the Cavern Club Beatles in celebration of 50 years of "revolving." When I met Klaus Voormann, I asked him to write "50th Anniversary" under his autograph on my copy of the *Revolver* album cover that he designed. I smiled when he asked me how to spell "anniversary."

The talent of the Beatles shines bright on this incredible release that has brought me many years of listening pleasure as a fan.

Dr. Jennifer Sandi

When *Revolver* was released in the U.S., I looked at the track listing and noticed that John sang lead on only two songs. I remember thinking at the time that this happened because Capitol wanted to either low key his involvement or punish John for his Jesus comments that had come out in the press a month earlier. I rarely listened to the American LP once I learned of the full content of the U.K. album.

Joe Pecorino

December 6, 1968 turned out to be a monumental day in my life. I was 12 years old and knew about the Beatles through my friends and radio, but had never purchased a Beatle record. No money. But that fateful Friday night I went shopping at a local a Radio Shack in New Haven, Connecticut. In those days Radio Shack sold a limited number of records in bins. As I looked through the selections I came across *Revolver*. I looked it over and wanted to buy it very badly so I asked my dad if I could buy it. He told me I could, but only if it cost a dollar or less. In desperation I changed the price to 99 cents and nervously walked up to the counter. The cashier, an older gentleman with a crew cut and glasses, looked at me and rang up the sale–my first Beatle album!

Two days later I received *Help!* as a gift. On Christmas Day I got *Yesterday And Today* and *Beatles VI*. The next day I bought *The Beatles' Second Album* and *Beatles '65*. By the end of the year I had all of the released Beatle albums.

Revolver is now my favorite album and has been for many years. But when I first bought it I was surprised that there were only two songs from John on the album. I did not know that the U.S. albums had different tracks from the British release until years later. When I eventually bought the British releases, *Revolver* became my favorite album due to the additional John songs. Until then, *Abbey Road* had been my favorite. I celebrate December 6, 1968 every year by playing *Revolver*—the album that opened my door to all the Beatles and solo albums, still going strong today.

John Schiraj

Now being in my early twenties, my introduction to the Beatles was via the *1* album when I was a toddler. The Red and Blue albums were my "next steps" into my adolescent Beatles obsession just prior to the Rock Band video game coming out. Then one day my dad's old buddy gave me a box of his old Beatles records, many with the seventies orange Capitol label. The box had most of the U.S. discography. *Revolver* was the glaring one missing.

This was around 2008 or so, just before the vinyl resurgence and before the 2009 remasters came out. The only way for me to get *Revolver* was to go snag the 1987 CD, which I did. Needless to say, I was flat-out floored. "She Said She Said" quickly became a favorite. This was also around the time I started playing bass, and the album's full of those rich Rickenbacker bass tones I've grown to love from Paul. Funnily enough, I first heard "Tomorrow Never Knows" as part of the *Love* album and was amazed even with that, but I wasn't prepared for hearing the original. I still haven't recovered.

Colin Pushchak

I am a second generation fan, so my copies of *Rubber Soul* and *Revolver* have the 1976 orange Capitol labels, but my copy of *Yesterday And Today* has the Apple label. I later got a copy of *Yesterday And Today* on the purple label because Capitol changed the mix of "I'm Only Sleeping." My singles from that time period are a mix of orange Capitol and light blue Capitol Starline labels.

I first heard *Rubber Soul* on an FM station that played whole albums at midnight. I had to go to school the next day, but stayed up late for the Beatles. I got *Yesterday And Today* and *Revolver* as presents on different birthdays. *The White Album* was my first Beatles album and *Revolver* and *Abbey Road* were my second and third albums (at the same time). I just loved the count-in for "Taxman" and was blown away by "Tomorrow Never Knows." Weird, but artistically a masterpiece. And I love the false starts on "I'm Looking Through You" on the Capitol album that are missing on the British-based CDs.

Tom Drill

I always loved the Beatles LP *Rubber Soul*—thought it was the best—until I purchased an import of *Revolver* in the early 1980s. It not only contained more songs than the U.S. version, but had a completely different feel. It blew me away. To this day it is not only my favorite Beatles album, but my favorite album of all time.

Mark Astorino

For me, both *Rubber Soul* and *Revolver* will always be associated with Christmas 1976. I'm a second-generation Beatles fan. I received the *Revolver* LP on Christmas Day and picked up *Rubber Soul* a couple of days later with Christmas money.

I had become a Beatles fan the summer before, as "Got to Get You Into My Life" and the *Rock And Roll Music* album flirted with the top of the charts. I set aside the comic books that had so engrossed me and became a 10-year-old Beatles obsessive. I played *Revolver* at least twice on Christmas Day—I had never heard anything quite like "Tomorrow Never Knows" before! I also received a new, relatively inexpensive turntable that Christmas, and I recall being fascinated by the stereo separation on my import copy of *Rubber Soul*.

Brad Hundt

I first listened to *Revolver* as a teenager in the mid-1990s (not the mid-1960s), but even then, it was an incredibly mind-blowing experience. I initially encountered it, of all places, in Haifa, Israel, while visiting my aunt and uncle there in Summer 1995. The only Beatles music I really knew until then were their radio hits and the Red and Blue albums, but noticing a CD of *Revolver* by their stereo, I decided to give it a spin. All I can say is — wow, what an incredible album! Sure, I recognized "Eleanor Rigby," "Yellow Submarine" and a couple of the other songs. But there was also "Taxman" and its groovy

guitar lines. "I'm Only Sleeping," which literally enticed me to feel sleepy. "Love You To"—whoa, Indian music on a Beatles album? "She Said She Said—what kind of drugs was John Lennon on? "For No One"—McCartney is a classical genius. "Tomorrow Never Knows"—just utterly speechless. After listening to this album, I wanted to hear a lot more Beatles music. Even 30 years on, they were clearly still the best rock band of all time.

Shane Stein

I grew up in Monterey, California. In September 1966, my older brother Jim was in high school and bought all the Beatles albums, including the recent *Revolver*. I couldn't afford buying LPs yet until Fall 1967 – just singles. I loved the album, but especially "Tomorrow Never Knows," which sounded so different than anything I heard before. I was starting 7th grade and played the LP every day.

One day, while waiting for the bus after school, standing near the band room windows, I had a magic moment with "Tomorrow Never Knows" that stayed with me ever since. My friends and I suddenly heard the opening whining chords of "Tomorrow Never Knows" coming out the windows via a record player, but the drums sounded even more thunderous—and live. We peered into the window and saw Jennifer, a 9th grader, a beautiful half-Asian girl who wore a brown beret and played drums in the band. I had a crush on her. There she was hitting the drums, in perfect beat with Ringo, her eyes closed as if in a trance and her head moving back and forth. I was mesmerized—by her, her drumming—and the song. I couldn't believe it. I was in love. With her—and the song.

Decades later Jennifer married another woman and her younger brother married my younger sister. Well, tomorrow never knows.

Martin Omoto

In My Life With The Beatles

by Jude Southerland Kessler, author of the John Lennon Series

In 1965, everything, it seemed, changed. My dad accepted a new position as the Dean of Education at Northwestern State University in Natchitoches, Louisiana, and we moved away from my hometown of Alexandria, Louisiana. On my first day at East Natchitoches Junior High, when I asked each person I encountered if he or she liked the Beatles, most responded with a nonchalant shrug or a polite nod. This dearth of enthusiasm rattled me.

At night, The Huntley Brinkley Report covered stories about the war in Vietnam and showed graphic film of civil rights protesters being knocked down by fire hoses. In school, we were required to read *You Can Trust the Communists...To Do Exactly What They Say*, a book predicting the unavoidable conquest of Communism over the free world. Then, just before Christmas, with the release of *Rubber Soul*, the Beatles – my one stability in a world shifting all around me – began changing as well.

Years and years later, Wall Street Journal contributor and freelance author, Mark Meyers, would express my teen angst quite eloquently: "For most American teens, the arrival of The Beatles' *Rubber Soul* ... was unsettling. Instead of cheer leading for love, the album's songs held cryptic messages about thinking for yourself, the hypnotic power of women, something called 'getting high' and bedding down with the opposite sex. Clearly, growing up wasn't going to be easy." But in Natchitoches, in December 1965 – knowing nothing about all the other teenagers who (according to Meyers) were feeling as alienated as I did – I listened to the Beatles new album and teared up, feeling utterly alone.

Granted, some of the songs on the LP struck a familiar chord. Having been an Elvis fan before I found the Beatles, I instantly recognized John Lennon's inspiration for "Run For Your Life" in Elvis' "Let's Play House." And the raucous Lennon song was a comfortingly familiar rocker in the vein of the boys' popular covers of "Long Tall Sally" and "Roll Over Beethoven."

Today, using 21st-century standards to judge a 20th-century song, outraged critics fault John's "Run for Your Life" for espousing chauvinism and even misogyny. But in the Sixties, songs like Joanie Sommers's "Johnny Get Angry" (about an inadequate boyfriend who refuses to get jealous and shout at his coquettish girlfriend when she purposely makes eyes at other boys) and "My Boyfriend's Back" (about a flirtatious rogue who is destined for a beating when the girl's absent boyfriend-hero returns to town) were all the rage. In 1965, "real men" smoked Marlboros and rode horses. "He's a rebel and he'll never be any good/He's a rebel 'cause he never ever does what he should!" was one hit song's measure of the manly man. James Dean, the surly "rebel without a cause" was a heartthrob. And in the film *Hud*, Paul Newman was full of scowling, muttering machismo. John Lennon had never been "the Cute Beatle" or "the Quiet One." He had always been the tough guy—the commanding, wide-stanced "Sexy Beatle." And "Run for Your Life" only solidified his long-established image. It was a song that felt gratifyingly typical, and I loved it.

The lyrics of "Girl" were also hauntingly familiar. "Once again," I remember thinking, "John's singing about HER." It was this album's outcry to the girl who had hurt him in "If I Fell," the girl who had abandoned him in "Not A Second Time," and the girl he'd lost in "I'll Cry Instead." She was the inaccessible ideal who never showed up at the party. She was the one who made him feel like a loser and not what he appeared to be. She was the girl who'd left him sitting on his own, although he'd given her everything he had. And here she was once again...the girl who came to stay. In 1965, I had no idea who she was. Until John's poignant "reveal" on The White Album, I couldn't even guess her identity. But I knew John was obsessed with her. And I knew that, as long as he had breath to sing, he would wail at the microphones of the world for this unattainable love. Finding her on this new album was no surprise at all. And, although I resented the way this woman had wounded John, I would've been shaken to discover her absence.

"It's Only Love" and "In My Life" were my favorite songs on the new Rubber Soul album. Even today, they run neck and neck.

Like "Yes It Is" and "This Boy," "It's Only Love" was an exquisite Lennon ballad that took my breath away. "Yes It Is" sang of a love lost, of passion "over and gone." And "This Boy" laid bare the agony of unrequited love. But "It's Only Love" confronted the day-to-day complications of a relationship, the struggles of an all-too-human couple working to keep love alive. I wondered if John was singing about his wife, Cyn. I wondered if the strain of Beatlemania and the constant touring was taking a toll on their marriage. But I also remember thinking that John had told their story so artistically. All of my life, I've loved poetry. In fact, I kept a small, brown spiral notebook filled with powerful phrases and quotable quotes. And just after New Year 1966, inside the cover of that book I scrawled, "It's only love." Nothing, I thought, was more eloquently under-stated than that phrase. I still feel that way.

I wouldn't truly understand "In My Life" until 1993 when I first walked the streets of Liverpool...visiting Liverpool College of Art, Gambier Terrace, Ye Cracke, The Grapes, the Whitechapel North End Music Store, Hessy's, and The Jacaranda. That day, John's Rubber Soul song became a "pop-up" book, his lyrics springing to life in kaleidoscopic 3-D. But as all great songs are meant to do, "In My Life" conjured up memories of my happy childhood in Alexandria, Louisiana...visions of Camp Calico and the icy City Park swimming pool and joyous nights rehearsing "The Sound of Music" in CenLa's Little Theater. All of the hometown folk I'd left behind and those (like my grandfather) whom I'd recently lost, were heralded in this simple, universal ballad of a life remembered. John, of course, was writing about himself. But the greatest strength of the Beatles was always their ability to make us feel as if they were looking right at us, singing for us, reciting our histories, and telling our stories. They seemed to understand (as no one else did) the moments of our lives.

But then there was "Norwegian Wood." For a girl who had just turned 13 and was the daughter of a former junior high principal and a Home Economics teacher, this song was bewildering. I lived a sheltered life in the Bible Belt and had no (zero!) knowledge of love affairs. I had no idea why this woman had announced to John: "It's time for bed." I couldn't understand why on earth he'd slept in the tub! And the final line of the song was a tremendous enigma! In fact, the only thing stranger than the lyrics of "Norwegian Wood" was its unusual music. The whole thing made me feel excluded.

This wave of ostracism was amplified when I heard George's "Think for Yourself." What did George mean by, "And though your mind's opaque, try thinking more, if just for your own sake..."? This song was clearly no "She Loves You." No "Dizzy Miss Lizzy." No "Twist And Shout." A distinct feeling of unease began to settle in.

Both "You Won't See Me" and "I'm Looking Through You" seemed angry, resentful and unhappy. And I didn't buy into a word of "Michelle." Even with its trimming of fine French lace, it seemed a bit of "forced rhyme" to me. French in a Beatles song? I just couldn't relate. But none of these slightly unnerving elements on *Rubber Soul* could prepare me for the over-arching oddity that was 1966's revolutionary *Revolver*.

After reading Robert Rodriguez's incredible book, *Revolver: How The Beatles Re-Imagined Rock'n'Roll*, I now like the innovative, creative, shake-up-the-world LP that *Revolver* continues to be. But from 1966 until the release of Rodriguez's work in 2012, I found very little to admire in that oddly bizarre collection of songs.

For years, I'd gravitated to John's gritty rock'n'roll covers and original numbers. And I loved his achingly sorrowful ballads. But on *Revolver*, there was nothing in John's catalogue that I could enjoy. "Tomorrow Never Knows" convinced me that he had summarily lost his sanity. And "She Said She Said" was solid evidence that, as our DARE instructor had constantly preached to us, drugs can "fry your mind." I was deeply concerned for John Lennon. He seemed to have vacated the known world for a land far beyond my horizon.

The afternoon that *Revolver* came out, I remember sighing to my friend Patty Dalme, "I guess I'll have to like Paul's 'For No One,' even though I've never ever picked a Paul song as 'best of record' in my entire life!" "Well," she said, "what about 'Eleanor Rigby'?" "Yeah, I could." I chewed my lip. "But...that's Paul, too." For a while, I even considered liking "Got To Get You Into My Life." But even though I played the trumpet in the school band, I despised horns in rock'n'roll.

A few hours ago, I got my *Revolver* platter out and looked it over. Not surprisingly, it's fairly free of scratches and wear marks. I'll bet I didn't play it 25 times. I dutifully wrote my name on the cover as my father had always directed me to do, and I'd added it to my collection. But to me, *Revolver* was merely the artistic symbol of the intense estrangement I felt in the late Sixties. It was the embodiment of the "odd woman out" feeling that washed over me as hippies flocked to San Francisco and urged us all to "tune in, turn on, and drop out." The times they were a-changin', and so were the Beatles. But terribly upset about it all, I went to college a year early, buried myself in scholastic endeavors, concentrated on the pursuit of two degrees, and watched the Students for a Democratic Society (SDS) chapter on my college campus with wary eyes.

I'm still that reserved, serious North Louisiana girl with a penchant for study, but now I understand (well, I understand better) what the Beatles were trying to say. Today, I realize that "the meaning of within is being." I unreservedly believe that "love is all" and "love is everyone." And although I still create a rigid list of "To Dos" for every 24-hour cycle, I attempt to "listen to the colour of [my] dreams." Bit by bit, I'm evolving.

Now, the Beatles weren't naive. They fully realized that these two albums would shake up their fan base. Paul said: "People have always wanted us to stay the same, but we can't stay in a rut. No one else expects to hit a peak at 23 and never develop, so why should we? *Rubber Soul* for me is the beginning of my adult life." Their late 1965 and 1966 albums were abrupt departures from the music of the Cavern Club; they were no longer that untamed band in worn, damp leathers and Cuban heels. *Rubber Soul* and *Revolver* were dramatic turn-abouts for the cheeky group who rocked 1963's Royal Command Performance and 1965's Shea Stadium. *Rubber Soul* and *Revolver* boldly ushered in "Beatles 2.0." And for those who were "cool enough" and/or free enough to follow the four pied pipers, I'm sure it was a thrilling journey. It took me 40 years to hitch a ride to this party. But at last, I've arrived. Let the music play!

A Fan's Notes: Summer of '66—A Quiet Revolution

by Bill King (edited from Beatlefan 101, July 1996, and other sources)

When people ask what made the Beatles great, I point to the music, their charismatic personalities and the way they tended to defy expectations. You couldn't ask for a better example than the summer of 1966 and the LP *Revolver*. Maybe that's one reason I've always favored that album over *Sgt. Pepper's Lonely Hearts Club Band*, which came along the next year.

Sgt. Pepper caught almost no one by surprise. Oh, sure, listening to it was a revelatory, spine-tingling experience. But you expected that given the album's psychedelic packaging and the advance word from Life magazine that this was a Beatles album like no other. In contrast, *Revolver*, released in a low-key (albeit strikingly arty) black and white cover in the wake of the "Butcher" cover flap, the hoopla over John's Jesus remarks, and another Beatles tour, didn't call attention to itself like *Sgt. Pepper* did, so a lot of folks didn't notice how revolutionary it really was.

Sgt. Pepper, after all, was unleashed with much fanfare and anticipation just as that heyday of pop culture experimentation known as the Summer of Love was reaching its full flower-power frenzy. It was no less than what we expected of the Beatles that year.

Revolver, to the contrary, quietly presented us with its trailblazing collection of songs—including the Beatles' first forays into psychedelia, though that term hadn't yet come into use—during a summer that was chiefly memorable for race riots, space shots and the dying vestiges of the Batman fad.

This was, frankly, not the height of Beatlemania. Many younger fans had been turned off by the folk-rock *Rubber Soul* LP with its distorted cover shot, and had turned their attention to new idols such as the Monkees when their NBC show premiered in September. There was no Beatles movie that summer, and show business pundits were noting that sales for their August stadium tour were off from the two previous summers.

We spent quite a few afternoons escaping the heat in the frigid air-conditioning offered by the three local cinemas, watching such fare as the Cold War satire "The Russians Are Coming, The Russians Are Coming," Dick Van Dyke in Disney's "Lt. Robin Crusoe, U.S.N" and "Born Free." Also big in theaters that summer were "Who's Afraid Of Virginia Woolf?" and "Torn Curtain."

My family signed up for this new thing called cable TV (which then meant interference-free reception of 12 channels from Atlanta, Augusta and the Carolinas). Our viewing habits pretty much conformed to that of the nation: Bonanza, Batman, The Andy Griffith Show, Bewitched, The Beverly Hillbillies, Hogan's Heroes, Green Acres, Get Smart and The Man From U.N.C.L.E.

For pop music viewing, Hullaballoo was in reruns through August, when it would go off the air for good, but there still was American Bandstand on Saturdays and Where the Action Is on weekday afternoons.

On the radio, the Beatles were big early that summer with "Paperback Writer" and "Rain" (which sounded a little different from your usual Beatles song), along with the Lovin' Spoonful's "Summer In The City," Simon and Garfunkel's "I Am A Rock," the Cyrkle's "Red Rubber Ball," Bobby Hebb's "Sunny" the Troggs' "Wild Thing," Sam the Sham and the Pharaohs' "Lil' Red Riding Hood," Paul Revere and the Raiders' "Hungry," the Association's "Along Comes Mary," Donovan's

"Sunshine Superman" and that annoyingly omnipresent novelty hit, "They're Coming To Take Me Away Ha Haaa!" by someone billed as Napoleon XIV.

The big fads among junior high kids that summer were colored sunglasses (like the Beatles wore in the "Paperback Writer" and "Rain" clips on The Ed Sullivan Show) and wearing "surfer crosses" (which looked like the Maltese cross) on a chain around your neck.

Being a college town, Athens, Georgia actually did have the beginnings of a hippie lifestyle, though we didn't call it that yet. Some long-haired types rented a house near the shopping district and would sleep on mattresses on the porch where they liked to play "You've Got To Hide Your Love Away" and Dylan songs.

When news about Lennon's "we're more popular than Jesus" comment hit, my mom was surprisingly tolerant, taking the British view that it was no big deal. And Athens, being a bastion of liberal thought, had no Beatle burnings, as they did in Alabama. I remember seeing Dick Clark on Bandstand trying to ride the fence as he noted that viewers could send in Beatles stuff to be burned if they wanted to, while he introduced the group's new single, "Yellow Submarine." As summer ended, radio was playing "Yellow Sub" and "Eleanor Rigby" heavily. The controversy quickly died. *Revolver* was a big hit on the charts—and on the hippies' front porch. Little did we know a new era had dawned.

I grew up on the Capitol albums, and that comes into play with *Revolver*, the last Beatles album on which the American and British track listings differed. Three of the British LP's tracks, "I'm Only Sleeping," "And Your Bird Can Sing" and "Doctor Robert," had been supplied to Capitol for its earlier *Yesterday And Today* album, and so were deleted from the U.S. version of *Revolver*. The fact that all three were Lennon songs, leaving him with only two of the 11 remaining tracks, skewed the American *Revolver*, making it appear even more of a Paul McCartney tour de force than the U.K. album. George Harrison had three songs, giving the group's junior songwriter a bigger footprint on the U.S. *Revolver* than Lennon. Still, the stylistic departure of the two Lennon songs included on the album left a strong impression on me and most other listeners.

Revolver marked the beginning of the golden age of the Beatles rhythm section, with Paul's bass playing standing out and Ringo's drum work absolutely superb.

I loved five of the tracks: "Eleanor Rigby," "Here There And Everywhere," "Yellow Submarine," "For No One" and "Got To Get You Into My Life," with its Motown-influenced horns and one of Macca's best vocals ever. My mom thought that "Here There And Everywhere" was one of the loveliest songs she'd ever heard. And, even though I was just entering ninth grade, I recognized how sophisticated the mournful French horn solo was on the achingly beautiful "For No One."

I enjoyed Harrison's "Taxman," but it took me a bit longer to warm up to his "I Want To Tell You." Also in my second tier were Paul's piano-led, bouncy "Good Day Sunshine" and John's "Tomorrow Never Knows." The other-worldly production on the latter track, the album-closer, presaged the band's approach on their next album. I liked, but didn't love, Lennon's rather strange "She Said She Said." I thought Harrison's raga rock "Love You To" was the album's weakest track.

All in all, I was knocked out by *Revolver*, and my opinion never has wavered; I think it is the Beatles overall best album, no matter whether you're talking the U.S. or U.K. versions. It's the band's great artistic leap forward, a stylistically diverse collection of tunes with mature, thoughtful lyrics and superb playing, all of which was imaginatively recorded. Packaged with the avant-garde Klaus Voormann cover, the end result marked the transition of the Beatles from teen idols to rock gods. And, at age 14, I was ready for that transition.

I Love the American *Rubber Soul* More

By David Leaf (*The U.S. vs. John Lennon*) www.leafprod.com

In the fall of 1965, I didn't know there was going to be an album called *Rubber Soul*. I didn't belong to a Beatles fan club. I didn't get the teen magazines. All I knew about the Beatles was what I heard on the radio (WABC, WINS and WMCA in New York) and saw on TV and at the movies.

The truth is, even had I known it was coming out, I wouldn't have done much more than shrug. You see, for me, at least, buying albums, even Beatles albums, hadn't become a habit. Yet.

I actually first heard the Beatles in the late fall of 1963, but that's another story. When "I Want To Hold Your Hand" exploded in early 1964, I was hooked. My older brother and I had *Meet The Beatles!* (who didn't?). And once we watched The Ed Sullivan Show along with 73 million other Americans, I bought all the previous singles on Swan and Vee-Jay, and almost all of the singles afterwards on Capitol, Tollie and Vee-Jay.

But long-playing albums? Nope. Except for *Neil Sedaka's Greatest Hits* LP, singles were still the coin of the realm for me as an 11- or 12-year-old Beatles fan. They were always under a dollar. Maybe 79 cents.

In the 1960s, I was completely clueless about the music business. And I certainly didn't know that Capitol was changing the track order on Beatles records. I remember standing in Caruso's Record shop on Main Street in New Rochelle, puzzling over *Introducing The Beatles*. I didn't buy it because I already had some of the songs. Obviously, I was hardly a "completest" then.

In 1965, I didn't understand when the girl next door, Robbie Singer, said she was going to see the Beatles at Shea. I thought, "Why would you go to a concert at a baseball stadium?" It would be a few years before I found out why. (And I'll always treasure seeing Paul, joined by Ringo, at Dodger Stadium in 2019.)

Anyway, by November 1965, I had seen *A Hard Days Night* once and *Help!* twice and was blown away by the music. So when my mother asked me what I wanted for Chanukah, I asked for the *Help!* soundtrack. That December, opening gifts one night, I tore off the paper on the 12" X 12" (okay, maybe 12.375") package, "knowing" what was inside. I thrilled at the sight of the *Help!* cover.

But the package was thicker than one album. Underneath *Help!* was *Rubber Soul*. I said to my mother something ungrateful and stupid like, "How could you buy this? I don't even know if the songs are any good."

Does that last sentence make any sense? Not today, of course. Not then, either. But in 1965, I was thinking economics. What if my mother had spent all that money and I didn't like the record? Her response to me was simply, "It was on sale." At the New York area discount department stores where I would eventually buy albums (Korvette's, S.J. Klein's and Alexander's), mono LPs were priced as low as $1.64, $2.14 for stereo. "Loss leaders," I guess.

I quickly learned that my ungrateful whining about an un-asked-for gift was probably the biggest musical misjudgment I would make in my life.

From the first moment I dropped the needle on *Rubber Soul* to this day, it remains my favorite. I'm fairly certain that I've played it more than any other Beatles record (with the possible exceptions of *Meet The Beatles!* and Side Two of *Abbey Road*). In 1976, (having slept overnight at the L.A. Forum to get tickets to all three Wings shows), I remember during the acoustic set being especially thrilled when Paul, Linda, Denny Laine and company played a foot-stomping version of "I've Just Seen A Face."

In the years since, whenever (Sir) Paul has played a song from *Rubber Soul* (e.g. "Michelle") in concert, it puts me back in that magical moment of discovery when *Rubber Soul* was brand new and I wanted to hear every song over and over again. And that remained true for over twenty years until the Beatles albums were released on CD.

When I first heard the U.K. track listing (as the Beatles intended) on CD, I wasn't happy. That's now how my *Rubber Soul* plays. I was annoyed, and I guess I wasn't the only one because Capitol would eventually release a 4-CD boxed collection of the American versions, including *Rubber Soul*. Not that I listened to that CD much. By then, I had adjusted to the Beatles U.K. track listing.

But ultimately, there is another, more significant thought than my petulance.

In 1965, when Brian Wilson heard *Rubber Soul* and was inspired and challenged by it, he was almost certainly talking about the American track listing. In interviews, he would say "a whole album with all good stuff" and through the years, he has said that the acoustic "folk rock" vibe was what challenged him and inspired him to create an album with a similar sonic consistency: *Pet Sounds*. It's in my biography of him and my liner notes for *Pet Sounds,* as well as *The Pet Sounds Sessions* box set books I wrote. And a million other places.

But what if Brian had first heard the UK *Rubber Soul* that opened with "Drive My Car"? Would he have been similarly inspired to create *Pet Sounds*? One of those "we'll never know" rock history mysteries, but my guess is that the answer is a qualified "No."

Fortunately, thanks to the inspiration of the U.S. *Rubber Soul* track listing, Brian's competitive nature, his compositional and arranging genius, and Tony Asher's pitch perfect lyrics, *Pet Sounds* would then inspire the Beatles. Paul points to "Here, There And Everywhere" on *Revolver*.

As Sir George Martin told tell me in an interview, "Without *Pet Sounds*, *Sgt. Pepper* wouldn't have happened. *Pepper* was an attempt to equal *Pet Sounds*."

At the Capitol Tower in Hollywood, the executives seemed to have had the same disregard for promoting *Pet Sounds* as they did for the Beatles original track listings. None of this "tower intrigue" crossed my radar.

I bought the "Nowhere Man" single (unaware that it and the B-side, "What Goes On," were from the U.K. *Rubber Soul*). I bought the *Yesterday And Today* LP when it came out, even though I had the "Yesterday," "We Can Work It Out"/"Day Tripper" and "Nowhere Man" singles. For me, the album had only five new songs. Although I didn't know it at the time, that album got me three tracks that would be on the U.K. *Revolver*.

Still being somewhat singles oriented, I bought the "Yellow Submarine"/"Eleanor Rigby" 45 when it came out, so I delayed buying the U.S. *Revolver* album because I already had two of its eleven songs. (Don't ask me to explain that economic decision!) Ultimately, the U.S. *Revolver* would get spun a lot in my world; it has several of my all-time favorite Beatles cuts ("Got To Get You Into My Life," "For No One," "Taxman" and the aforementioned "Here, There And Everywhere" and "Eleanor Rigby.")

But back then the album itself didn't, pun intended, rock my world the way *Rubber Soul* did. *Rubber Soul* changed my life if not my record buying habits.

Now, when I look back, especially from my place as a fan, a professor and something of a rock historian, it's clear now how *Rubber Soul* and *Revolver* changed the industry from a singles-oriented business to one that focused on albums. They did that by showing other artists that making albums was the artistic statement.

For me, as much as I love most of *Abbey Road* and *The White Album*, I consider *Rubber Soul*, *Revolver* and *Sgt. Pepper* to be the Beatles artistic apex as a group.

Similarly, Dylan had his mid-1960s run (*Bringing It All Back Home* ending with *Blonde On Blonde*) that he would never top. The Beach Boys from *Beach Boys Today* to *Summer Days* to *Pet Sounds*. Simon and Garfunkel from *Parsley Sage* to *Bridge Over Troubled Water*. And the Who (depending upon your taste but for me) the list would have to include *The Who Sell Out*, *Tommy* and *Who's Next*.

There are so many others, which is why I talk with my students in my "Songwriters on Songwriting" course about the 1960s being an era that can be described as the beginning of a "rock renaissance."

Of course, it didn't begin or end in the 1960s. Each decade has given birth to legendary figures, and, it seems to me, a time when artists reach their peak over a three or four consecutive albums streak. Endless arguments can be started and never resolved by fans as to who is even worthy of conversation let alone which albums to include on their all-time greatest lists.

In the 1970s, I think of Elton John (his incredibly prolific six-album run that begins with 1970's *Elton John* through *Honky Chateau* and cresting with 1973's double LP *Goodbye Yellow Brick Road*) and Billy Joel (I'll pick *Turnstiles*, *The Stranger* and *52nd Street*). Marvin Gaye's *What's Going On* and *Let's Get It On* was a remarkable pair. As were Crosby, Stills and Nash's debut (yeah, I know it was 1969) and CSNY's *Déjà Vu*. And, if they had stayed together, the best of their solo albums for the next five years, from Nash's *Songs For Beginners*, Stills' first solo album and the *Manassas* double LP, Crosby's *If I Could Only Remember My Name*

and Neil Young's *After The Gold Rush*, *Harvest* and more would have created another half-dozen spectacular records. Given how outspoken they could be, how in touch with the Zeitgeist they were, they could have been the American Beatles.

We all have different tastes. In terms of true greatness, Joni Mitchell was to her era what Dylan had been to the mid-1960s, the best singer-songwriter around, her "commercial" period ending with 1974's studio classic *Court and Spark* and that same year's live summation, *Miles Of Aisles*. There are/were so many singer-songwriters to love but few put together three great albums in a row (Randy Newman being my favorite notable exception).

The 1970s was when I renewed my passion for the Bee Gees, starting with *Main Course* through *Spirits Having Flown*. That decade was my favorite era of Bruce Springsteen records, from *The Wild, The Innocent & The E Street Shuffle* through *Darkness On The Edge Of Town*. Traffic (my favorites include *John Barleycorn Must Die* and *The Low Spark Of High Heeled Boys*) and Steve Winwood are on my all-time list of favorites. In those youthful days, there was room for everybody, John Coltrane and Miles Davis and Pink Floyd and Derek & the Dominoes. Poco and the Eagles.

The 1970s was my biggest decade for new musical love affairs: at various times I was deeply into James Taylor (especially his Apple album), Paul Simon, the Moody Blues, Yes, Queen and Fleetwood Mac.

Elvis Costello and the Police/Sting would bridge the 1970s/1980s for me. But my biggest crushes in the 1980s were the obvious ones: Michael Jackson (*Off The Wall*, *Thriller* and *Bad*), U2 (in the mid-1980s including *War*, *The Unforgettable Fire* and *The Joshua Tree*) Prince (starting with *1999* through *Sign O' The Times*.) There was room in my collection for Squeeze, Crowded House, XTC and Peter Gabriel, but *London Calling* by the

Clash was there too. Clearly, I'm more of a pop person than a rocker. In 1988, I spent almost six months working to promote Brian Wilson's first solo album, which was, to me, his best new work.

I would follow R.E.M. across the decade, and Radiohead was big for me, but by the 1990s, my musical hard drive was getting quite full. That said, I was the writer on The Party Machine, the first broadcast hip-hop show, and for a decade, The Billboard Awards, so I had to be in tune with what was going on. Obviously, Hip-Hop was finally part of the mainstream, as was punk. But Oasis, Scotland's the Pearlfishers and L.A.'s Wondermints were more my style.

What I remember most about the 1990s is being really angry when Kurt Cobain killed himself. In the late 1990s/early 2000s, Rufus Wainwright became a massive new favorite. *American Idiot* made me a mad Green Day fan.

Everybody's taste is different. You might have been a Led Zeppelin or a funk or punk fan. Or liked none of the above. I appreciate Hip Hop, but I like to sing along.

When I was old enough to understand how hard it was to not just be great, but consistently great, maybe the ultimate artistic streak ever was Stevie Wonder's peak run from *Talking Book* to *Innervisions* to *Fulfillingness' First Finale* to his ultimate masterwork, *Songs In The Key Of Life*. Stevie, who really did it all (and set the stage for Prince), has to be singled out. And seeing him perform his *Songs In The Key of Life* live–double album start-to-finish in concert–was as powerful, thrilling and rewarding a night of music as I've ever experienced.

I'm sure fans of every artist and group will all have their golden era of albums. The albums they cherish the most. Yet it was the Beatles who opened my ears to those and so many artists. It's what opened so many artists' ears.

But re-inventing yourself? The solo Beatles had to do it. Stevie Wonder had to wait until he turned 21 to do it. Paul Simon's break up with Art lead to a remarkable career evolution that took him from "Mother And Child Reunion," "American Tune" and "Still Crazy After All These Years" to *Graceland* and beyond is unmatched.

But none of those other artists would have come into my life in such a meaningful way had the Beatles not showed me what a great album could be.

My lifetime of love for the Beatles makes them my forever favorite group (me and about 500 million others). As for the solo years, John was really powerful right out of the box, as was George. As a listener, in my opinion, neither they nor Ringo sustained consistently great recording careers, although the Wilburys were certainly as welcome a gift as any during that time.

I do have to single out Sir Paul because his first two solo albums (is *Ram* the most underrated album ever?) are still in heavy rotation, and then, with Wings, from *Band On The Run* to *London Town*...so many great cuts. I've gone to see him on every single American tour (usually multiple times) and bought every album he's ever made, many that I especially adore (like *Tug Of War*, *Flowers In The Dirt* and *Flaming Pie*).

But in 1965, *Rubber Soul* was the album that would change everything for me. Ironically, looking at the track listing of U.K. *Help!* album, I see my journey might have begun there had the American department stores carried the U.K. albums with the original track listings. But all those "woulda, coulda, shouldas" about U.K. vs. U.S. track listings don't matter much anymore.

This much I know for sure. When Bruce Spizer asked me to write about *Rubber Soul* and *Revolver,* I instantly dropped everything I was supposed to be doing. Because just seeing those titles on a page brings me so much joy. I think I better go listen to them both right now.

The *Nowhere Man* EP

During the three years from July 1963 through July 1966, EMI had issued a dozen Beatles extended play (EP) discs. These records played at 45 RPM and had two songs on each side. They cost more than a single, but less than an album, giving purchasers the option of buying a disc with four quality songs from an album for less than the cost of the album itself. The first five Beatles EPs each sold over a quarter million units and were awarded silver discs. The next seven, including the *Nowhere Man* EP, had varying degrees of success, with three failing to top the EP chart. EMI saw the writing on the wall and would issue no additional Beatles EPs with recycled songs in the sixties, making *Nowhere Man* the last of its kind.

EMI waited seven months after the release of the Beatles *Rubber Soul* LP to issue an EP featuring songs from the album. By the time the *Nowhere Man* EP was released on July 8, 1966, *Rubber Soul* had sold over a half million units. As many Beatles fans already had the EP's songs from their purchase of the album, the pool of potential purchasers was significantly smaller than that for a new Beatles single or album. Despite having four solid songs, each with the potential to top the charts, sales were disappointing. The disc peaked at number four during its 18-week run on the Record Retailer EP chart. The glory days of the EP format were fading fast.

Side 1 contains "Nowhere Man" and "Drive My Car." Side 2 has "Michelle" and "You Won't See Me." The record's title track had been issued in America as a single on February 15, 1966. Although the record stalled at number three in Billboard, Cash Box charted the song at two and Record World at one. It sold a million copies. "Michelle" and "Drive My Car" were issued as an export single on Parlophone DP 564. "Michelle" was successfully covered, with David and Jonathan having a top 20 hit in both the U.K. (#11) and U.S. (#18) and the Overlanders taking the song to the top of the British charts for three weeks in early 1966. Anne Murray's version of "You Won't See Me" charted in the U.S. at number eight in 1974.

The front jacket to the EP features a color photo of the group taken on May 20, 1966, by Robert Whitaker at Chiswick House and Gardens during the filming of the "Paperback Writer" and "Rain" promo clips (see page 230). If you look closely to the left of George, you can see a young schoolboy in shorts and knee-high socks sitting on a tree limb behind the group. The psychedelic font used for the group's name and the EP title previously appeared on the Capitol album *Yesterday And Today* (see page 51). The back cover lists the song selections and the six most recent Beatles EPs under the heading "You will also enjoy these swinging EP recordings by the Beatles."

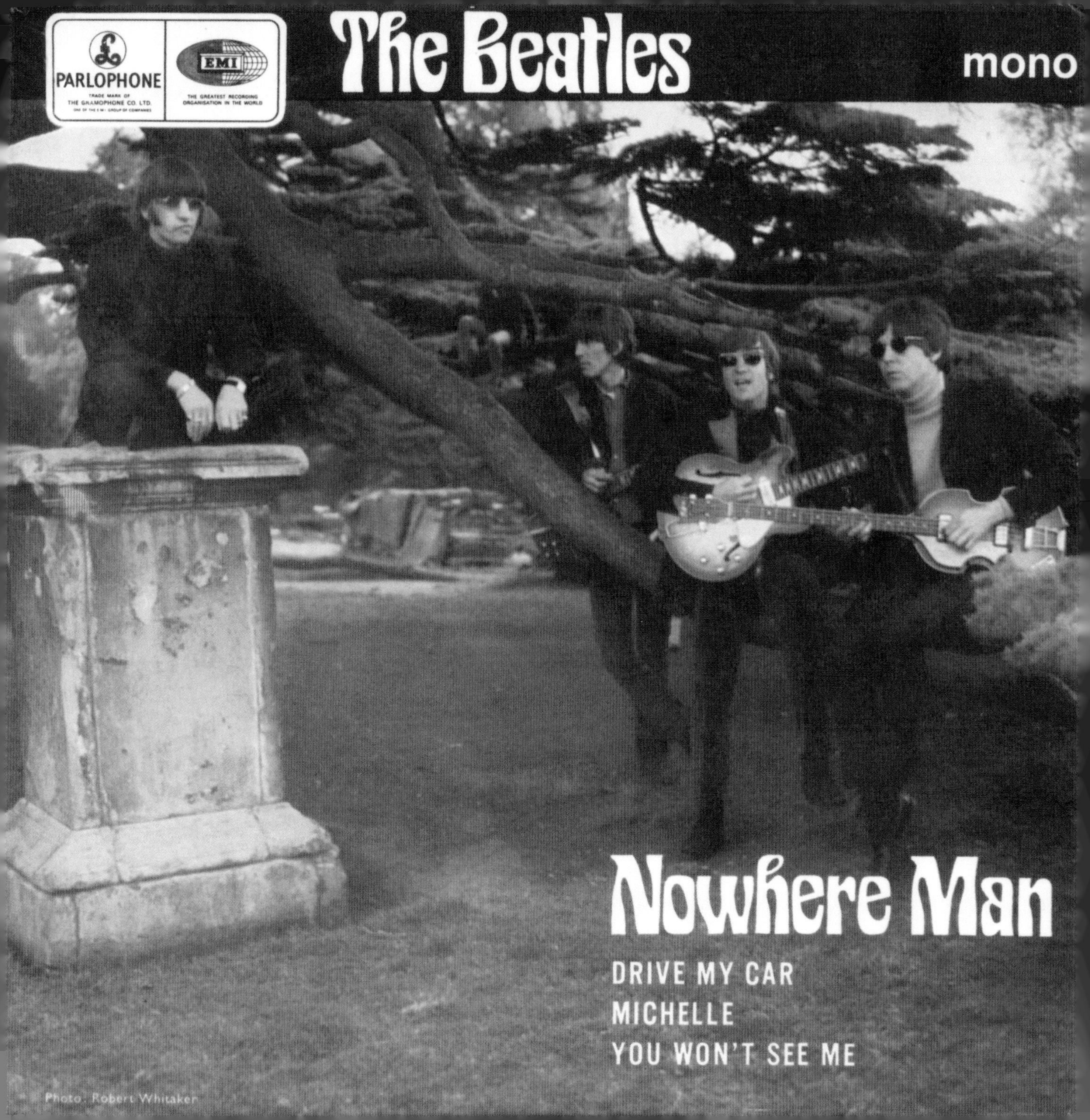

PARLOPHONE
TRADE MARK OF
THE GRAMOPHONE CO. LTD.
ONE OF THE E.M.I. GROUP OF COMPANIES

EMI
THE GREATEST RECORDING
ORGANISATION IN THE WORLD

The Beatles

mono

Nowhere Man

DRIVE MY CAR

MICHELLE

YOU WON'T SEE ME

Photo: Robert Whitaker

A Collection Of Beatles Oldies

In October 1966, EMI was informed by Brian Epstein that, for the first time in the Beatles career, the group would not have an album of new material for the Christmas holiday season. The previous year the Beatles had delivered their groundbreaking *Rubber Soul* LP and a double A-side single despite waiting until October 12 to start recording. But this year there would be no miraculous musical marathon. The most EMI could hope for was the group coming together to record a single in time for the Christmas trade. In order to fill the void, EMI turned to its archives.

The November 17, 1966 Record Retailer reported a December 9 release date for a Beatles oldies LP featuring most of the group's major hits and one new track, "Bad Boy." This marked the first time EMI attempted a Beatles hits album. EMI marketing manager Roy Featherstone told the magazine, "We feel that the 16 tracks, including one unreleased song, is a good package for Christmas." He explained that some hits collections have a long selling life and thought, "Maybe the Beatles will do the same."

A Collection Of Beatles Oldies entered the Record Retailer chart at number 23 on December 8 while *Revolver* was at number six and *The Sound Of Music* was at the top. After a week at 14 and two weeks at 11, the Beatles hits LP reached its peak position of number seven on January 5, 1967. The album charted for 18 weeks during 1966-67 and re-charted for 16 more weeks during 1970-72.

Melody Maker charted the album for six weeks, with a peak at number four. Disc also showed a peak of four, while NME reported the album at six.

While the disc was not a failure, EMI must have been disappointed with its sales. That Christmas season, the Beatles oldies LP was outperformed by two other hits collections: *Best Of The Beach Boys*, which peaked at number two, and the Rolling Stones' *Big Hits (High Tide And Green Grass)*, which worked its way up to four.

The Beatles showed no enthusiasm towards the album, which was put together without their input and was issued at a time the group was breaking away from their fab four mop top days. According to Beatles press manager Tony Barrow, the Beatles disliked the timing of this oldies-but-goodies bundle since they would have preferred to get their new album out first to show off their latest material before re-warming their early tracks.

The album is missing the group's first two hits, "Love Me Do" and "Please Please Me," but has all of the remaining singles starting with "From Me To You" and continuing through "Yellow Submarine" c/w "Eleanor Rigby," all of which topped the charts. Seven of the singles had yet to appear on a British LP. It also includes two Beatles album tracks that were hits by other artists—"Yesterday," a number eight hit for Matt Monro, and "Michelle," which the Overlanders took to the top of the charts. Beatles fans were given additional inducement to purchase the disc by the inclusion of "Bad Boy," a Larry Williams song from the Beatles early days stage show. It was recorded by the group for the 1965 Capitol album *Beatles VI* and had not previously been available in the U.K.

The front album cover features a drawing by David Christian. Its bright colors and mod imagery portray the swinging sixties. The back cover features a color photo of the group taken in their hotel suite in Tokyo, Japan by Robert Whitaker on June 30 during the Beatles 1966 world tour.

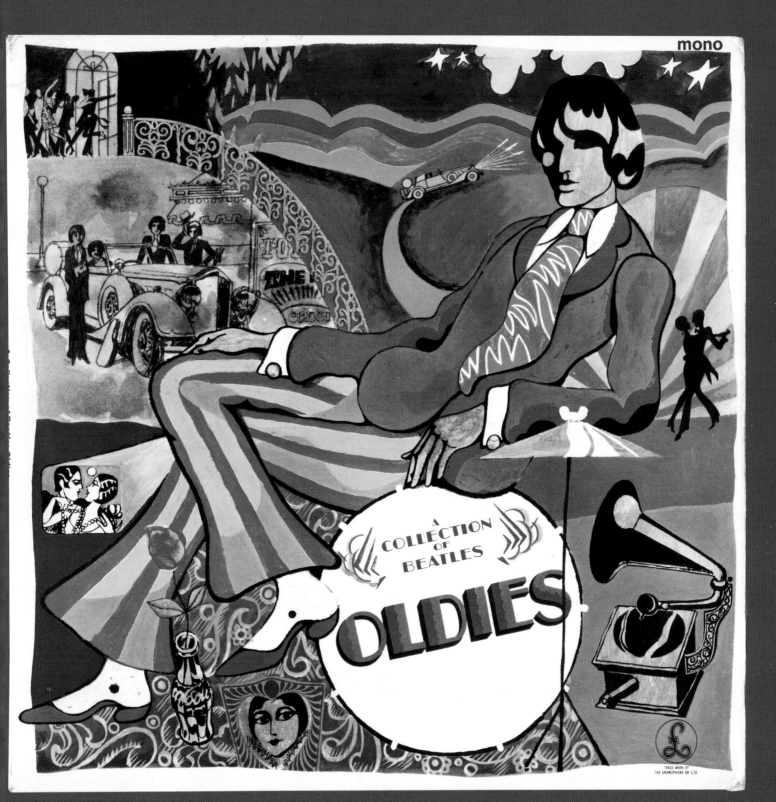

Two More Innovative Covers

Continuing with a trend dating back to the Beatles second Parlophone album, *With The Beatles*, the cover photo for *Rubber Soul* was assigned to Robert Freeman. This would be his fifth and final cover for the group.

The striking front cover features a deliberately distorted tight portrait of the group showing little more than their faces taken in front of a tall, dark green rhododendron bush. The group members are wearing dark polo neck (turtleneck) shirts and suede leather jackets, although only John's jacket is clearly visible. Freeman recalls looking for "another angle on the group and a different tonality – greens, browns and black, but with an almost monochrome look."

Although some sources state that the picture was shot in the woods, Freeman and Paul recall the photo being taken at John's Weybridge home, Kenwood. This is most likely the case, as the album's back cover (shown on page 194) has a picture of John taken at Kenwood in front of the same type of bush.

The Beatles got the idea for the cover's distorted image due to a mishap that occurred when the group met with Freeman to review the slides from the photo shoot. Paul remembers Freeman projecting the photos on an album-sized white piece of cardboard so that the group could see exactly what the pictures would look like on an album cover. Just after selecting the picture for the cover, the card fell backwards, elongating the photograph. According to Paul: "It was stretched and we went, 'That's it, *Rubber So-o-oul*, hey hey! Can you do it like that?" Freeman indicated he could and duplicated the distortion effect by tilting the image in the enlarger and copying it onto a larger transparency.

Freeman contacted graphic designer Charles Front to prepare a title logo for the album's cover. According to the text accompanying the Bonhams' auction listing of Front's draft design of the cover lettering, the album title *Rubber Soul* "suggested to Front the image of a globule of latex or other viscous substance being pulled downward as if by the force of gravity (mirroring the distortion in Freeman's photograph)." Although its imagery has been associated with psychedelic drugs, Front was not into LSD and denied that drugs had anything to do with his design. In an interview with Lisa Bachelor in the June 17, 2007 edition of The Guardian, Front stated: "It was all about the name of the album title. If you tap into a rubber tree then you get a sort of globule, so I started thinking of creating a shape that represented that, starting narrow and filling out." The designer recalled being paid 26 guineas and five shillings (slightly over 27½ pounds) for his work. After the Beatles approved the print of Freeman's photo and Front's title logo, the designer made minor modifications to the lettering and spacing.

The album's front cover has the *Rubber Soul* title logo in the upper left corner space above the group's elongated heads. The Parlophone £ logo is in the lower right corner. Both are orangish-brown. For the first time on a Beatles album, the group's name does not appear on the front cover. (The front cover to the Rolling Stones first U.K. album from 1964 has neither the group's name or album title.) Most of the *Rubber Soul* front covers do not have a mono or stereo designation, although a very limited number of U.K. covers have "stereo" printed in silver or black.

The back cover features eight photographs, two of each Beatle, taken by Freeman. The album title logo, the group's name and the song details are in a rectangular box surrounded by photos on all sides but the top. The lower portion has the usual information appearing on back covers of EMI albums.

Up to this point, Capitol's Beatles albums bore little resemblance to the British releases. While *Meet The Beatles!* had the same cover photo and many of the songs from Parlophone's *With The Beatles*, all subsequent Capitol albums had unique cover art and track selections.

Perhaps recognizing that the Beatles had prepared a special album that should not be dissected beyond recognition, the decision was made to keep the album's British title and cover art work. This decision was undoubtedly influenced by pressure exerted by the Beatles. By memorandum dated August 31, 1965,

Capitol president Alan Livingston informed Dave Dexter of the group's desires: "In a meeting with Brian Epstein yesterday, he expressed the very strong hope that we would consider using the same art work for our Beatle album covers as England does." Capitol's Voyle Gilmore, who had received a copy of the memo, sent a memo to Livingston and Dexter on September 2 stating that it was a good idea to use the same art work used by EMI. He also thought Capitol's albums should have the same songs and release date as the British albums.

Dexter disagreed and defended his handling of the Beatles catalog. "Firstly, no Capitol LP is ever identical in repertoire to the British LP. This affects billing, pose of artists, etc. Timing is another (and perhaps the most frequent factor) in our going ahead and rushing out a Beatles album with our own art. Because EMI persists in the 14-track package we will never ever be in position to release with them simultaneously." He also thought Capitol's art work was better: "We consider our art work in virtually every case superior to the English front cover art, artistically as well as commercially. Ours is slanted more to the merchandising end; we also use more color than EMI. Our billing is vastly different. Their type on front cover is smaller, underplayed, at some cases at the side or bottom of the cover instead of at the top as we must do."

Despite Dexter's views, the front of the Capitol album is very similar to the U.K. release, except for the location of the company logo, the colors being slightly darker and the *Rubber Soul* logo being brown. Both back covers have the same photo layout, but the text box on the Capitol LP has two columns rather than one and "THE BEATLES" appears in large slanted block letters above the box and pictures. The mono back covers have the Capitol/EMI logo, while the stereo covers have the company logo as part of a stereo information rectangle.

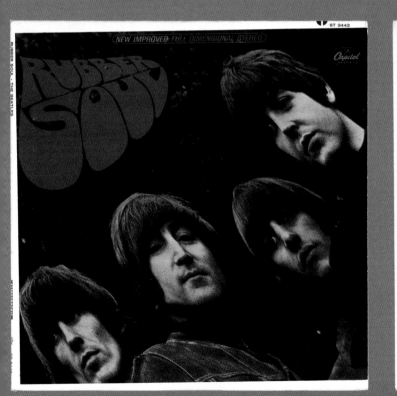

Robert Freeman's streak of designing and photographing the front cover of Beatles albums came to an end with *Revolver*. Although Freeman initially got the assignment, the group rejected his black and white photo montage of the faces of the group contained within a circle the same size as a vinyl LP disc. Freeman's design was inspired by the album's title, which was based on the idea that a spinning disc is a "revolver." The montage featured over 150 faces of the Beatles and comprised of circular rows of faces, with each row getting smaller moving from the outer band to the center.

John then went to Klaus Voormann, a graphic designer who had been friends with the Beatles since 1960 when he saw the band perform in Hamburg. After going to Abbey Road to hear the album's tracks, Klaus came up with 10 to 15 ideas which he presented to the group. The one that got the most favorable response was based on the group's hair. He wanted a cover suitable for the record's avant-garde sound. The cover would be the opposite of the colorful images of the day. It would be a stark black and white pen and ink drawing.

Voormann took a couple of weeks to draw the faces and hair. In addition to the four primary faces, there are other images of the Beatles in the flowing hair and one face peering out of Paul's ear. After having difficulty drawing George, he cut out a mouth and eyes from a newspaper and pasted them on. Assisted by John, Paul and Pete Shotton, he added cut-out photos from newspapers and magazines. Ironically, many of the pictures in the collage were taken by Robert Freeman. Klaus signed his name in George's hair below John's chin.

Once again, the group's name does not appear on the cover. The title "REVOLVER" is printed in thick block letters at the bottom. The Parlophone £ logo is above the album's name. The mono or stereo designation appears in the upper right corner.

The back of the jacket features a Robert Whitaker photograph of the group taken at Abbey Road on May 19, 1966, during the videotaping of promotional videos for the "Paperback Writer"/"Rain" single (see pages 230-31). The group members are wearing sunglasses. The back cover has a black background with white text. "REVOLVER" is centered towards the top in large block letters. The group's name is in small uppercase letters above the "RE" in the title. Side One's song titles, along with songwriter, time and lead singer information, are to the left of the album title. The same information for Side Two is to the right. Production, cover design and photo credits are at the top. EMI information is at the bottom.

The Capitol album jacket is essentially the same, but with the Capitol logo and information. The innovative cover won the Grammy for Best Album Cover, Graphic Arts for 1966.

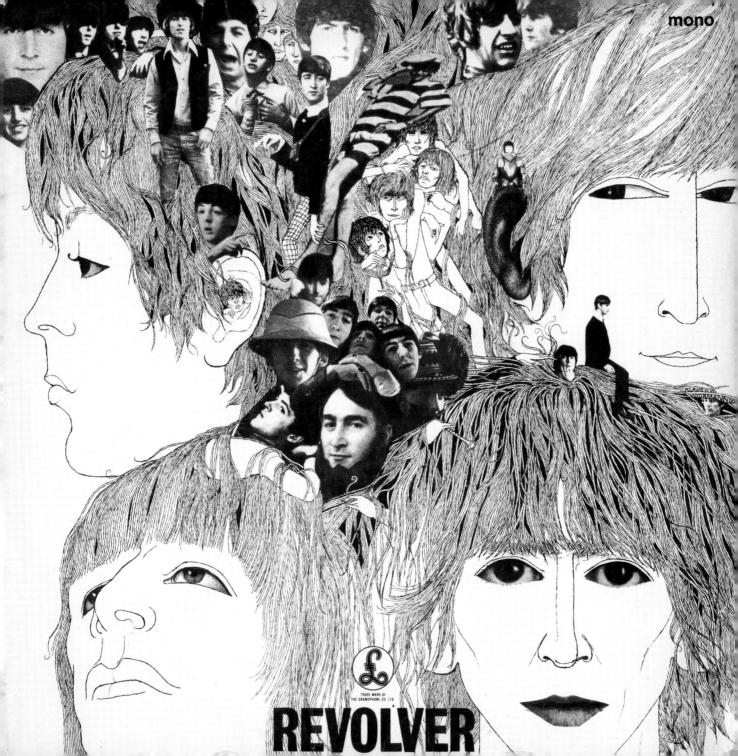

mono

REVOLVER

TRADE MARK OF
THE GRAMOPHONE CO LTD

KLAUS O. W.
VOORMANN

The *Rubber Soul* and *Revolver* Sessions

In the Beatles *Anthology* book, George Harrison says, "I don't see too much difference between *Revolver* and *Rubber Soul*. To me, they could be Volume One and Volume Two." There is some truth to this thinking as both albums set new standards for rock and pop records. But there are clearly noticeable differences between the songs and sounds that each has to offer.

Work on the Beatles album for the 1965 holiday season began on October 12, 1965, at EMI Studios on Abbey Road, with all sessions in Studio Two. The group was coming off a well-deserved break of nearly six weeks (providing time to write new songs), which followed their second North American tour. Due to the limited time available to get the album into stores by early December, the Beatles had to work quickly. During the next month, the group was in the studio for 100 hours over 15 days, producing a 14-track album and the double A-side single, "We Can Work It Out" c/w "Day Tripper." During these sessions, which wrapped up on November 11, the Beatles began experimenting with different instruments, including harmonium, Hammond organ and sitar, as well as creating new instrumental sounds such as fuzz bass. Several tracks featured acoustic guitars, continuing with the folk-rock sound found on some of the tracks on *Help!* such as "I've Just Seen A Face," "It's Only Love" and "You've Got To Hide Your Love Away." They produced a remarkable and diverse body of work, all the more amazing given the time constraints.

While the Beatles prior albums had been collections of great performances, *Rubber Soul* is best appreciated when considered as an entire record—one that set a new standard for the Beatles and rock albums. George Martin's reflections indicate that the record's wholeness and innovative nature was intentional: "It was the first album to present a new, growing Beatles to the world. For the first time we began to think of albums as art on their own, as complete entities." This is not meant to take anything away from the songs themselves; many of the tracks on the disc are among the group's finest. The proof of the quality of the songs is that six of its 14 songs were included on *The Beatles 1962-1966* hits collection, the most from any Beatles album. If the two songs recorded for the singles market during the sessions are included, then half of the 16 songs recorded during the *Rubber Soul* sessions are on the hits collection.

While *Rubber Soul* is remembered as a cohesive collection of great songs, *Revolver*'s most striking feature is its sound. George Martin fondly recalls: "With the new sounds on *Revolver* it was basically an attempt to get more color into our records. I mean, the Beatles were always looking for new sounds and they were always looking to a new horizon. And it was a continually happy journey, even though it was also a continual strain to try to provide new things for them. They were always wanting to try new instruments and new sounds."

The Beatles groundbreaking *Revolver* album was recorded and mixed from April 6 through June 22, 1966, at EMI Studios on Abbey Road. During these sessions, which logged 300 hours, the Beatles, assisted by George Martin and the Abbey Road engineers, were constantly experimenting with new recording techniques. Geoff Emerick, who had previously worked on prior Beatles sessions as second engineer or tape operator, was elevated to balance engineer. In response to John complaining about having to double-track his vocals, engineer Ken Townsend came up with a revolutionary recording technique he called Artificial Double Tracking ("ADT"). Townsend's idea was to create the sound of a double-tracked voice without having to record two separate vocal parts. This was accomplished by delaying a copy of the vocal track by a few milliseconds and then superimposing the delayed vocal track over the original vocal. ADT added depth and texture. The group was so impressed with this new technique that ADT was used on many of the group's subsequent recordings on vocals and instruments.

Although listeners are drawn into *Revolver* by its unique sound images, one should not ignore the brilliance of its songs. The Beatles were not engaging in studio wizardry to cover weaknesses; they were looking for new sounds to enhance their songs. According to Martin: "They were always thinking of fresh ideas and new things, and each song that came out seemed to be a good one. I don't think they really started developing their best songwriting skills, in a really strange way, until *Revolver*. I think that was the beginning of the breakthrough, and certainly "Tomorrow Never Knows," on the end of *Revolver*, was the beginning of the so-called psychedelic bit, which was the forerunner of *Sgt. Pepper*."

Drive My Car

Recorded: October 13, 1965 (Abbey Road Studio 2)
Mixed: October 25 (mono); October 26 (stereo)

Producer: George Martin
Engineers: Norman Smith; Ken Scott

Paul: Lead vocal; bass guitar; piano; slide guitar solos (Casino)
John: Lead vocal; tambourine
George: Backing vocal; lead guitar (Fender Stratocaster)
Ringo: Drums; cowbell

The British version of *Rubber Soul* opens with "Drive My Car." It is a clever and effective rocker that grabs the listener's attention. The music for the song was written by Paul, who initially came up with lyrics full of corny things such as the chorus "you can give me golden rings." He knew the words were a disaster, but liked the melody. Paul sought John's assistance at Lennon's home in Weybridge. After a fruitless attempt to salvage the song, the two took a break and then came up with "drive my car" to replace "golden rings." The story quickly evolved into a movie-star wanna-be offering the singer the opportunity to drive her car. The theme worked well for the duo as "drive my car" was an old blues expression for sex. In the end the girl admitted she had no car, but had "found a driver and that's a start."

The writing of the song is a classic example of how John and Paul brought out the best in each other. In this case, transforming a potential "One And One Is Two" into a song worthy of opening a both a British (*Rubber Soul*) and American (*Yesterday And Today*) Beatles album.

"Drive My Car" was completed in a single night session on October 13, 1965, that started at 7:00 p.m. and ran until 12:15 a.m. This was the first time the Beatles recorded past midnight, a practice that soon become the norm. The group took four takes to complete the basic backing track, which was then embellished with overdubs. The backing includes Ringo's drums providing the beat for George on his Fender Stratocaster and Paul on bass playing, in tandem, a line similar to the bass part played by Donald "Duck" Dunn on the 1965 Otis Redding song, "Respect." Other instruments include tambourine, cowbell, Paul's piano and Paul's slide guitar played on his Epiphone Casino, which is heard during the song's introduction, middle solo and ending. Paul, in a soulful-sounding voice, sings the lead with John. George supplies backing vocals. The song's fade-out is reminiscent of the ending passage to "Ticket To Ride," but with "My baby don't care" replaced with "Beep, beep, beep, beep, yeah."

Norwegian Wood (This Bird Has Flown)

Recorded: October 12 & 21, 1965 (Studio 2)
Mixed: October 25 (mono); October 26 (stereo)

Producer: George Martin
Engineers: Norman Smith; Ken Scott

John: Lead and backing vocals; acoustic guitar (Jumbo)
Paul: Backing vocal; bass
George: Acoustic 12-string guitar; sitar
Ringo: Drums (crash cymbal and bass drum); tambourine

"Norwegian Wood" was originally titled "This Bird Has Flown" when it was recorded on October 12, 1965, during the first day of recording for the album. Although completed in one take, the basic backing track was subject to numerous overdubs. The finished recording from this early session features John's double-tracked lead vocal accompanied by his Gibson J-160 E "Jumbo" acoustic guitar, Paul's backing vocal harmonies and bass, George's double-tracked sitar and Ringo tapping his fingers on his crash cymbal and his drum sticks on the rim of his snare drum, along with overdubbed maracas and tambourine. "Norwegian Wood" would be the first released rock song to feature a sitar.

The lyrics are equally interesting. According to John: "I was trying to write about an affair without letting me wife know...so it was very gobbledegook. I was sort of writing from my experiences, girls' flats." The song had been around for awhile before being completed and recorded. A picture taken during the group's 1964 North American Tour shows a piece of paper containing John's drawing of a girl, the title "This Bird Has Flown" and the song's opening lyrics: "I once had a girl, or should I say, she once had me, she showed me her room, isn't it good, Norwegian Wood." George Martin recalls hearing John play the song on acoustic guitar during a January 1965 Alpine skiing holiday in St. Moritz, Switzerland.

In Barry Miles' *Many Years From Now*, Paul explains how the song basically wrote itself from John's classic opening line, "I once had a girl, or should I say, she once had me." The song evolved into a story of an evening at a woman's flat where the principal decor was wood—cheap pine, often referred to as Norwegian wood. (Thus, the title of the song refers to the room's furniture.) After being led on by the girl and then forced to sleep in the bath tub, the singer awakes in the morning to find himself alone. Although the ending lyric could be interpreted to mean lighting a fire to keep warm, Paul states that it meant the singer burned down the house as an act of revenge.

While the group's initial October 12 recording of the song is quite remarkable, the Beatles completely re-recorded the song nine days later as John was dissatisfied with the results. The previously unissued Take 1 was later released on *Anthology 2*.

The remake and finished master of "Norwegian Wood" was recorded on October 21. The day's third attempt at the song (Take 4) proved to be the charm. The basic track consists of John's lead vocal and acoustic guitar, Paul's backing vocal and bass, and George's acoustic 12-string guitar. George overdubbed his sitar part. Other embellishments include tambourine, claps (or someone tapping their thighs) and Ringo's bass drum and crash cymbal faintly heard at the end of the song. The session tape reveals that John had difficulty with the song's acoustic guitar opening. After two false starts, John mutters the word "wrong" and gamely proceeds. At the successful completion of the song, John triumphantly declares, "I showed ya!," to which George Martin replies "great." And, indeed it is.

You Won't See Me

Recorded: November 11, 1965 (Studio 2)
Mixed: November 15 (mono and stereo)

Producer: George Martin
Engineers: Norman Smith; Ken Scott

Paul: Lead vocal; piano; bass guitar
John: Backing vocal; tambourine
George: Rhythm guitar
Ringo: Drums
Mal Evans: Hammond organ

"You Won't See Me" was recorded in two takes at the November 11, 1965, final recording session for the album. The song features Paul on lead vocal, piano and overdubbed bass, with backing vocals from John and George. Ringo is on drums, while George provides a chopping rhythm guitar part and John adds tambourine. The album's song credits on the back cover list Mal "organ" Evans on Hammond organ, which can be heard providing a sustained A note throughout the last verse.

The song was written by Paul over his frustration with his girlfriend, Jane Asher, for moving out of her London home, where Paul was living at the time, for her career. In *Many Years From Now*, Paul described the track as "very Motown-flavoured" due to his bass playing, which has a "James Jamerson feel." He admired the Motown bass player, "who did all those great melodic bass lines."

Nowhere Man

Recorded: October 21 & 22, 1965 (Studio 2)
Mixed: October 25 (mono); October 26 (stereo)

Producer: George Martin
Engineers: Norman Smith; Ken Scott

John: Lead vocals; acoustic guitar (Jumbo); lead guitar (Strat)
Paul: Backing vocals; bass
George: Backing vocals; lead guitar (Stratocaster)
Ringo: Drums

"Nowhere Man" was the first Beatles-composed song with no reference to love. As such, it has been subjected to much interpretation, with some suggesting it was written about a particular person or as commentary on the loss of faith in modern society. The song's origin is actually much simpler. According to John, the song resulted from the pressure of having to come up with more songs for the album. "I'd spent five hours that morning trying to write a song that was meaningful and good and I finally gave up and lay down." This lowered John's self-esteem. "I thought of myself as Nowhere Man– sitting in his nowhere land." The song, "words and music, the whole damn thing," then came quickly.

In Miles' *Many Years From Now*, Paul noted: "It was really an anti-John song. He told me later, he didn't tell me then, he said he'd written it about himself, feeling like he wasn't going anywhere. I think it was actually about the state of his marriage. It was in a period where he was a bit dissatisfied with what was going on; however, it led to a very good song. He treated it as a third-person song, but he was clever enough to say, 'Isn't he a bit like you and me?' – 'Me' being the final word."

The group's first attempt at the song took place towards the end of the October 21 session. After a series of rehearsals, two takes were recorded. The first was an immediate false start, and the second left much to be desired, so the group called it a night. The following afternoon the Beatles recorded three more takes (numbered 3-5), with Take 4 being the best. The initial backing consisted of acoustic guitar, bass and drums. George and John then overdubbed Fender Stratocaster parts, including the song's melodic middle eight guitar duet that ends with a fifth-fret harmonic. At the group's request, the electric guitars were given extra full treble sound by the Abbey Road engineers. John, Paul and George then double-tracked their harmony vocals over two tracks, with John singing lead. The group added the song to its set list for the December 1965 U.K. tour.

Think For Yourself

Recorded: November 8, 1965 (Studio 2)
Mixed: November 9 (mono and stereo)

Producer: George Martin
Engineers: Norman Smith; Ken Scott

George: Lead vocals; electric guitar (Stratocaster)
Paul: Backing vocals; bass; fuzz bass
John: Backing vocals; organ; tambourine
Ringo: Drums; maracas

The lyrics to George's "Think For Yourself" have an overall sour and bitter feel with a touch of semi-constructive criticism and optimism thrown in at the end. "Although your mind's opaque/Try thinking more if just for your own sake/The future still looks good/And you've got time to rectify all the things that you should." In his book *I Me Mine*, George stated that he was not sure who inspired the song. "'Think For Yourself' must have been written about somebody from the sound of it—but all this time later I don't quite recall who inspired that tune. Probably the government."

"Think For Yourself" was completed in one take with overdubs during a late night session on November 8, 1965. The song, originally identified as "Won't Be There With You," features George on lead vocal, with backing harmonies from John and Paul. The backing track consists of George on guitar, Paul on bass, John on tambourine and Ringo on drums. The overdubs include additional guitar by George, Paul matching his bass part played for the overdub through a fuzz box, John on Vox Continental organ and Ringo on maracas. In *Anthology*, George explained that the fuzz sound came about accidentally in the Phil Spector-produced track "Zip-A-Dee-Doh-Dah" (by Bobby Sox and the Blue Jeans) when the engineer overloaded the microphone on the guitar part causing a distorted sound. The fuzz box was invented to duplicate that sound. He added, "We had one and tried the bass through it and it sounded really good."

Prior to the recording of the song, the tapes rolled while the group rehearsed the song and rambled on about various topics including what they watched on television the previous evening. A brief snippet of George, John and Paul practicing their vocal harmonies ("And you've got time to rectify all the things that you should") was used in the film *Yellow Submarine*. One of the more humorous remarks captured on tape is one of the Beatles asking "I wonder if Ron Richards is free tomorrow," as if the group wanted to replace George Martin with Ron Richards as their producer.

The Word

Recorded: November 10, 1965 (Studio 2)
Mixed: November 11 (mono); November 15 (stereo)

Producer: George Martin
Engineers: Norman Smith; Ken Scott

John: Lead vocals; guitar
Paul: Backing vocals; piano; bass
George: Backing vocals; guitar
Ringo: Drums; maracas
George Martin: Harmonium

"The Word" was the first Beatles song to preach the message of love ("it's so fine, it's sunshine, it's the word love"), a sort of predecessor to John's anthem for the 1967 Summer of Love, "All You Need Is Love." In *Anthology*, John commented: "It sort of dawned on me that love was the answer, when I was younger, on the *Rubber Soul* album. My first expression of it was a song called 'The Word.' The word is 'love', in the good and the bad books that I have read, whatever, wherever, the word is 'love'. It seems like the underlying theme to the universe."

John claimed that, although he collaborated with Paul on "The Word," the song was primarily his. In *Many Years From Now*, Paul described the writing session: "We smoked a bit of pot, then we wrote out a multicoloured lyric sheet, the first time we'd ever done that. We normally didn't smoke when we were working. It got in the way of songwriting because it would just cloud your mind up...It's better to be straight. But we did this multicoloured thing."

The song was completed in three takes on the second to last day of recording songs for the *Rubber Soul* album on November 10, 1965. The initial instrumental backing consists of John on rhythm guitar, George on lead guitar, Paul on piano and Ringo on drums.

As was the case with other later-recorded tracks for the album, Paul chose to overdub his bass part. This enabled him to come up with more melodic bass lines to add to the backing. It also helped increase the definition of the bass sound on the group's records. This practice of Paul overdubbing his bass would carry over to the *Revolver* sessions. Other overdubs to the song included maracas (probably played by Ringo) and George Martin on harmonium. John's lead vocal is double-tracked, as are the backing vocals of Paul and George.

The Capitol stereo album used a November 11 mix, whereas the British stereo LP used a later November 15 mix.

Paul plays his acoustic guitar part for "Michelle" on his Epiphone Texan. The guitars on the floor are Paul's Rickenbacker 4001S bass guitar and George's José Ramírez Guitarra de Estudio nylon string classical guitar. An Epiphone Casino is leaning against a chair. The paper on the floor lists the order of the song's structure.

Michelle

Recorded: November 3, 1965 (Studio 2)
Mixed: November 15 (mono and stereo)

Producer: George Martin
Engineers: Norman Smith; Ken Scott

Paul: Lead vocal; acoustic guitar; bass guitar
John: Backing vocal; nylon-string acoustic guitar
George: Backing vocal; 12-string acoustic guitar; electric guitar
Ringo: Drums

The first side of *Rubber Soul* ends with the Paul McCartney ballad "Michelle," which was recorded on November 3, 1965. Paul had composed the chord structure and melody several years earlier, but did not come up with proper lyrics until 1965 when John suggested he prepare the song for a Beatles album. The words are a charming mixture of English and French. Jan Vaughan, wife of Ivan Vaughan, the man who introduced Paul to John, came up with "Michelle, ma belle." She provided Paul with the French translation "sont les mots qui vont tres bien essemble" for "these are words that go together well." John's contribution to the song was the "I love you" middle eight, which was influenced by Nina Simone's recording of "I Put A Spell On You," a moderate U.K. hit (#49) in August 1965. John did this to give the ballad a "bluesy edge." According to Paul, the song's guitar part was inspired by Chet Atkins.

The basic backing was completed in one take with Paul on his Epiphone Texan acoustic guitar, George on the Framus Hootenanny 5/024 acoustic 12-string guitar and Ringo on drums, all on Track 1, and Paul's vocal on Track 2. Backing vocals by Paul, John and George were overdubbed onto Track 3 and then double-tracked on Track 4. The four-track master was then copied to a new tape with Tracks 1 and 2 transferred to Tracks 1 and 2, and the backing vocals on Tracks 3 and 4 mixed down to Track 3 to leave Track 4 open for overdubs. This was identified as Take 2. Paul then overdubbed bass, played on his new Rickenbacker 4001S bass guitar (with a capo on the fifth fret) through a Fender Bassman amp, George superimposed a guitar solo on his Epiphone Casino, and John added nylon-string acoustic guitar, all onto Track 4 to complete the recording. According to George Martin, he came up with the guitar solo, writing down the notes and playing the sequence for Harrison so that he could duplicate what Martin had composed.

The Capitol mono album used a November 9 mix of "Michelle," whereas the Parlophone mono LP used a later November 15 mix.

What Goes On

Recorded: November 4, 1965 (Studio 2)
Mixed: November 9 (mono and stereo)

Producer: George Martin
Engineers: Norman Smith; Ken Scott & Graham Platt

Ringo: Lead vocal; drums
John: Backing vocals; rhythm guitar
Paul: Backing vocals; bass
George: Lead guitar

The second side of the British *Rubber Soul* album opens with "What Goes On," a charming country rocker sung by Ringo. According to John, the song was one of his earlier efforts, written before the group was known as the Beatles. He acknowledged that Paul later contributed to the song. The Beatles first gave serious consideration to recording "What Goes On" at a session held on March 5, 1963, after they completed their new single "From Me To You" and "Thank You Girl." In addition, the group dusted off another early Lennon-McCartney tune, "One After 909," which was recorded but not released until *Anthology 1* in 1995. Because that session's runthrough of "What Goes On" was not recorded, it is not known what the tune originally sounded like. Two years and eight months later, when the group realized that Ringo was not featured as a lead vocalist on any song recorded for *Rubber Soul*, John and Paul resurrected the song.

According to Beatles road manager Neil Aspinall, in order to show Ringo how the song sounded, Paul made a home demo multi-track tape with Paul singing and playing lead guitar, bass and drums. Ringo listened to the tape and added his own ideas before the recording session. Although Ringo characterized his contribution as "about five words," he was generously given co-writer's credit by John and Paul, making "What Goes On" the only song credited to Lennon-McCartney-Starkey.

The song was recorded in one take on November 4, 1965. Like many of the songs featuring Ringo as lead vocalist, "What Goes On" has a country & western sound. The backing track consists of George's lead guitar on his Gretsch Tennessean, John's rhythm guitar on his Rickenbacker Capri, Paul on bass and Ringo on drums. Ringo apparently provided an off-mike guide vocal during the recording of the instrumental backing. Ringo's lead vocal and the backing vocals of Paul and John were superimposed at the end of the late night session.

Girl

Recorded: November 11, 1965 (Studio 2)
Mixed: November 15 (mono and stereo)

Producer: George Martin
Engineers: Norman Smith; Ken Scott

John: Lead vocals; acoustic guitar (Jumbo)
Paul: Backing vocals; bass
George: Backing vocals; acoustic guitars
Ringo: Drums

"Girl" was the last new song recorded for the album. It was written primarily by John, who recalled: "This was about a dream girl. When Paul and I wrote lyrics in the old days we used to laugh about it like the Tin Pan Alley people would. And it was only later on that we tried to match the lyrics to the tune. I like this one. It was one of my best." But the dream girl Lennon sings about is less than ideal: "She's the kind of girl who puts you down when friends are there you feel a fool/When you say she's looking good she acts as if its understood she's cool." Despite this, "She's the kind of girl you want so much it makes you sorry/Still you don't regret a single day."

John told of the song's religious side in an interview published in early 1970 in Rolling Stone. "I was just talking about Christianity in that – a thing like you have to be tortured to attain heaven. I'm only saying that I was talking about 'pain will lead to pleasure' in 'Girl' and that was sort of the Catholic Christian concept – be tortured and then it'll be all right, which seems to be a bit true but not in their concept of it. But I didn't believe in that, that you have to be tortured to attain anything, It just so happens that you were."

The song was completed in two takes on November 11, 1965. The backing track consists of John and George on acoustic guitars, Paul on bass and Ringo on drums. Although George Martin recalls Harrison playing bouzouki (a Greek string instrument) on "Girl," Paul doesn't remember it that way. In describing the "Zorba-like" Greek-influenced instrumental passage at the end of the song, Paul says that he got the idea for the line while on vacation with Ringo in Greece in September 1963, and that the group "did it on acoustic guitars instead of bouzoukis." John's lead vocal is double-tracked, as are the backing vocals of Paul and George. The Abbey Road engineers used a special compressor on John's vocals to enable his breathing to be heard on the chorus following the word "girl." During the bridge of the song, the boys can be heard singing "tit, tit, tit, tit" behind John's lead vocal.

I'm Looking Through You

Recorded: October 24, November 6, 10 & 11, 1965 (Studio 2)
Mixed: November 15 (mono and stereo)

Producer: George Martin
Engineers: Norman Smith; Ken Scott

Paul: Lead vocals; bass guitar
John: Backing vocal; acoustic guitar (Jumbo)
George: Tambourine; lead guitar (Casino)
Ringo: Drums; Hammond organ; percussion (taps on matchbox)

"I'm Looking Through You" was written by Paul at a time when he was bitter about then-girlfriend Jane Asher leaving him to go to Bristol for her acting career. These same emotions inspired another song recorded later in the sessions, "You Won't See Me," which was also written by Paul in his room at the Asher family home on Wimpole Street, London. Like "Norwegian Wood," "I'm Looking Through You" went through a complete remake.

The group's first version of the song was recorded on October 24, 1965. The basic rhythm track was completed in one take, with numerous overdubs added. This terrific performance features a great vocal from Paul, backed by nylon-string acoustic and electric guitars, bass, organ, maracas and extremely effective hand claps. At this stage, the song did not have any lyrics during its bridge. Although the group later re-recorded the song from scratch, there is nothing wrong with this version. Paul, ever the perfectionist, just believed the song could be improved. Take 1 is included on *Anthology 2*.

The group returned to the song on November 6, with Paul adding lyrics to the bridge. Once again, the group completed the song, this time in two takes, but Paul still was not satisfied with the recording. Four days later, on November 10, the band went through its third go at the song, with the vocals superimposed the following evening. This performance is the final master that appears on the album. The backing track consists of John on acoustic guitar, Paul on bass, Ringo on drums and George on tambourine. George superimposed a distorted lead guitar on his Casino. Ringo added Hammond organ to emphasize the beat heard after each verse and during the fade-out ending. He also tapped on a box of matches. John provides backing vocals behind Paul's double-tracked lead vocal.

The Capitol stereo LP contains a short false start on acoustic guitar that was edited out for the Parlophone stereo release. The false start is not on the mono album.

In My Life

Recorded: October 18 & 22, 1965 (Studio 2)
Mixed: October 25 (mono); October 26 (stereo)

Producer: George Martin
Engineers: Norman Smith; Ken Scott

John: Lead vocal; electric guitar (Casino)
Paul: Backing vocal; bass
George: Backing vocal; lead guitar (Casino)
Ringo: Drums
George Martin: Piano

"In My Life" is one of the album's highlights. It was the first song John wrote that was consciously about his life. His original lyrics described his favorite childhood haunts:

There are places I'll remember
All my life tho' some have changed
Some forever but not for better
Some have gone and some remain
Penny Lane is one I'm missing
Up Church Road to the Clock Tower
In the circle of the Abbey
I have seen some happy hours
Past the tram sheds with no trams
On the 5 bus into town
Past the Dutch and St. Columbus
To the Dockers Umbrella that they pulled down
In the parks I've spent some good times
Calderstones was good for summer
But if you really want to find...
All these places have their memories
Some with love...
Some are dead & some are living

In addition to Penny Lane, John wrote about Church Road, which runs from Penny Lane up to Picton Clock (a popular meeting place) and the Abbey Cinema, the Smithdown Road tram sheds (located by Penny Lane), the Dutch café, St. Columba's Church (which John calls "St. Columbus"), the docker's umbrella (an overhead electric railway at Seaforth Docks that dock workers used for shelter when it rained until it was removed in 1958) and Calderstones Park (another popular meeting place).

John realized that his references to Liverpool places would mean nothing to most listeners, making the song "the most boring sort of 'what I did on my holidays' bus trip song." Because he believed "it wasn't working at all," John rewrote the song. His revised lyrics focused on his recollections of friends and lovers, both dead and living, but without getting specific and naming names (although Pete Shotton says that John told him that former Beatle Stuart Sutcliffe was among the dead and that he was among the living). By making it general, everyone could relate by thinking of their own places, friends and lovers. He also turned it into a love song with the line "In my life, I love you more."

Lennon wrote the song at Kenwood, his house in Weybridge, England. In his Rolling Stone interview published in 1970 John said: "I wrote it upstairs, that was one where I wrote the lyrics first and then sang it. That was usually the case with things like 'In My Life' and ['Across The] Universe' and some of the ones that stand out a bit..."

John and Paul had different memories as to the extent of Paul's contribution to the song's music. John said Paul helped on the bridge, while Paul recalls writing the melody, described by him as "inspired by the Miracles," on John's Mellotron. "So it was John's original inspiration, I think my melody, I think my guitar riff."

"In My Life" was recorded in three takes on October 18, 1965. The backing track consists of John and George on electric guitars, Paul on bass and Ringo on drums. John's lead vocal and the backing vocals of Paul and George are all double-tracked. Overdubs from the session include tambourine and additional electric guitar, which may have originally provided the song's solo. It is possible that the group tried a guitar duet by George and John for the song's instrumental passage before deciding that keyboards would be more appropriate.

On October 22, George Martin added the song's breathtaking piano solo. Martin first attempted his solo on a Hammond organ, but wasn't satisfied with the sound. He then got the idea to play the solo on piano at half speed and an octave below its desired sound so that upon playback at full speed the solo would flow rapidly and be in the proper octave. The plan worked to perfection, making his baroque-influenced interlude sound as if it were played on harpsichord. John was quite pleased with the recording, calling the song his "first real major piece of work." He added: "Up till then it had all been sort of glib and throwaway. And that was the first time I consciously put my literary part of myself into the lyric. Inspired by Kenneth Allsop, the British journalist, and Bob Dylan."

Wait

Recorded: June 17 & November 11, 1965 (Studio 2)
Mixed: November 15 (mono and stereo)

Producer: George Martin
Engineers: Norman Smith; Phil McDonald (June); Ken Scott (Nov)

John: Lead vocals; rhythm guitar; tambourine
Paul: Lead vocals; bass guitar
George: Electric guitar; tone pedal guitar
Ringo: Drums; maracas

"Wait" was recorded on June 17, 1965, during the *Help!* LP sessions. Although a finished master with John and Paul on lead vocals was completed in four takes, the song initially suffered the same fate as "If You've Got Trouble" and "That Means A Lot," making it one of three *Help!* session songs left off the British album. When it was realized that another song was needed for *Rubber Soul*, the "Wait" tape was resurrected for additional tweaking. On November 11, 1965, towards the end of the *Rubber Soul* sessions, the group overdubbed tambourine, maracas, tone pedal guitar by George and additional vocals on the previously finished master.

If I Needed Someone

Recorded: October 16 & 18, 1965 (Studio 2)
Mixed: October 25 (mono); October 26 (stereo)

Producer: George Martin
Engineers: Norman Smith; Ken Scott

George: Lead vocals; electric 12-string guitar (Rickenbacker)
John: Backing vocals; rhythm guitar (Fender Stratocaster)
Paul: Backing vocals; bass guitar
Ringo: Drums; tambourine

"If I Needed Someone" was written by George, who said that it was "like a million other songs written around the D chord. If you move your finger about you get various little melodies." He later told Derek Taylor that he was influenced by two songs recorded by the Byrds: "The Bells Of Rhymney" (a Pete Seeger adaptation of a poem written by Idris Davies) and "She Don't Care About Time" (written by Gene Clark of the Byrds). This brought things full circle since the Byrds sound was heavily influenced by George Harrison's use of a Rickenbacker 12-string electric guitar on the songs featured in *A Hard Day's Night*. "If I Needed Someone" became part of the Beatles 1966 set list.

The backing track was recorded in one take on October 16, 1965. It features George playing lead guitar on his Rickenbacker 12-string, John playing rhythm guitar on his Fender Stratocaster, Paul on bass and Ringo on drums. Two days later, George overdubbed his double-tracked lead vocal. John and Paul supplied backing vocals, and Ringo played tambourine.

Run For Your Life

Recorded: October 12, 1965 (Studio 2)
Mixed: November 9 (mono); November 10 (stereo)

Producer: George Martin
Engineers: Norman Smith; Ken Scott

John: Lead vocal; acoustic guitar (Jumbo)
Paul: Backing vocal; bass guitar
George: Backing vocal; electric guitar
Ringo: Drums; tambourine

The album's closing track, "Run For Your Life," was the first song recorded for *Rubber Soul*. It was completed in five takes on the afternoon of October 12, 1965, and features John on lead vocal backed by Paul and George. The backing track includes John on his Jumbo acoustic guitar, George on electric guitar, Paul on bass and Ringo on drums, along with overdubbed tambourine.

The song's opening line, "I'd rather see you dead little girl than to be with another man," was taken from Arthur Gunter's "Baby Let's Play House," which was written and recorded by Gunther in 1954, although John knew the song from Elvis Presley's Sun recording from the following year. In England, Presley's version of the song was the B-side to "Rip It Up," which charted at number 27 in March 1957. The lifted line came from: "Now listen to me baby/ Try to understand/I'd rather see you dead, little girl/Than to be with another man/Now baby/Come back, baby, come/Come back, baby, come/Come back, baby/I wanna play house with you."

John's song was much more menacing than the R&B song it evolved from. Lennon had previously sung of jealousy in "You Can't Do That," but in that song, he only threatened to "let you down" and "leave you flat." Here, infidelity could lead to murder.

John thought of the recording as a "throwaway song," one that he "just knocked off." Although John told Rolling Stone "I always hated 'Run For Your Life,'" his negative feelings towards the song are not universally shared. The song was praised by British reviewers and was one of George Harrison's favorite Beatles songs.

We Can Work It Out

Recorded: October 20 & 29, 1965 (Studio 2)
Mixed: October 29 (mono); November 10 (stereo)

Producer: George Martin
Engineers: Norman Smith; Ken Scott

Paul: Lead vocals; bass guitar; harmonium
John: Backing vocals (bridge); acoustic guitar (Jumbo); harmonium
George: Tambourine
Ringo: Drums

"We Can Work It Out" was written primarily by Paul, who wrote the verses and chorus on acoustic guitar at the house he had purchased for his father in Heswall, Cheshire, known as Rembrandt. The song's inspiration may have been an argument with Jane Asher. In *Many Years From Now*, Paul explained: "The lyrics might have been personal. It is often a good way to talk to someone or to work your own thoughts out. It saves you going to a psychiatrist, you allow yourself to say what you might not say in person." He added: "I had the idea, the title, had a couple of verses and the basic idea for it, then I took it to John to finish it off and we wrote the middle together. Which is nice: 'Life is very short. There's no time for fussing and fighting, my friend.'" John's impatient observations during the song's pessimistic bridge ("life is very short") serve as an intriguing counterpoint to Paul's optimistic upbeat chorus ("we can work it out"). The contrasting perspectives of John and Paul would later appear again in the song "Getter Better" on *Sgt. Pepper*.

"We Can Work It Out" was recorded on October 20, 1965. According to Paul: "It was George Harrison's idea to put the middle into waltz time, like a German waltz. That came on the session, it was one of the cases of the arrangement being done on the session." The afternoon was used to perfect the instrumental backing of John on acoustic guitar, Paul on bass, Ringo on drums and George on tambourine, with harmonium most likely overdubbed by Paul. That evening Paul and John superimposed their vocals, with John's contribution mainly being on the bridge. Additional vocals and a second harmonium part (most likely played by John) were added on October 29.

The studio session tapes include a breakdown and the finished master with a few seconds of additional music and studio chatter. The most interesting thing about the session tape is the mix, which features the harmonium more prominently than on the released master. The song was issued as a single simultaneously with the LP.

Day Tripper

Recorded: October 16, 1965 (Studio 2)
Mixed: October 29 (mono); October 26 (stereo)

Producer: George Martin
Engineers: Norman Smith; Ken Scott

John: Lead vocal; rhythm guitar (Casino); lead during break (Strat)
Paul: Lead vocal; bass
George: Backing vocal; lead guitar (Casino)
Ringo: Drums; tambourine

"Day Tripper" was written primarily by John, who came up with the idea, the lick and the guitar break. The song, completed with Paul under pressure for the singles market, is dominated by a memorable riff played in tandem by George on lead guitar and Paul on bass. John's rhythm guitar is pushed to the back of the mix. The rhythm track was recorded on the afternoon of October 16, with vocal overdubs that evening. Highlights include John and Paul's double-tracked vocals, Ringo's drumming and strategically placed tambourine and the exciting instrumental break, accompanied with backing vocals, that boils over into the return of the dominant riff. The session tape includes two breakdowns and the finished master without its fade-out ending. The song was part of the 1966 concerts.

12-Bar Original

Recorded: November 4, 1965 (Studio 2)
Mixed: November 30 (mono)

Producer: George Martin
Engineers: Norman Smith; Ken Scott & Graham Platt

George: Lead guitar (Fender Stratocaster with tone pedal)
John: Rhythm and lead guitar (Epiphone Casino)
Paul: Bass guitar
Ringo: Drums
George Martin: Harmonium

In addition to 14 album tracks and two songs released as a single, the Beatles recorded an instrumental titled "12-Bar Original" during the *Rubber Soul* sessions on November 4, 1965. The recording, credited to Lennon-McCartney-Harrison-Starkey, has George on his Fender Stratocaster with a tone pedal, John playing lead and rhythm on his Epiphone Casino, Paul on bass, Ringo on drums and George Martin on harmonium. Take 2 ran for over six and a half minutes. The song was first issued in edited form (2:54) on *Anthology 2*.

I've Just Seen A Face

Recorded: June 14, 1965 (Studio 2)
Mixed: June 18 (mono and stereo)

Producer: George Martin
Engineers: Norman Smith; Phil McDonald

Paul: Lead vocal; nylon-string acoustic guitar
John: Acoustic guitar (Jumbo)
George: 12-string acoustic guitar
Ringo: Drums; maracas

"I've Just Seen A Face" was selected by Capitol Records to be the lead track for its version of *Rubber Soul*, replacing "Drive My Car." The song was recorded during the *Help!* sessions and appeared on the British version of the *Help!* LP. It was written by Paul at the Asher family home on Wimpole Street. Paul had the tune prior to the lyrics and originally named the song "Auntie Gin's Theme" because his aunt liked the music.

The Beatles recorded "I've Just Seen A Face" in six takes at the same June 14, 1965 McCartney-dominated session that produced "Yesterday" and "I'm Down." Paul's lead vocal is double-tracked. The instrumental backing includes Paul on nylon-string acoustic guitar playing the song's intricate introduction, George on 12-string acoustic guitar, John on acoustic guitar and Ringo on drums. The song also includes maracas.

It's Only Love

Recorded: June 15, 1965 (Studio 2)
Mixed: June 18 (mono and stereo)

Producer: George Martin
Engineers: Norman Smith; Phil McDonald

John: Lead vocal; acoustic guitar (Jumbo)
Paul: Bass guitar
George: 12-string acoustic, 6-string & 12-string electric guitars
Ringo: Drums; tambourine

"It's Only Love" was selected by Capitol to lead off the second side of its *Rubber Soul* LP, replacing "What Goes On." The song was recorded towards the end of the *Help!* sessions on June 15, 1965. The song's acoustic guitar-dominated sound meshes perfectly with the tunes recorded four months later for *Rubber Soul*. It was completed in six takes. The song features five guitars: acoustic 6-string, acoustic 12-string, electric, George's 12-string Rickenbacker and one of George's Gretsch guitars. George played his lead parts through a tone pedal. Other instruments include bass, drums and tambourine. John's lead vocal is double-tracked. *Anthology 2* contains the brief false start from Take 3 edited to the beginning of Take 2, which is presented in its entirety.

George Martin's instrumental version of the song on his *Help!* LP is titled "That's A Nice Hat (Cap)," which was apparently the song's working title prior to the lyrics being written. "It's Only Love" holds the distinction of being the first Beatles song that refers to getting high, although in a somewhat innocent way ("I get high when I see you go by, my oh my"). John, who wrote the song, thought its lyrics were "abysmal."

Stereo Mixes, Banding and Mastering

Nearly all of the stereo mixes for the songs recorded during the *Rubber Soul* sessions have the vocals almost exclusively in the right channel and the instruments in the left channel. This drastic stereo separation was a result of George Martin experimenting with the mixes in hopes of achieving mixes for stereo records that would sound good when played on mono equipment. In an interview with Allan Kozinn, Martin indicated that his "attempts on *Rubber Soul* were to find a decent mono result from a stereo record." Martin explained that "if you put something in the center, it comes up four dB louder in mono than it does in stereo." So he balanced things between one side and the other knowing that with most home stereo record players "the speakers were about three feet apart, and the stereo picture was very near mono anyway." Martin said he "exaggerated the stereo to get a clearer effect."

George Martin came up with the running order for *Rubber Soul* on November 16, 1965. The following day, Harry Moss cut the lacquers, which were immediately sent to Hayes for manufacture of the metal parts to press the records. Shortly into the run, EMI decided that Moss had mastered the album too loud and ceased production. After Moss re-cut mono lacquers on November 19, new metal parts were made and Hayes resumed pressing the album. Moss cut the stereo lacquers on November 23.

The Capitol albums were mastered at the Capitol Tower in Los Angeles on November 16, 1965. The mono album was mastered by Billy Smith and the stereo by Hal Muhonen. With the exception of "Michelle" on the mono LP and "The Word" on the stereo disc, Capitol used the sames mixes found on the British albums.

Taxman

Recorded: April 21 & 22 & May 16, 1966 (Studio 2)
Mixed: June 21 (mono and stereo)

Producer: George Martin
Engineers: Geoff Emerick; Phil McDonald

George: Lead vocal; rhythm and lead guitar
Paul: Backing vocals; bass guitar; lead guitar with solos (Casino)
John: Backing vocals
Ringo: Drums; tambourine; cowbell

Revolver opens with a slow, lazy "One, two, three, four, one, two" count-in by George augmented by tape sounds and a cough. Paul's original count-in for the song's backing track can be heard as well, just as Harrison ends his count. It is a far cry from Paul's youthful, exuberant "One, two, three, faaa!" count-in that preceded "I Saw Her Standing There," the opening track on the group's first Parlophone LP, *Please Please Me*, and the second song on Capitol's *Meet The Beatles!* LP. In comparing those early albums to *Revolver*, the music and lyrical themes from that follow are as different as the count-ins.

George's "Taxman" is a bitter yet humorous social commentary on the high taxes imposed by the British government. It was written upon his realization that even though the group was earning a lot of money, most of it was going to the government in the form of taxes. John assisted with the lyrics, providing one of the song's best-known lines, "Now my advice for those who die/Declare the pennies on your eyes." Although Capitol's *The Beatles' Second Album* features George as the lead vocalist on its opening track, "Roll Over Beethoven," *Revolver* is the first and only British Beatles LP to open with a Harrison lead vocal.

"Taxman" was essentially completed in 11 takes on April 21, 1966, although some overdubs were made the following day and on May 16. The song is an attention-grabbing rocker with stinging lead guitar and social commentary. Paul's stop-and-start bass guitar riff and Ringo's energetic drumming, joined by George's distorted rhythm guitar, propel the song into a rock groove that borders on what would later be known as funk music. Paul's bass playing is in the style of James Jamerson, bassist for the Funk Brothers, the core session musicians who provided the instrumental backing for most of Motown's best recordings during the sixties. George's lead vocal and the backing vocals of John and Paul are double-tracked. Ringo superimposed tambourine and cowbell.

The song's impressive guitar solo was overdubbed by Paul on his Epiphone Casino. While this may have caused some awkwardness at the time for Paul to play the lead guitar solo on George's song, the final result was worth it. According to Paul: "George let me have a go for that solo because I had an idea. I was trying to persuade George to do something...feedback-y and crazy. And I was showing him what I wanted, and he said, 'Well, you do it.'" Although George may have capitulated with a taste of resentment and sarcasm, he was later appreciative, saying: "I was pleased to have Paul play that bit on 'Taxman.' If you notice, he did like a little Indian bit on it for me."

Anthology 2 contains Take 11, the final take from the first day of recording. At this stage, the backing vocals in the last verse consisted of the fast-paced gibberish "Anybody got a bit of money, anybody got a bit of money?" refrain rather than the stately references to political leaders Mr. Wilson and Mr. Heath. (Harold Wilson was the Prime Minister, and Edward Heath was head of the opposition party.) The song also lacked the cowbell overdub and ended on a hard break, which would later be edited with a repeat of the song's guitar solo for a fade-out ending. Final mixing and editing of the song were completed on June 21. It was during this session that the decision was made to end the song with an edit containing a reprise of Paul's aggressive guitar solo.

Eleanor Rigby

Recorded: April 28 & 29, June 6, 1966 (Studio 3 except 2 on Apr 28)
Mixed: June 22 (mono and stereo)

Producer: George Martin
Engineers: Geoff Emerick; Phil McDonald

Paul: Lead and backing vocals
John: Backing vocals
George: Backing vocals

Outside musicians: Violins (Tony Gilbert, Sidney Sax, John Sharpe and Jurgen Hess); violas (Stephen Shingles and John Underwood); cellos (Derek Simpson and Norman Jones)

George's indictment of the British tax system is followed by Paul's haunting "Eleanor Rigby," which was issued simultaneously with the album as part of a double A-side single throughout the world. The song is another remarkable showcase of talent. Paul's stirring and memorable lyrics of isolation and loneliness are melded beautifully with a string arrangement scored by George Martin.

The song's protagonist started out as Daisy May Hawkins, but later evolved into Eleanor Rigby. Paul recalls getting the first and last names from separate sources: actress Eleanor Bron, who starred with the Beatles in *Help!*; and a business sign for Rigby & Evans Ltd. Wine & Spirit Shippers. The name may also have come from Paul's subconscious mind. There is a tombstone (shown on the following page) at St. Peter's Parish in Woolton, Liverpool, that bears the name Eleanor Rigby. It was at this church where Paul was introduced to John on July 6, 1957.

Paul finished the storyline for the song at John's Kenwood home in Weybridge, assisted by John, George, Ringo and Pete Shotton, who, as the washboard player in the Quarrymen, was present at the church fete where Paul met John. The priest in the song was initially named Father McCartney, but the name was changed to Father McKenzie to eliminate people thinking it was a reference to Paul's dad. Ringo came up with "darning his socks in the night" and George contributed "Ah, look at all the lonely people."

The musical backing was recorded by eight outside musicians on April 28, 1966. It marked the first time a Beatles song was recorded with no Beatle playing an instrument. While Paul and John sat in the control room, George Martin conducted a double string quartet consisting of four violins, two violas and two cellists. The instruments were spread over four tracks. It took 14 takes to perfect the instrumental backing.

Martin's score has a strident sound, which was inspired by the film scores of American Bernard Herrmann. Although Martin cites the soundtrack to the François Truffaut film *Fahrenheit 451* as his inspiration, this is unlikely because that film was not released until September 16, 1966, more than four months after the song was recorded. The more likely source is the 1960 Alfred Hitchcock film *Psycho*. The string backing from this session prior to the addition of Paul's vocals can be heard on *Anthology 2*.

The instrumental backing was mixed down to one track, leaving three tracks for Paul, John and George to superimpose their vocals. This was done the following evening. After Paul sang lead on one of the tracks, he joined John and George to sing harmony on the "Ah, look at all the lonely people" refrains on another track. He also added harmony to a few of his lead lines. The vocals were recorded with the tape machine running at 49 cps. When played back at the normal speed of 50 cps, the vocals were 3 semitones higher. On June 6, Paul added a counterpoint vocal embellishment to the end. The song was mixed for mono and stereo on June 22.

I'm Only Sleeping

Recorded: April 27, 29, May 5, 6, 1966 (Studio 3 except 2 on May 6)
Mixed: May 12 (U.S. mono), June 6 (U.K. mono) & May 20 (stereo)

Producer: George Martin
Engineers: Geoff Emerick; Phil McDonald

John: Lead vocals; acoustic guitar (Jumbo)
Paul: Backing vocals; bass guitar (Rickenbacker)
George: Backing vocals; electric guitars, including backwards solos
Ringo: Drums

"I'm Only Sleeping" was another song co-written by John and Paul at John's house, this time based on an idea by John. It was written and arranged in one session. Although the writing of the song went quickly, the recording was another story.

The initial session began at 11:30 p.m. on April 27, 1966. Eleven takes were recorded until a satisfactory backing track was obtained consisting of acoustic guitars, bass and drums. After taking time off to record "Eleanor Rigby," the group returned to the song on April 29. For the recording of John's vocal, the tape machine was run at 45 cycles rather than 50. This caused John's voice to sound faster on playback. And to further complicate matters and change the texture of the music, the speed of the backing rhythm track was also varied.

The song's unique electric guitar passages are also the result of studio tricks. Paul's recollection is that during the superimposition of George's guitar solo, the tape operator accidentally put the tape on tails out during playback. This caused the guitar part to be played backwards. The group thought it sounded fantastic and asked George Martin if it could be intentionally recorded that way. After Martin told them it could be done, Harrison began work on his backwards guitar parts.

Engineer Geoff Emerick recalls Harrison going through the laborious process of working out the notation forwards, writing it out backwards and then playing it in reverse order so that when the tape was played backwards, the notes were in the correct order. That way, his guitar passages had the unique backwards effect while retaining the integrity of the intended melody. Harrison separately recorded regular and fuzz guitar passages, which were then merged. Paul fondly recalls: "It was a beautiful solo actually. It sounds like something you couldn't play." The session, which marked the group's discovery of the backwards guitar, took place on May 5. The following day, John, Paul and George added their vocal harmonies.

IN LOVING ☩ MEMORY OF

MY DEAR HUSBAND
JOHN RIGBY,
WHO DEPARTED THIS LIFE
OCT 4TH 1915, AGED 72 YEARS.
"AT REST".
ALSO FRANCES, WIFE OF THE ABOVE,
DIED APRIL 3RD 1928, AGED 85 YEARS.
ALSO DORIS W. DAUGHTER OF
F & E RIGBY, DIED DEC. 24TH 1927,
AGED 2 YEARS & 3 MONTHS.
ALSO ELEANOR RIGBY,
THE BELOVED WIFE OF THOMAS WOODS,
AND GRANDDAUGHTER OF THE ABOVE
DIED 10TH OCT. 1939, AGED 44 YEARS.
ASLEEP.
ALSO FRANCES,
DAUGHTER OF THE ABOVE
DIED 2ND NOVEMBER 1949,
AGED 71 YEARS.

Anthology 2 contains selections from the April 29 session of the group attempting a remake of "I'm Only Sleeping." During an instrumental rehearsal, the song was performed with vibraphone, acoustic guitar and drums. Fortunately, a brief portion of the run through was preserved at the end of the tape containing the proper takes from the session. The group recorded five takes of the song with John and Paul sharing lead vocals while being backed by acoustic guitars and percussion. Prior to the start of the remake, John announces "I'm Only Sleeping, Take One," even though 11 takes had been recorded two days earlier. This experiment was quickly discarded and all subsequent recordings of the song were overdubbed onto Take 11 from the initial April 27 session.

"I'm Only Sleeping" was one of three songs recorded for *Revolver* that were sent to Capitol for its *Yesterday And Today* album. A mono mix was made for Capitol on May 12. A different mono mix was made on June 6 for the U.K. album. Stereo mixes were made on May 20, with Remix 1 sent to Capitol and Remix 2 for the U.K.

Love You To

Recorded: April 11 (Studio 2) & 13 (Studio 3), 1966
Mixed and edited: April 13 (mono) & June 21 (stereo)

Producer: George Martin
Engineers: Geoff Emerick; Phil McDonald (April 11) & Richard Lush (April 13)

George: Lead vocal; acoustic and fuzz guitar; sitar
Paul: Backing vocals; bass
Ringo: Tambourine

Outside musicians: Tabla (Anil Bhagwat); svaramandal; tamboura

"Love You To" is the first song George consciously composed with Indian instruments in mind. "I wrote 'Love You To' on the sitar, because the sitar sounded so nice and my interest was getting deeper all the time. I wanted to write a tune that was specifically for the sitar. Also it had a tabla part, and that was the first time we used a tabla player."

When the basic track was recorded in six takes on April 11, 1966, George had not come up with a title for the tune. The song was initially called "Granny Smith," in honor of the Granny Smith apple. Two years later a green Granny Smith apple would become the logo of the Beatles venture, Apple Corps, Ltd.

Take 1 of the song featured George on lead vocal and acoustic guitar, with Paul providing backing vocals. Later takes added fuzz guitar, bass, Indian string instruments (svaramandal, tamboura and sitar) and tabla (a pair of Indian hand-played drums) played by Anil Bhagwat, who is given credit on the record cover. The sitar was probably played by George, although it is possible that an outside musician contributed sitar to the recording. On April 13, George re-recorded his lead vocal, Ringo played tambourine and Paul added a harmony vocal, which was omitted from the final mix.

Here, There And Everywhere

Recorded: June 14, 16 & 17, 1966 (Studio 3)
Mixed: June 21 (mono and stereo)

Producer: George Martin
Engineers: Geoff Emerick; Phil McDonald

Paul: Lead vocal; electric guitar (Casino); bass; finger snaps
John: Backing vocals; finger snaps
George: Backing vocals; 12-string electric guitar; finger snaps
Ringo: Drums; finger snaps

"Here, There And Everywhere" was written primarily by Paul while sitting by the swimming pool at John's Kenwood home. Paul views the beautiful ballad as one of his favorite compositions as does John, who, in his Playboy interview, called the tune "one of my favorite songs of the Beatles."

The song was recorded in 14 takes spread over three sessions June 14, 16 and 17, 1966. The group recorded four takes at the first session, with only the fourth being complete. These takes were recorded at a faster tempo than the finished master and featured the "oohs" and "aahs" backing vocals, but no lead vocal by Paul. Nine more takes were recorded on June 16, with the final one, Take 13 being used for the master. The backing track features Paul on his Casino electric guitar, George on 12-string electric guitar and Ringo on drums. Overdubs included the group snapping their fingers, gentle brush drumming by Ringo on his cymbals and Paul on bass. Paul, John and George double-tracked their backing harmony vocals. A reduction mix, designated Take 14, was made to allow Paul to overdub his lead vocal. The following evening Paul doubled-tracked his lead vocal.

George Martin, who arranged the song's beautiful vocal harmonies, described his work as follows: "The harmonies on that are very simple, just basic triads which the boys hummed behind and found very easy to do. There's nothing very clever, no counterpoint, just moving block harmonies. Very simple to do... but very effective."

The 1966 "Real Love" Maxi CD single, issued shortly before *Anthology 2*, contains a newly-created edit and mix of "Here, There And Everywhere." The track begins with Take 7 (the backing track with Paul's guide vocal) and concludes with a remix of the backing vocal harmonies superimposed onto Take 13.

Yellow Submarine

Recorded: May 26 (Abbey Road Studio 3) and June 1, 1966 (Studio 2)
Mixed: June 3 (mono); June 22 (stereo)

Producer: George Martin (June 1 only)
Engineers: Geoff Emerick; Phil McDonald

Ringo: Lead vocal; drums
John: Backing vocals and effects; acoustic guitar ("Jumbo")
Paul: Backing vocals and effects; bass guitar
George: Backing vocals and effects; tambourine
Mal Evans: Backing vocals; bass drum

Outside musicians: Brass band instruments (names unknown)
Sound effects: John Skinner and Terry Condon (swirling chains in a water-filled metal bathtub); Brian Jones (clinking glasses and playing an ocarina, a vessel flute wind instrument); John Lennon (blowing bubbles in a bucket of water); George Harrison (swirling water in a metal bathtub); ships' bells; whistles; mechanical sounds (engines and gears); shouts, party chatter and more.
Other voices on the chorus: Brian Jones, Marianne Faithfull, Pattie Harrison, George Martin, Geoff Emerick, Neil Aspinall, Alf Bicknell

"Yellow Submarine" was released simultaneously as an album track and single throughout the world, paired as a double A-side disc with "Eleanor Rigby." In contrast to the haunting themes of isolation and loneliness and the strident musical backing of its flip side, "Yellow Submarine" is a joyous sing-along highlighted by sound effects, clever improvisations and backing vocals, a catchy chorus and an overall party atmosphere. It's a song that sounds like it was as much fun to make as it is to hear. And, like many of the tracks recorded during the sessions for *Revolver*, it was totally different from anything previously released by the group.

In *Anthology*, Paul recalled how he got the idea for the song. "I remember lying in bed one night, in that moment before you're falling asleep – that little twilight moment when a silly idea comes into your head – and thinking of 'Yellow Submarine': 'We all live in a yellow submarine....I quite like children's things; I like children's minds and imagination. So it didn't seem uncool to me to have a pretty surreal idea that was also a children's idea. I thought also,

with Ringo being so good with children – a knockabout uncle type – it might not be a bad idea for him to have a children's song, rather than a very serious song. He wasn't that keen on singing."

In *Many Years From Now*, Paul added: "I just made up a little tune in my head, then started making a story, sort of an ancient mariner, telling the young kids where he'd lived and how there'd been a place where he had a yellow submarine...I think John helped out; the lyrics get more and more obscure as it goes on but the chorus, melody and verses are mine." Prior to recording the song, Paul visited Donovan and asked him if he could fill in a missing line. Donovan came up with "sky of blue, sea of green."

The basic rhythm track was recorded on May 26, 1966, with Judy Martin at the console in place of husband George Martin, who was suffering from food poisoning. The backing track, featuring John on acoustic guitar, Paul on bass, George on tambourine and Ringo on drums, was completed in four takes, all of which had an extended instrumental introduction that was later edited out. Ringo's lead vocal, along with backing vocals by John, Paul and George, were then recorded (as Take 5) at 47½ cycles per second (cps) so the vocals would be sped up when played back at 50 cps.

Recording resumed six days later on June 1, with George Martin back in the recording booth. The 12-hour session added numerous sound effects (bells, whistles, engines, gears, bubbles, crashing waves, clinking glasses and more), John's shouting ("Full speed ahead Mister Boatswain, full speed ahead") and response vocals (on the third verse), brass instruments (by outside session musicians) and backing vocals on the chorus (including Brian Jones of the Rolling Stones, George's wife Pattie Harrison, Beatle assistants Neil Aspinall and Mal Evans, George Martin and the Beatles themselves). The Abbey Road studio log indicates that the party ended at 2:30 a.m.

The "Real Love" Maxi CD single contains a newly created and interesting mix of "Yellow Submarine." It begins with a previously unheard introduction with Ringo, and briefly John, Paul and George, speaking over the sound of marching feet (simulated by shaking a cardboard box full of coals) the following passage: "And we will march 'til three the day to see them gathered there, from Land O'Groats to John O'Green, from Stepney do we tread, to see his yellow submarine, we love it." The mix contains more sound effects than the released version of the song. The 1996 mix of the 1966 song reveals how creative the band could be when turned loose in the studio.

She Said She Said

Recorded: June 21, 1966 (Studio 2)
Mixed: June 22 (mono and stereo)

Producer: George Martin
Engineers: Geoff Emerick; Phil McDonald

John: Lead vocals; rhythm guitar; Hammond organ
George: Backing vocals; lead guitar
Paul: bass guitar (probably)
Ringo: Drums; shaker

Side One closes with "She Said She Said," whose inspiration dates back to the Beatles 1965 North American tour. The key line came from an incident at a party thrown by the group at their rented Mulholland Drive house in the Benedict Canyon, Los Angeles. John recalls: "Peter Fonda came in when we were on acid and he kept coming up to me and sitting next to me and whispering, 'I know what it's like to be dead.'" Fonda's memory is slightly different, saying that he was trying to calm George, who was on LSD and thought he was going to die. "I told him there was nothing to be afraid....I said that I knew what it was like to be dead because when I was 10 years old I'd accidentally shot myself in the stomach and my heart stopped beating three times while I was on the operating table....John was passing at the time and heard me saying 'I know what it's like to be dead'. He looked at me and said, 'You're making me feel like I've never been born. Who put all that shit in your head?'"

George Harrison, who helped Lennon complete the song, recalled: "I was at his house one day – this is the mid-Sixties – and he was struggling with some tunes. He had loads of bits, maybe three songs, that were unfinished, and I made suggestions and helped him to work them together so that they became one finished song, She Said She Said. The middle part of that record is a different song."

The heavy guitar-dominated song was recorded at the end of the *Revolver* sessions on June 21. The basic rhythm track of two guitars, bass and drums was spread over two tracks and was completed in three takes. Paul recalls getting into a "barney" (argument) with John and leaving the studio, but he most likely played bass before he left. John and George double-tracked vocals over the remaining two tracks, which were mixed down to a single track to free up a track for another guitar part by George and organ played by John. These were added during Take 4. Although the song's lyrics are full of drug references, the group's increasing use of mind-altering drugs was not public knowledge at the time of the album's release.

Good Day Sunshine

Recorded: June 8 & 9, 1966 (Studio 2)
Mixed: June 9 (mono); June 21 (stereo)

Producer: George Martin
Engineers: Geoff Emerick; Phil McDonald

Paul: Lead vocal; piano; bass; handclaps
John: Backing vocals; handclaps
George: Backing vocals; handclaps
Ringo: Drums; handclaps
George Martin: Piano solo

The second side of *Revolver* opens with "Good Day Sunshine," which was written primarily by Paul, with assistance from John, at Lennon's Kenwood home. In *Many Years From Now,* McCartney acknowledged that the song was "very much a nod to the Lovin' Spoonful's 'Daydream,' the same traditional, almost trad-jazz feel." He also indicated that "Daydream" was the Beatles favorite song by the New York group.

"Daydream" was written by John Sebastian, the lead vocalist and guitarist of the Lovin' Spoonful. The song was released as a single in the U.S. on February 19, 1966, reaching the top spot in Cash Box and number two in Billboard and Record World. When issued in the U.K. in April, "Daydream" went to number two. Based on the timing of the song's British chart performance, Paul most likely wrote "Good Day Sunshine" well into the *Revolver* sessions.

The song, then titled "A Good Day's Sunshine," was recorded on June 8 and 9, 1966 in EMI's Studio 2. After several rehearsals, the basic rhythm track of Paul on piano and Ringo on drums was recorded. Although three takes were recorded, Take 1 was deemed the best. Paul then overdubbed his bass guitar and later his lead vocal, with John and George supplying backing harmony vocals. John can be heard echoing Paul's "She feels good" at 1:27 into the song.

The next day of recording added a second drum part by Ringo, a honky-tonk-style piano solo by George Martin and handclaps by the entire group. As was the case with Martin's solo on "In My Life," his piano part was recorded at a slower speed, which made it sound brighter when played back at the normal speed of 50 cps. Although Paul's handwritten lyrics for the song reference a guitar solo, none was recorded for the song. John, Paul and George also added a segment consisting of them harmonizing the song's title multiple times, which appears at the end of the song.

And Your Bird Can Sing

Recorded: April 20 & 26, 1966 (Studio 2)
Mixed: May 12 (U.S. mono), June 6 (U.K. mono) & May 20 (stereo)

Producer: George Martin
Engineers: Geoff Emerick; Phil McDonald

John: Lead vocals; rhythm guitar; handclaps
Paul: Backing vocals; lead guitar (Casino); bass guitar; handclaps
George: Backing vocals; lead guitar (Casino); handclaps
Ringo: Drums; tambourine

Although John described "And Your Bird Can Sing" as "another of my throwaways," it is a catchy and energetic rocker full of memorable harmonic guitar riffs. Paul believes he helped with the verses and the middle eight, but views the song as being 80% John's work. The lyrics are somewhat cryptic, perhaps influenced by Bob Dylan's style of wordplay. It is also possible that the song is a gentle jab at the Rolling Stones, with the "bird" in the song being singer Marianne Faithfull, who at the time was Mick Jagger's girlfriend.

The initial recording session for the tune took place on April 20, with two takes being completed. Take 2, featuring lead and rhythm guitars and drums, was deemed the best, and was adorned with numerous overdubs, including tambourine, bass and several vocal parts by John, Paul and George. During one of the vocal overdubs, John and Paul get the giggles and end up laughing their way through much of the song while the previously recorded voices continue unabated behind them. This enjoyable version of the song is on *Anthology 2*.

The Beatles returned to the song on April 26, deciding to scrap their previous efforts and start anew. After completing Takes 3 through 13, it was determined that Take 10 was the best rhythm track. The harmony guitar runs heard throughout the song were played by Harrison and McCartney on their Epiphone Casinos. John's lead vocal, along with backup from Paul and George, tambourine by Ringo and handclaps by John, Paul and George, were superimposed onto Take 10. Paul's distinctive run of bass notes at the end of the song was edited to the finished master from Take 6.

The song was initially mixed and edited for mono on May 12 and for stereo on May 20. The May 12 mono mix was used on Capitol's *Yesterday And Today* album. The U.K. mono *Revolver* has a different mix, made on June 6 and edited on June 8. "And Your Bird Can Sing" received additional exposure when it was used as the opening song for the 1966-67 season of the Beatles cartoon series.

For No One

Recorded: May 9 & 16 (Studio 2) & 19 (Studio 3), 1966
Mixed: June 21 (mono and stereo)

Producer: George Martin
Engineers: Geoff Emerick; Phil McDonald

Paul: Lead vocal; piano; clavichord; bass guitar
Ringo: Drums (recorded over); hi-hat; maracas; tambourine
Alan Civil: French horn

"For No One" was written by Paul in March 1966 while on vacation with Jane Asher at the Swiss ski resort of Klosters. At the time it was titled "Why Did It Die?" The song's first two verses shown on Paul's original lyrics sheet were recorded as is. Discarded lines include: "Why did it die?/you'd like to know/Cry and blame her;" "But you wait/You're too late/As you're deciding why the wrong one wins/the end begins and you will lose her;" "Why let it die/I'd like to know?/Try to save it;" and "You want her/You need her/So make her see that you believe it may work out one day/you need each other."

Paul's rewrite is much more effective as he eliminates the blame and removes any hope of saving the relationship. The song's painful words of lost love are sung over a simple melody that is as memorable as the woman the singer won't forget.

The backing track was recorded in ten takes on May 9, with Paul on piano and Ringo on drums. Paul overdubbed an additional keyboard part on George Martin's clavichord, which was brought to the studio by the producer from his home. Ringo added hi-hat and maracas. Paul recorded his lead vocal on May 16 with the tape machine running at 47½ cps. The song was then given a reduction mixdown (Take 14), during which time Ringo's original drum part was removed from the mix.

The song's baroque-style French horn solo, played by and credited on the album's back cover to Alan Civil, was added on May 19. At the time, Civil was the lead horn player with the New Philharmonic Orchestra and was know by George Martin as a top notch musician. While Martin recalls providing Civil with a written score based on what Paul sang to him, Civil claims there was nothing written down and that he came up with the motive on his own after multiple attempts with Paul encouraging him to "Try something a bit higher." The horn solo perfectly captures the mood of the song.

After Civil's work was done, Paul overdubbed his bass, and Ringo added tambourine. Neither John nor George played or sang on "For No One," which John called "a nice piece of work."

Doctor Robert

Recorded: April 17 & 18, 1966 (Studio 2)
Mixed: May 12 (U.S. mono), June 21 (U.K. mono) & May 20 (stereo)

Producer: George Martin
Engineers: Geoff Emerick; Phil McDonald

John: Lead vocals; rhythm guitar; harmonium
Paul: Backing vocals; bass guitar (Rickenbacker); piano
George: Backing vocals; maracas; lead guitar
Ringo: Drums

"Doctor Robert" is a song about a medical doctor (most likely Dr. Robert Freymann of New York) who gave his patients various injections and pills. According to Paul: "The song was a joke about this fellow who cured everyone of everything with all these pills and tranquilizers. He just kept New York high." In *Many Years From Now*, McCartney explained: "John and I thought it was a funny idea: the fantasy doctor who would fix you up by giving you drugs, [the song] was a parody on that idea. It's just a piss-take. As far as I know, neither of us ever went to a doctor for those kinds of things. But there was a fashion for it and there still is. Change your blood and have a vitamin shot and you'll feel better."

The song was written by John, although Paul may have helped with the bridge. When asked about the song, John recalled: "Another of mine. Mainly about drugs and pills. It was about myself. I was the one that carried all the pills on tour. Well, in the early days. Later on the roadies did it. We just kept them in our pockets loose. In case of trouble."

The song's backing track, consisting of John on rhythm guitar, Paul on bass, Ringo on drums and George on maracas, was recorded in seven takes on April 17, 1966. Overdubs included Paul on piano, John on harmonium and George's lead guitar played through a Leslie.

The following day, John, Paul and George superimposed their vocals onto Take 7. The guitar-driven rocker clocked in at nearly three minutes, but was edited down to 2:13 on May 12 for all releases.

"Dr. Robert" was initially mixed for mono and edited on May 12 for inclusion on the Capitol album *Yesterday And Today*. Two stereo mixes were prepared on May 20, with Remix 1 sent to Capitol (although the label initially created a fake stereo duophonic mix for its stereo LP), and Remix 2 used for the stereo U.K. pressing of *Revolver*. The song was remixed for the U.K. mono *Revolver* LP on June 21.

I Want To Tell You

Recorded: June 2 & 3, 1966 (Studio 2)
Mixed: June 6 (mono) and June 21 (stereo)

Producer: George Martin
Engineers: Geoff Emerick; Phil McDonald

George: Lead vocal; lead guitar (through Leslie); handclaps
Paul: Backing vocals; piano; bass guitar; handclaps
John: Backing vocals; tambourine; handclaps
Ringo: Drums; maracas

George's third song on the album, "I Want To Tell You," is, according to its composer, "about the avalanche of thoughts that are so hard to write down or say or transmit." In his book *I Me Mine*, George added: "The mind is the thing that hops about telling us to do this and do that—when what we need is to lose (forget) the mind. A passing thought."

Harrison's lyric sheet for the song shows that the second verse was going to start with: "How can I tell you/About the things I'm thinking of." This was changed to "When I get near you/The games begin to drag me down." The words in the song's bridge are: "But if I seem to act unkind/It's only me, it's not my mind/That is confusing things." In *I Me Mine*, Harrison said that if he were to re-write the bridge, the words would be changed to: "Although I seem to act unkind/It isn't me, it is my mind/That is confusing things."

"I Want To Tell You" was recorded on June 2, 1966, with a final overdub on June 3. Once again, George had trouble coming up with a title. John suggested the song be titled "Granny Smith Part Friggin' Two" in reference to the initial "Granny Smith" title given to "Love You To." Engineer Geoff Emerick suggested another brand of apple, "Laxton's Superb." This became the title for the day, but was soon changed to "I Don't Know." The new title was George's response to the nagging question of what the song was going to be called. By the time the song was mixed on June 6, Harrison had settled on "I Want To Tell You."

The group recorded five takes of the rhythm track consisting of George on guitar, Paul on piano, Ringo on drums and John on tambourine. Take 3 was selected as the best and given numerous overdubs, including George's lead vocal, backing vocals by John and Paul, maracas, handclaps and additional piano. The following evening, Paul added his bass part, and the song was given an initial mono mix.

Got To Get You Into My Life

Recorded: April 7, 8 & 11, May 18 & June 17, 1966 (Studio 2 except April 7, Studio 3)
Mixed: June 20 (mono); June 22 (stereo)

Producer: George Martin
Engineers: Geoff Emerick; Phil McDonald

Paul: Lead vocal; bass guitar (Rickenbacker)
John: Rhythm guitar; organ
George: Lead guitar
Ringo: Drums; tambourine
Outside musicians: Trumpets (Eddie Thornton, Ian Hamer and Les Condon); Tenor saxophones (Peter Coe and Alan Branscombe)

"Got To Get You Into My Life" was written by Paul. Although John thought the song was about Paul's experience taking LSD, Paul calls the song "an ode to pot, like someone else might write an ode to chocolate or a good claret."

The Beatles began work on the song on April 7. The first take with vocals was Take 5, which was completed that night. This first incarnation of the song has a totally different feel than the finished master. The song opens with George Martin on organ and Ringo's hi-hat. John and George are on acoustic guitars, and Paul is on bass. Paul sings a bluesy lead vocal backed by John and George. *Anthology 2* contains this fascinating version of the song.

The next evening, the group rearranged the song and recorded three new takes with John and George on fuzz guitars on one track, and Paul on bass and Ringo on drums on another track. Take 8 was selected as the best. Paul then overdubbed his lead vocal on one track. The remaining track was used for backing vocals and a second bass part by Paul. A guitar overdub was added on April 11, and the song was put on hold for over five weeks.

The Beatles returned to "Got To Get You Into My Life" on May 18 for a 12-hour session to complete the song. To give the song its Motown sound, five outside musicians were brought in to add brass and saxophones. The lineup included Eddie Thornton, Ian Hamer and Les Condon on trumpet, and Peter Coe and Alan Branscombe on tenor sax. Thornton and Coe were members of Georgie Fame and the Blue Flames. The brass was recorded in two separate performances over the two tracks that had the fuzz guitars, backing vocals and Paul's second bass. (Although the fuzz guitars were later recorded over, they are slightly audible as bleed over on the drum track.) The brass was mixed down to one track, freeing up a track for Paul's double-tracked lead vocal, John's organ and George's tambourine.

Electric guitar parts were then punched into the track. The song was mixed for mono at the end of the session.

An additional dual guitar overdub was added on June 17. The song was then remixed for mono. Three days later, the brass was beefed up in the mono version of the song by making a copy of the most recent mix and then superimposing, slightly out of sync, the May 18-recorded brass parts onto the tape. When the song was mixed for stereo on June 22, the brass was brought sufficiently up to the front of the mix, thus eliminating the need to superimpose additional brass. The vocals towards the end of the song differ slightly between the mono and stereo mixes.

Tomorrow Never Knows

Recorded: April 6 & 7 (Studio 3) & 22 (Studio 2), 1966
Mixed: June 6 (mono); June 22 (stereo)

Producer: George Martin
Engineers: Geoff Emerick; Phil McDonald

John: Lead vocals; organ; tape loops
Paul: Bass guitar (Rickenbacker); lead guitar; tape loops
George: Tamboura; tape loops
Ringo: Drums; tambourine; tape loops
George Martin: Piano

The album's closing track, John's "Tomorrow Never Knows," was actually the first song recorded during the *Revolver* sessions. It sounded unlike anything the Beatles or anyone else had ever recorded. The song came to life on April 6, 1966, under the working title of "Mark I." Its lyrics were inspired by the Tibetan Book of the Dead as interpreted by LSD advocates Timothy Leary and Richard Alpert in their book, *The Psychedelic Experience*. John had grown from "Love, love me do/You know I love you" to: "Turn off your mind, relax and float down stream/It is not dying, it is not dying/Lay down all thought, surrender to the void/It is shining, it is shining."

On paper, the song's structure is simple, consisting of only one chord and a basic melody. On tape, it is one of the group's most complex recordings. With studio trickery, multiple overdubs and use of tape loops, it is a song that could not be duplicated in the studio much less on stage. The recording sheets indicate that the song was recorded in three takes, with Take 2 breaking down. Take 3, the finished master, was subjected to numerous overdubs.

Take 1 of "Mark 1" is a dense, echo-drenched dirge. The foundation of the recording is a relentlessly repeating tape loop consisting of an electric guitar fed through a rotating Leslie speaker (whose normal use produced a swirling sound for Hammond organ) in its fast vibrato mode, another electric guitar played through a fuzz pedal, and a tom-tom beat. While the tape loop played back at half-speed, Ringo and Paul added their drum and bass parts while John simultaneously sang his lead vocal fed through the rotating Leslie speaker in its slower choral mode. John's acoustic guitar, which is occasionally given a strum, as well as Ringo's drums, bleed through John's vocal mike.

This incredible first attempt at the song is on *Anthology 2*. Its mix has John's vocal buried under a wall of sound murkier than anything achieved before by Phil Spector. While some songs sound as if they were recorded in a cave, and reverb-dominated surf songs sound as if they were recorded under water, Take 1 sounds like it was recorded deep inside a cave at the bottom of an ocean.

The finished master opens with the whining sound of a tamboura (an Indian string instrument), which is quickly joined by Ringo on drums and Paul on bass, both playing in tandem. Ringo relentlessly plays the same pattern over and over again, as if part of a tribal ritual. His drums have a deadened, earthy sound achieved by placing the microphone close up to the bass drum stuffed with paper plus the use of limiters and compressors. The tape loop sound effects, which were added the next day on April 7, make their first appearance prior to John's vocal, and phase in and out throughout the entire song. Other sounds include a tambourine, an organ, a backwards guitar solo played through a Leslie speaker and a honky-tonk piano solo during the song's fade-out ending.

John's vocal presented a challenge for George Martin and the studio engineers. Martin recalls John telling him, "I want to sound as though I'm the Dalai Lama singing from the highest mountain top." Others say that John wanted the song to sound like four thousand monks chanting in the background. When John's vocal returns after the song's instrumental break, it sounds distant and swirling, as if coming down from the mountains. This effect was achieved by running John's voice through a rotating Leslie speaker. The group was so fascinated by the sound this gave guitars and vocals that they later experimented with running pianos and drums through a Leslie.

Work on Take 3 began towards the end of the April 6 session with the recording of Ringo's drums and Paul's bass on Track 1, and John's vocal, fed through the Leslie speaker during the second half of the song, on Track 4. After the session ended at around 1:30 a.m., Paul went home and recorded brief tape loops of guitar, sitar and various other instruments and vocal sounds. He brought them to the studio the next day with the idea that the tape loops could be randomly faded in and out of the song.

The tape loops were added to Track 3 during one of the most unique sessions ever held at Abbey Road. George Martin described the session as follows: "We did a live mix of all the loops. All over the studio we had people spooling them onto machines with pencils while Geoff [Emerick] did the balancing. There were many other hands controlling the panning."

In *Recording The Beatles*, the authors identify the five tape loops, in order of appearance, as: (1) a laughing male voice played double speed that sounds like seagulls; (2) a B-flat major chord played by an orchestra (lifted from a classical recording); (3) a sitar phrase reversed and played double speed; (4) a phrase performed on mandolin or acoustic guitar played double speed; and (5) a scalar sitar line, reversed and played double speed.

After taking a two-week break from the song, the Beatles superimposed additional vocals and instruments on April 22. John re-recorded his vocal on Track 4, once again fed through the Leslie speaker for the second half of the song. The tamboura, heard most clearly at the song's introduction, was simultaneously recorded onto Track 4. Track 3 was then filled with John's double-tracked lead vocal for the first half of the song, tambourine, organ and, at the end of the song, piano (a 1964 Challen upright "tack" piano). George Martin claims that he played piano on the song, though some credit it to Paul. A backwards guitar solo, most likely played by Paul, was dropped in on Track 3 during the instrumental break, wiping out the organ and tambourine during that part of the song.

The recording, still known as "Mark 1," was given nine mono mixes on April 27, with Remix 8 deemed the best. By the time the song was remixed for mono on June 6, it finally had an appropriate title, "Tomorrow Never Knows," taken from one of Ringo's expressions. That evening, three more mono mixes were made, with Remix 11 marked as the best. The song was mixed for stereo on June 22. A small number of the initial pressings of the U.K. mono album have Remix 11 of "Tomorrow Never Knows," which was quickly replaced with Remix 8. All mono pressings of the Capitol album have Remix 8.

Although "Tomorrow Never Knows" was the first song the Beatles recorded for *Revolver*, it was wisely placed at the end of the LP. For listeners wondering what the Beatles would do to follow up their amazing new disc, the album's closing statement said it all—Tomorrow Never Knows.

Paperback Writer

Recorded: April 13 & 14, 1966 (Studio 3)
Mixed: April 14 (mono); October 31 (stereo)

Producer: George Martin
Engineers: Geoff Emerick; Richard Lush (April 13);
Phil McDonald (April 14)

Paul: Lead vocals; lead guitar (Casino); bass guitar (Rickenbacker)
John: Backing vocals; rhythm guitar (Gretsch Chad Adkins 6120)
George: Backing vocals; tambourine; guitar (Gibson SG)
Ringo: Drums

"Paperback Writer" was the first song written by Paul that departed from the standard boy/girl love theme. It was written in response to one of Paul's aunts asking if he could write a song that wasn't about love. The song tells the story of a novelist submitting his work to a publisher in hope of becoming a paperback writer. It is written in the style of a letter, bringing back memories of "P.S. I Love You." But the two songs sound light years apart.

In *Many Years From Now*, Paul told how the song evolved: "I arrived at Weybridge and told John I had this idea of trying to write off to a publisher to become a paperback writer, and I said, 'I think it should be written like a letter.' I took a bit of paper out and I said it should be something like, 'Dear Sir or Madam, as the case may be...' and I proceeded to write it just like a letter in front of him, occasionally rhyming it. And John, as I recall, just sat there and said, 'Oh, that's it,' 'Uhuh,' 'Yeah.'...And then we went upstairs and put the melody to it. John and I sat down and finished it all up...."

Recording on the song "Paperback Writer" took place during the second week of the *Revolver* sessions. Its exciting instrumental track features a new bass-dominated sound unlike anything previously recorded by the group. This was partly attributable to Paul's continued use of his Rickenbacker 4001S bass, which first supplanted his Hofner during the *Rubber Soul* sessions. In addition, Abbey Road engineer Ken Townsend came up with a new technique for boosting the bass guitar sound by placing a large White Elephant speaker in front of Paul's bass amplifier and using it in reverse as a large microphone to capture the bass signal.

The Beatles began work on the song on April 13, 1966, in Abbey Road's Studio Three with Paul playing lead guitar on his Epiphone Casino, joined by John on his new Gretsch Chet Adkins signature 6120 hollow-body electric guitar (shown on page 218), George on tambourine and Ringo on drums. This was recorded live onto one track. Ringo kept time with his hi hat and Paul strummed chords during the parts of the song that would later be filled with the a capella vocal refrain of "Paperback writer, writer, writer." This was completed on the second take, the first attempt having broken down. Paul's lead vocal along with John and George's backing vocals were then recorded twice, filling up two more tracks.

The group returned to the studio the next day to fill the remaining track with Paul's bass and other embellishments. The first attempt included Paul on bass and George Martin on piano played through a Leslie speaker. Next, the group did a run through with John and George adding falsetto backing vocals. Paul then got the idea to have John and George sing "Frère Jacques" (from the French nursery rhyme) in the background during the second and third verses. This was first attempted with Paul on bass and Martin on piano. The next pass was similar, but Martin switched to Vox organ and Harrison added guitar. After playback revealed that keyboards were not needed, the final track was filled with Paul's bass, John and George's "Frère Jacques" backing vocals and additional guitar by George on his Gibson SG at the end of each a capella vocal refrain.

The song was then mixed for mono, with Repeat Echo applied to the word "writer" at the end of the a capella refrain. This was then treated with Artificial Double Tracking, with the tape echo ADT slowed down during the fade. The hard work and tweaking on "Paperback Writer" paid off. The song opens with the intricate three-part harmony of Paul, John and George (in the style of the Beach Boys) singing the song's title, treated with echo. Ringo then hits his snare drum and the rest of the band storms in. The song is propelled by Paul's powerful intricate bass lines behind his catchy guitar riff, all held together by Ringo's steady beat. The vocals are superb.

Although "Paperback Writer" was recorded by the Beatles during the *Revolver* sessions, it was not on the album because it was issued as a single in America on May 30, 1966, and in the U.K. on June 10, prior to the completion of the album. The single was a not-so-subtle hint that the group's next album would be strikingly different than their previous efforts as to lyrical content and sound. The song was performed by the group during its 1966 concerts.

Because neither EMI nor Capitol Records had any initial plans to issue "Paperback Writer" on an album, the song was only mixed for mono during the sessions. "Paperback Writer" got its first stereo mix on October 31, 1966, when EMI decided to place the song on its upcoming album *A Collection Of Beatles Oldies*.

Rain

Recorded: April 14 (Studio 3) & 16 (Studio 2), 1966
Mixed: April 16 (mono); December 2, 1969 (stereo)

Producer: George Martin
Engineers: Geoff Emerick; Phil McDonald

John: Lead vocals; guitar
Paul: Backing vocals; bass guitar
George: Backing vocals; guitar
Ringo: Drums; tambourine

After completing "Paperback Writer" on April 14, the group began work on the single's exciting flip side, "Rain." John described it as "a song I wrote about people who are always moaning about the weather all the time." In *Anthology*, Paul asserted his contribution: "We sat down and wrote it together. It was John's vocal and John's feel on the song, but what gave it its character was collaboration."

Pictures taken at the session for The Beatles Book show, at least for rehearsals, John (Gretsch 6120) and Paul (Casino) playing the same guitars they used on "Paperback Writer" with George on a Burns Nu-Sonic bass. If George did play bass on the recording, it was later wiped when Paul overdubbed his bass part.

Having experimented with recording at a non-standard speed during the "Paperback Writer" session and learning that the texture and depth of instruments change when the tape is slowed down, the Beatles deliberately played the rhythm track for "Rain" at an overly fast pace. When the tape's speed was adjusted to run the song at a slower pace, the song took on a deeper, richer textured sound. John's lead vocal also was recorded that way.

The group took five takes to obtain a suitable basic track highlighted by John's lead vocal and distorted guitar (through a WEM Rush Pep Box) and Ringo's drums. Two days later, on April 16, the group superimposed Ringo's tambourine, Paul bass and backing vocals from John, Paul and George onto Take 5. Another studio trick was John's weird-sounding vocal at the end of the song, which was achieved by running a tape of his voice backwards and superimposing it over the backing track. John was proud of this effect, calling it: "The first backwards tape on any record anywhere. Before Hendrix, before The Who, before any fucker." His lead vocal was also given ADT treatment. The tone and style of Ringo's drumming and Paul's bass playing, along with the vari-speed recording technique, gave "Rain" a totally unique "heavy" sound that influenced countless heavy metal bands of lesser talent.

Mixes, Banding and Mastering

Final mixing for the *Revolver* LP took place on June 22, 1966. Shortly thereafter, George Martin worked out the running order for the tracks. When the mono album was banded, Remix 11 of "Tomorrow Never Knows" was mistakenly inserted instead of Remix 8, which had been determined to be the best. Harry Moss cut the mono and stereo lacquers in early July. After a relatively small number of mono discs were pressed, George Martin became aware of the error on the mono disc and directed Moss to recut the lacquer using Remix 8 for the song. All subsequent pressings have Remix 8, as does the Capitol mono album.

The initial mono discs have the matrix number XEX-606-1 in the trail off area of Side 2, while the later discs have XEX-606-2. The primary difference between the two mixes is the additional piano heard during the fade out of Remix 11 of "Tomorrow Never Knows."

The Capitol version of *Revolver* is essentially the same as its British counterpart except that it lacks the three songs previously issued by Capitol on its *Yesterday And Today* album, "I'm Only Sleeping," "And Your Bird Can Sing" and "Dr. Robert." The running order remains the same but for the deleted tracks.

The stereo Capitol LP was mastered on July 15, 1966. The mono Capitol album was mastered by Wally Traugott on July 18, 1966. Both have the same mixes as the U.K. album.

Capitol's *Yesterday And Today* album has mixes for its *Revolver* tracks that differ from those on the British LP. George Martin mixed the three *Revolver* preview songs for mono on May 12, 1966, and immediately sent the tape to Capitol. The next day, Billy Smith mastered the mono LP. Because Martin later remixed the songs, the Capitol LP has different mixes for these tracks. The British mix of "I'm Only Sleeping" has more backwards guitar, particularly in the second verse. The British mix of "Dr. Robert" is similar to the Capitol mix except the guitar is louder on the earlier Capitol mix. On "And Your Bird Can Sing," the handclaps and guitars are louder on the Capitol mix. Due to its mastering, the Capitol tracks have less bass.

Although Martin would make stereo mixes of the songs on May 20, Capitol chose not to wait and made duophonic (fake stereo) mixes for these songs. The Capitol stereo disc was mastered by Hal Muhonen and Wally Traugott on May 13, 1966. All stereo pressings of the album from the sixties have the duophonic mixes (although tape versions of the album have the May 20 stereo mixes, which differ slightly for U.K. mixes of "I'm Only Sleeping" and "Dr. Robert").

Promotional Videos

From the start of their recording career, the Beatles effectively used television appearances to promote their new singles. But towards the end of 1965 the group had become weary of these performances. Furthermore, their popularity was so great that they could not meet the demand of all of the networks that wanted the group to appear on their shows. This problem was solved by producing their own promotional videos for distribution to television networks in England and foreign markets such as America and Japan.

To understand how innovative this concept was, one must realize this took place 15 years before MTV. As 1965 drew to a close, only a handful of promotional clips had been produced by recording artists. The closest thing to a rock video had been the scenes of the Beatles performing their songs in *A Hard Day's Night* and *Help!*

During the *Rubber Soul* sessions, the Beatles took a break from recording to participate in a Granada TV special titled The Music Of Lennon & McCartney. The show, filmed in Studio 6 of Granada TV Centre in Manchester, England on November 1 and 2, 1965, was broadcast in London on December 16, 1965, and throughout the U.K. the following day. It featured various recording artists performing Lennon-McCartney songs such as: the George Martin Orchestra ("I Feel Fine" and "Ringo's Theme (This Boy)"); Peter & Gordon ("World Without Love"); Lulu ("I Saw Him Standing There"); Marianne Faithful ("Yesterday") with Paul miming the first verse; Antonio Vargas ("She Loves You" in a Spanish flamenco version); Billy J. Kramer with the Dakotas ("Bad To Me"); Cilla Black ("It's For You"); Henry Mancini ("If I Fell" on piano); Ester Phillips ("And I Love Him"); and Peter Sellers ("A Hard Day's Night" in a spoken performance in the style of Lawrence Olivier performing Shakespeare's *Richard III*).

The Beatles mimed their way through both sides of their new single, "We Can Work It Out" and "Day Tripper." These were straight performance clips with the group wearing black suits. John is on his Rickenbacker 325, Paul plays his Hofner violin bass, George is on his Gretsch Tennessean and Ringo plays his new Ludwig Super Classic oyster black pearl drum kit. The "Day Tripper" clip, which opens with dancing go-go girls, is on *The Beatles 1+* video disc.

A week after the completion of the *Rubber Soul* LP, the Beatles went to Twickenham Film Studios (where several scenes from their movies had been filmed) on November 23, 1965, to shoot videos for five songs, including both sides of their new single. Joe McGrath directed the clips, which were shot onto two-inch black and white video tape and later transferred onto 16mm film for stations that did not have the then-new video format. His crew had four cameramen, a lighting man, a sound man and a runner. The sets were designed by Nicolas Ferguson. Tony Bramwell oversaw the session for NEMS.

The Beatles lip-synced their way through three versions each of "We Can Work It Out" and "Day Tripper." They also made video clips for prior singles, including two takes of "I Feel Fine" and one each of "Help!" and "Ticket To Ride." George brought his new Gibson ES-345TD hollow body electric guitar, while the others played the same instruments as on the TV show.

The first two versions of "We Can Work It Out" feature the Beatles, dressed in black suits and turtlenecks, miming the song in a performance setting, with Ringo on a drum riser and John playing harmonium. They are having fun, with John flashing exaggerated smiles to the camera and the others smiling and laughing. Version 2 has George sitting on the drum riser starting with the middle eight of the song and John playing harmonium with one finger for the ending chords, causing a semi-disapproving reaction from Paul. Version 2 of "We Can Work It Out" is included on *The Beatles 1* video disc.

In Version 3 of the song, the group is on the same set, but now wearing their Shea Stadium jackets over the black turtlenecks. The clip opens with a photo of John's face with a flower covering one of his eyes. For this performance, George is seated on the drum riser. Once again, the group is cracking up during parts of the performance. As the song comes to an end, Paul begins to laugh and John swings his left foot on top of the harmonium's keyboard. This clip is included in *The Beatles 1+* video collection.

The first two versions of "Day Tripper" are also performance clips. Once again the group is dressed in black, but Paul is wearing a black dress shirt instead of a turtleneck. All members are on platforms, with George to the left of Ringo and Paul and John to the right. Version 2 of "Day Tripper" is on *The Beatles 1* video collection.

In Version 3, the group, in their Shea jackets, is behind a flat board set. George and Ringo look through the window of a old train car, while Paul and John are shown over a vintage airplane. Ringo plays tambourine through the open train window. He also plays air drums and saws the set. This clip is on *The Beatles 1+* video.

The BBC showed videos of "We Can Work It Out" and "Day Tripper" on Top Of The Pops on December 2, 1965, the night before the single was released in the U.K. The videos of these songs were not aired in the United States until January 3, 1966, when they were featured on NBC's Hullabaloo.

The Beatles also shot a series of promotional clips for their single from the *Revolver* sessions, "Paperback Writer" and "Rain." Once again, the group took time off from their recording to produce the clips. The group did not have to travel far for the first day of filming on May 19, 1966. They, along with director Michael Lindsay-Hogg and crew, gathered in Studio One of EMI Studios on Abbey Road at 10:00 a.m. The Beatles were familiar with Lindsay-Hogg from Ready, Steady, Go!, a British pop/rock TV show broadcast on Friday nights from August 1963 through December 1966. They would later hire him to direct the promotional films for "Hey Jude" and "Revolution" in September 1968 and their January 1969 rehearsals and recording session that became known as the *Get Back/Let It Be* project.

The videos shot at Abbey Road Studios were straightforward performance clips of the group miming both sides of the single. John strummed his sunburst Epiphone Casino hollow body electric guitar, while George played lead on his new cherry red Gibson SG Standard. Paul used his Hofner violin bass, although by this time he was recording with a Rickenbacker, and Ringo was on his Ludwig kit.

The first part of the session was shot by color TV cameras for video tape. As color clips of the songs would be sent to The Ed Sullivan Show for broadcast on June 5, 1966, the group taped an introduction for the show. It opens with each of the Beatles holding a colored lighting gel in front of his face. They then drop the gels and say "Hello" to Ed. Ringo then introduces the songs with: "Well I'm sorry we can't be there in person, you know, to do the show, but everybody's busy these days with the washing and the cooking, and er, we hope you like it, and, er, one's called 'Rain' and one's called 'Paperback Writer.'" This intro is on *The Beatles 1+* video.

Taping for the color clip for "Rain" began at 10:40 a.m. It opens with a dimly lit studio with only Ringo visible. When John starts his vocal, he is lit up. Similarly, Paul and George are shown in light when they begin their backing vocals. There are several close-ups of John's face. The group then watched a playback on the color monitor and had a belated Beatles breakfast of boiled eggs and bread and butter.

The group then shot the color clip for "Paperback Writer," with all members wearing sunglasses. It opens with a downward angle shot of the group and then cuts to individual members of the band. Paul is seated on a stool, while George and John are sitting on a piano. Early on, Paul can be seen holding a clear plastic folder holding a few color butcher transparencies. This is followed by normal performance shots. The video ends as it starts, with a shot of the entire group taken from above. This clip is on *The Beatles 1+* video.

After a steak and croquette potato lunch at Genevieve, the group completed black and white clips for the songs, starting with "Paperback Writer." Version 2 (continuing with the numbering from the color clip) shows the group seated. It opens with close-ups of Paul's face and John's guitar. For Versions 3 and 4, Paul, John and George are standing. The group does a fairly decent job of miming in both, although the occasional laugh sneaks in.

The black and white clips for "Rain" are designated Takes 1 and 2. Both open out of focus before sharpening in on the band miming the song. John is wearing sunglasses and Ringo is set up on a small riser. John and George occasionally laugh and smile into the camera. Version 1 keeps going after the song fades out, showing Paul and George removing their guitars and placing them on the floor. John tries to lip-sync his backwards vocal in Version 2. Both end with the camera going out of focus as it was at the beginning. One of these versions was shown on the June 3 Ready, Steady, Go! *The Beatles 1+* video contains a newly-edited clip of both versions.

The second day, May 20, was filmed in color, starting with free-form shots of band that would be edited with bits of the Beatles miming both sides of their new single. The guitarists brought their same instruments along, but Ringo showed up empty handed without even his drum sticks.

The "Rain" outdoor film includes: shots of Ringo walking away from an entrance gate across the lawn; a close up of John singing; Ringo sitting on the top of an empty stone column keeping the beat with his hands while the others sit on low hanging branches of a tree (a photo of this was used on the cover of the *Nowhere Man* EP shown on page 189); the group walking through a conservatory; various tree shots with small children climbing the branches in the background; and the group singing and relaxing in the gardens. This clip was broadcast in black and white on the June 9 Top Of The Pops. It appears in color on *The Beatles 1+* video disc. The *Anthology* video has a new edit of "Rain" combining the color video with some black and white studio shots and color outtakes.

The "Paperback Writer" outdoor film includes: closeups of each Beatle; the group miming the song in a garden with statues and large stone urns; the group miming the song in the conservatory (Ringo sits on the stone floor); and the group sitting on a bench. Paul keeps singing after the sound fades away. This clip was broadcast in black and white on the June 2 and June 23 Top Of The Pops. It appears in color on *The Beatles 1* video. In all clips, Paul's chipped front tooth (a result of a moped accident) is visible when he sings.

VISIT
www.beatle.net
for more books by Bruce Spizer

SUBSCRIBE TO BRUCE'S EMAIL LIST

FOR MORE EXCLUSIVE BEATLES ARTICLES AND CONTENT

THE BEATLES ALBUM SERIES ALSO AVAILABLE IN DIGITAL, HARD COVER AND SPECIAL COLLECTOR'S EDITIONS

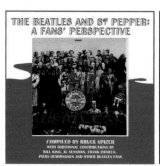

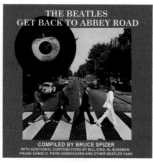

OTHER TITLES: DIGITAL EDITIONS, FIRST EDITION HARDCOVER AND SPECIAL COLLECTOR'S EDITIONS

stereo

REVOLVER

TRADE MARK OF
THE GRAMOPHONE CO. LTD.